THE GLORY YEARS

Volume Four of a Series
on the Historic Birthplace of California

THE HISTORY OF SAN DIEGO

GLORY YEARS

Written By
RICHARD F. POURADE

EDITOR EMERITUS, THE SAN DIEGO UNION

Commissioned By
JAMES S. COPLEY

CHAIRMAN OF THE CORPORATION, THE COPLEY PRESS, INC.

Published By The Union-Tribune Publishing Company

PREVIOUS BOOKS

"The Explorers," published 1960
"Time of the Bells," published 1961
"The Silver Dons," published 1963

CONTENTS

LIST OF ILLUSTRATIONS

DEDICATION

As we reflect upon "The Glory Years" of San Diego, we have reason to look with curiosity into the mirror of time to see what manner of men and women were playing their dramatic roles on the stage of Southern California in the days when there were "busts" as well as "booms".

It is a rare quality of actors of "The Glory Years" that we find reflected in the mirror of time. Each is a player of many roles and all contributing in a manner then as new to the 19th Century as those now strange in the miracles we see in the 20th Century.

So we find reflections from time intriguing and essential to the making of history.

JAMES S. COPLEY

*If it can be said that anyone envisioned a
future, certainly Alonzo Horton did. There
was nothing, but in his mind he saw a city.*

Introducing a Story
Without An Ending

In Southern California the past is so close that monuments and
graves do not belong to history. In an old graveyard, where are
buried so many of the pioneers who helped to found and build San
Diego, many headstones are broken or lying on their side, names
eroded by weather. Others are well-marked, if seldom visited.

There is the grave of Father Antonio Ubach, with a stately
monument. He was the last of the padres; a native of Spain, born
1835, died 1907. Nearby is the grave of Cave Johnson Couts, born
in Tennessee, 1821, a graduate of West Point. Lying beside him is
his wife, Ysidora Bandini de Couts, the daughter of a Spanish Don. The names tell of the melting together of two peoples.
There lies María Guadalupe de Smith and over there, Serafino
Stewart Serrano.

This melting had come to an end when a new generation of
pioneers reached the mountain passes. They came from New England and Ohio, from Ireland and Germany, and even Austria and
Poland, in the great tides of humanity that flooded across a continent in the later 1800's, to find their resting places under
eucalyptus trees on a barren hill overlooking a harbor that few
people in the world had ever heard of.

We find the names of Ames, of O'Brien, of Lyons, of McCoy, of
Clark, of Hinton, and of Warnock. In another cemetery are the
names of Sherman, of Wildy, of Cleveland, of Pauly, of Jorres and
Babcock. There is a thin spire-like monument for Alonzo Erastus
Horton, who founded a city, with the wrong date, and elsewhere a

belated plaque. Not far away is the grave of Ephraim W. Morse, who is deserving of almost as much from history as Horton, as our story will show, and the headstone merely notes that he rendered "faithful service to city and neighbor."

There are a few wood slats with numbers instead of names, but even these people cannot yet be erased from a story that is still unfolding, the astonishing growth of Southern California.

From the end of the Civil War to the beginning of the Twentieth Century it was one boom after another. They were glorious years, of success and failure, and always the opportunity to try again. There was wealth to be won in land, in railroads, in industry, in agriculture, in mining, and in oil, and cities to be built, if you could do it.

These things happened so recently, and events in Southern California are still moving so swiftly, that few have had time to look back and wonder how it all came about and who were the people who started it all in the first place.

This book brings together the stories of many of these builders and of a city commanded to rise from nothing. The story of San Diego is typically the story of Southern California and much of the Southwest. This book is the fourth in a series on the history of the region from the vantage point of the first white settlement on the Pacific Coast. The others have been *The Explorers, The Time of the Bells* and *The Silver Dóns.*

The records of the men who built Southern California, in the "boom and bust" years between 1865 and 1900, even of those who are not entitled to a name over their graves, are as fresh as letters from home. Newspaper files and libraries and museums abound with their words and deeds. The San Diego Historical Society, San Diego State College Library, Henry E. Huntington Library, Bancroft Library of the University of California at Berkeley, the library of the University of California at Los Angeles, California Historical Society, California Society of Pioneers, California State Library, Los Angeles County Museum, San Diego Public Library, and Title Insurance and Trust Company are rich sources of research.

This is a looking back into an era that perhaps has had no parallel. They were exciting years, but even more, they were meaningful years we need to know more about. For, as an Indian chief once said, a people without a history is like the wind on the buffalo grass.

Richard F. Pourade

IT ALL BEGAN WITH
FATHER HORTON

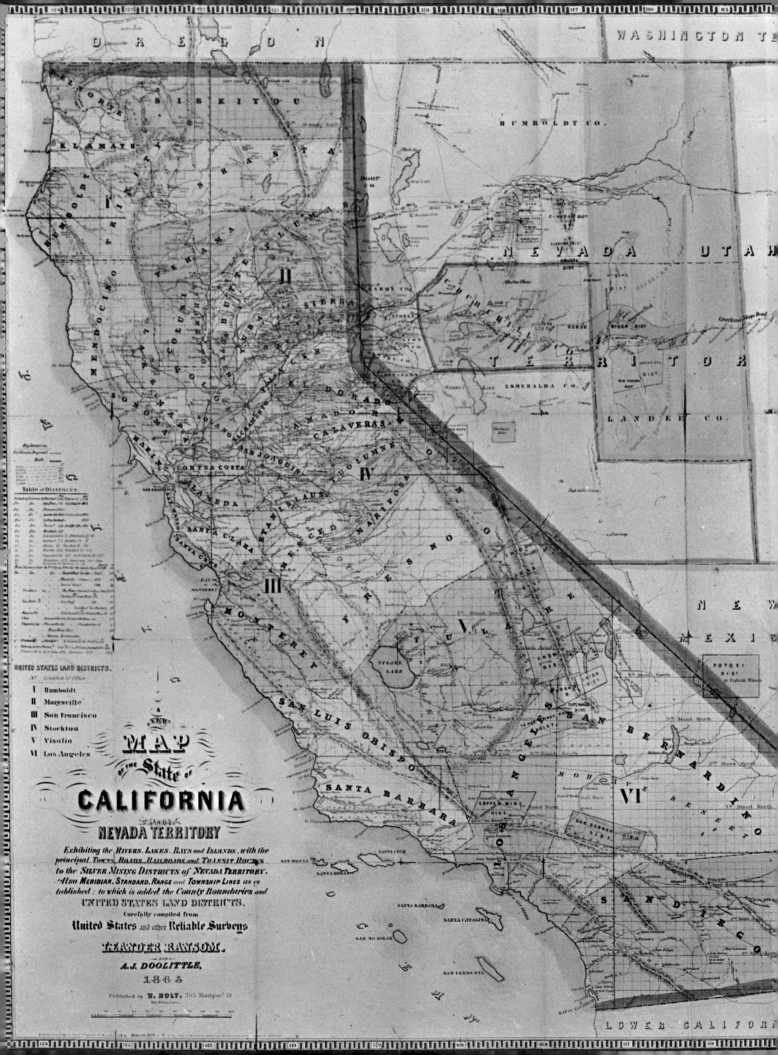

OREGON

WASHINGTON TE

DEL NORTE

SISKIYOU

HUMBOLDT CO.

KLAMATH

SHASTA

NEVADA — UTAH

HUMBOLDT

TRINITY

PLUMAS

TEHAMA

MENDOCINO

II

BUTTE

SIERRA

TERRITORY

CHURCHILL CO.

LANDER CO.

ESMERALDA CO.

COLUSA

YUBA

NEVADA

PLACER

SUTTER

YOLO

EL DORADO

SONOMA

NAPA

SOLANO

SACRAMENTO

AMADOR

CALAVERAS

ALPINE

MARIN

CONTRA COSTA

SAN JOAQUIN

TUOLUMNE

MONO

ALAMEDA

IV

STANISLAUS

SANTA CLARA

MERCED

MARIPOSA

NEW

MEXICO

FRESNO

MONTEREY

III

POTOSI
DIST

SAN LUIS OBISPO

TULARE

SAN BERNARDINO

COPPER MINE
DIST

SANTA BARBARA

MOHAVE DESERT

VIᵉ

LOS ANGELES

SAN BERNARDINO DIST.

SAN MIGUEL

SANTA CRUZ

SANTA ROSA

SAN DIEGO

SANTA BARBARA

SANTA CATALINA

SAN NICOLAS

SAN CLEMENTE

LOWER CALIFORNIA

UNITED STATES LAND DISTRICTS.

Nᵒ Location of Office
I   Humboldt
II Marysville
III San Francisco
IV Stockton
V   Visalia
VI Los Angeles

A NEW

MAP

of the State of

CALIFORNIA

and

NEVADA TERRITORY

Exhibiting the RIVERS, LAKES, BAYS and ISLANDS, with the
principal TOWNS, ROADS, RAILROADS and TRANSIT ROUTES
to the SILVER MINING DISTRICTS of NEVADA TERRITORY.
Also MERIDIAN, STANDARD, RANGE and TOWNSHIP LINES as es-
tablished; to which is added the County Boundaries and
UNITED STATES LAND DISTRICTS,
Carefully compiled from
United States and other Reliable Surveys
by
LEANDER RANSOM,
AND
A. J. DOOLITTLE,
1865.
Published by W. HOLT, 305 Montgom.ᵉ St
San Francisco.

This was California in 1865. San Diego County extended all the way to the Colorado River, an overwhelming area of many climates.

CHAPTER I

The Civil War had come to a close. The wagons of thousands of immigrants again were on the trails to California. From San Francisco, the Central Pacific Railroad was being pushed eastward across the High Sierra to meet the Union Pacific driving westward from Omaha.

Though the Gold Rush had long been over, the lure of California had kept growing with the years. To those seeking adventure and opportunity, it was a land of promise; to the disheartened and the ailing it was a land of sunshine and curative powers. New Englanders left their grim soil and pioneers the cold marsh lands of Wisconsin. Along the old Southern Trail from Texas to California came ruined plantation owners and merchants with their women and children, abandoning a ravaged South. They were joined by discharged soldiers and deserters of the Union and Confederate Armies, and by frontier people who were ever moving farther West. Behind them, a relentless wave of immigration from Europe washed up on the Eastern seaboard, poured into the cities, and trickled out across the prairies and lapped at the foot of the Rockies.

At one end of the Southern Trail was San Diego, at the southwest corner of the United States where Gaspar de Portolá of the Spanish Army and Fr. Junípero Serra had founded the first white settlement and Franciscan mission in California in 1769. Almost

3

geographically isolated by high mountains, deserts and the arid lands of northwestern Mexico, although open to the sea, San Diego had not prospered as had San Francisco, or even Los Angeles, and the Civil War and a prolonged drought had reduced its population to less than two-hundred persons.

It was a land that almost overwhelmed the traveler with its variety, beauty and surprises. Its rivers mostly ran underground. The coastal climate was semi-arid, but floods could alternate with droughts. Theodore S. Van Dyke, in his book, *Southern California,* published in 1886, described how the land rises to a height of a mile at about sixty miles from the coast, and by looking back from high Cuyamaca Peak, it can be seen "tumbling, tumbling, on the north and on the south and on the west, tumbling in long alternations of hills and slopes and valleys away to a distant coast." Continuing, he wrote:

It is easy to understand how a land thus rising a mile in fifty or sixty miles, rising away from the coast and falling off abruptly a mile deep into the driest and hottest of American deserts, could have a great variety of climates. And such is the County of San Diego . . . a land of climates within another land of climates. Only ten miles away on the east the summers are the hottest, and

Southern California was born of Spain and mothered by Mexico. The old ways, as shown in this 1857 etching of Los Angeles, persisted through the Civil War and then swiftly faded under the impact of Western migration.

only sixty miles on the west the coolest known in the United States . . . and between these is every combination that mountains and valleys can produce.

The county extended at its longest point about 75 miles northward and at its widest nearly 200 miles eastward to the Colorado River, an empire of 14,969 square miles. There were more than 6,000,000 acres subject to settlement or purchase, though most of it was in the mountainous interior. Another 2,500,000 acres lay in a merciless desert. Old San Diego, or Old Town, occupied but a few blocks of 48,557 acres of pueblo lands that had been originally granted to the community by the King of Spain. There were not more than sixty-five structures, perhaps half of them of the adobe that characterized a Spanish tradition. The population was about evenly divided between Americans and those of Spanish and Mexican descent. There wasn't even a newspaper. The original Royal Presidio of the great days of Spain was marked by heaps of mud on the hill above the town. At one time it had contained more people than were then residing in Old Town.

In the East, however, there was considerable discussion about a second transcontinental railroad to begin at the Mississippi River and run along the 32nd parallel and terminate at San Diego.

Ephraim W. Morse as a young man

In San Francisco, the Southern Pacific Company, with a charter from the state to build a railroad down the coast to San Diego, held out the possibility of connecting there with the Memphis and El Paso transcontinental line proposed by Gen. John C. Frémont, who had played a dramatic role in the early American Army explorations of California and its conquest in the war with Mexico in 1846.

Change was in the air. The immigrant wagons coming to the Colorado River at Yuma were struggling over the desert and up and into the mountains through San Felipe Pass to Warner's Ranch, and then down the hilly rock-strewn trails to San Diego. Land, not gold, was the primary desire of the newcomers who had responded to the exciting stories of the vast and fertile homestead lands awaiting everyone in California. The immigrants at first brought but little increase in prosperity for merchants and ranchers who had remained through the trying years of war and drought. Ephraim W. Morse, for one, had come to San Diego from San Francisco during the Gold Rush, and now was a merchant and a deputy sheriff and heavily in debt to his San Francisco suppliers. He had resisted the appeals of his father to return to Amesbury, Massachusetts, where he had been a teacher and farmer.

He believed in the future of San Diego. He was intrigued by the prospects of gold in the county, and knew that if a shorter road could be found between Yuma and San Diego, and if eventually the mountain barrier also could be conquered by a railroad, the stream of immigrants would become a river.

He did not agree with those who said that San Diego had no backcountry, that its mountains and deserts precluded its becoming a heavily populated area and a center of production and wealth. He had driven by wagon to the rim of the mountains, at Jacumba Pass, near the international border, and had looked out over what is now Imperial Valley, a part of the vast Colorado Desert, and it was an inspiring sight. He felt that if water could be diverted onto this basin of silt deposited over the ages by the Colorado River, it could be turned into a rich and productive land that would bring business and wealth to San Diego as well. But, as he wrote to his father:

> I'm still keeping store here but not making money. There is but little business here, the place not being so large as it was ten years ago . . . there are only two men in San Diego that don't occasionally get drunk and they are McCoy, the sheriff, and myself.

The land the immigrants had crossed a continent to reach was yet a frontier. The military rule of the Civil War had come to an end and the soldiers had withdrawn from San Diego. Military deserters and adventurers of many breeds lived by the gun and bandits from Sonora and Lower California raided across the border. The pages of the newspaper *Alta California,* published in San Francisco, reflected the harshness of the times. For crimes unmentioned, three Indians were taken from the San Diego jail and "lynched or killed." At Yuma, four men were hanged by vigilantes. A San Diego attorney, identified only as Smart, and described as young and dissolute but of good family, shot a youth named Gilbert, stole a horse and fled. He was captured by a posse at Las Flores, near Oceanside, and when he attempted to escape, or so it was reported, was himself killed. Joseph Smith, who had gone into partnership with Ephraim Morse on a sheep ranch on what was known as Smith mountain and later Palomar Mountain, was found murdered. A hired hand, a deserter from a British ship, who some say coveted Smith's Indian wife, was captured by ranchers and hanged from a tree.

A solution was offered to the murder of William James, the justice of the peace at Warner's and a clerk in Cyrus Kimble's store on the immigrant trail up from San Felipe Valley, which had so stirred San Diego in 1865. It had been feared that James had been murdered by mistake by Southern sympathizers who had been after Kimble, an outspoken Republican, and this suspicion had been strengthened by the subsequent slaying of Kimble and a companion along the Santa Ana River on the road to Los Angeles. The governor of Lower California, however, according to the *Alta California,* captured a band of guerrillas, and among other crimes, they acknowledged the murder and the robbery at Kimble's store. Six of the band were executed and the rest banished from the territory.

The situation began to improve with the arrival of new settlers and the assignment of United States Cavalry to patrols in the mountain and desert areas. The San Diego correspondent for the *Alta California* reported:

> People have got quieted down so that they can get along without "bagging a man before breakfast" every day, as was the case not long ago.

Judge Oliver S. Witherby

The ranchos of the Spanish and Mexican days were being diverted to raising sheep as well as cattle, and some already were being broken up into smaller farms for sale to the new settlers. Gold flakes were being found in the washes and gold ore was being taken out of the ground on El Rincón del Diablo Rancho

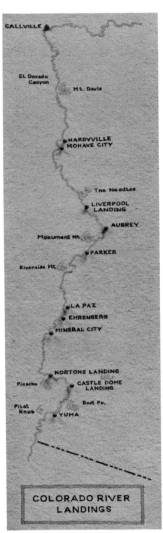

Steamboat landings on
Colorado River

J. J. Warner

owned by O. S. Witherby. The mine was two miles southeast of the present city of Escondido. Four miles north of Rancho San Dieguito, now known as Rancho Santa Fe, a copper strike was reported along Escondido Creek.

San Diego had great hopes for its port and foresaw a rapidly rising trade with Boston and a large wharf and warehouse were being considered to accommodate a line of clipper ships. San Diego was alert to point out that it was 500 miles closer to New England than was San Francisco. Steamers and sailing ships were bringing merchandise for the local market and for Fort Yuma on the Colorado River, and supplies and machinery to be transshipped to the gold mines of the river region around La Paz north of Yuma and the new copper mining developments in Lower California. In return, large quantities of copper ore were being brought to San Diego from Lower California, and application was being made to have San Diego declared a port of entry and a United States Naval Station. The California Steamship Navigation Company was operating three steamers and barges up the Colorado delta to Fort Yuma, La Paz and the Colorado River mines. Two of its steamers, the *Senator* and *Pacific*, the brig *J. D. Ford* and the schooner *Alert* were calling at San Diego.

There was a rising excitement over the prospects for the future. San Diego received word that Gen. William S. Rosecrans, one of the incorporators of the Southern Pacific Railroad that was to run down the Pacific Coast to San Diego, would arrive on the next steamer and that the company president himself might arrive at any time to make final arrangements for the construction of buildings, shops and a depot. On April 14, 1866, Gen. Rosecrans arrived and was greeted by a 100-gun salute. The *Alta California* reported that the whole town turned out to see him, and he made a short speech of thanks. However, he left almost immediately with Capt. W. A. Winder to inspect copper mines in Lower California.

Regardless of the fate of the railroad, San Diego knew that it must have an improved road over the mountains. Up until shortly after the end of the Civil War, the main 220-mile wagon route had followed the old Butterfield Stage line from Yuma on the Colorado River and turned northwest up the gently sloping San Felipe Valley to Warner's Ranch and then back down to San Diego. By 1865 there was a 195-mile wagon road open to Fort Yuma which went up the Tia Juana River Valley, though below the international border, to Tecate, Mexico, and descended the mountains along the border on the Mexican side of the line. This saved twenty-five miles between Yuma and San Diego and was known as the Kern route. It had been used occasionally during the Gold Rush period.

In 1866, Ephraim Morse, on his wagon trip through the backcountry and mountains, had used an odometer in measuring another route which went up the Tia Juana River Valley to Las Juntas, twenty miles west of Mountain Springs, then passed Cottontree Springs, crossed back into the United States near Jacumba, and descended the steep Jacum, or grade, in the Mountain Springs area, which, at some places, fell off thirty percent. The rain-starved hills as they slid off eastward toward the desert floor were steep and slashed by grim canyons choked by reddish rock heaved up in some angry outburst of nature. That anyone was confident that an adequate road could be hacked out of such a starved wilderness, and a railroad built, was a tribute to pioneering zeal. But, to the Army, it was the most practical route, being the shortest, and they foresaw San Diego as the main point of supply for posts all over the Southwest.

As the Army was without funds for such purposes, a campaign in the community led by Col. E. B. Williston raised $500 to improve the Jacumba Pass, and a short time later he reported he had driven a train of heavily-loaded wagons pulled by six-mule teams over the route and had encountered no trouble whatsoever. By fall, with the arrival of the steamer *Orizaba* on the first trip of a regular schedule, with forty-three passengers and 140 tons of freight, J. J. Tomlinson & Company had its stages on the San Diego-Yuma run, carrying passengers and light freight and making the journey in forty-eight hours.

In a letter to the *San Francisco Bulletin,* for which he was San Diego correspondent, Rufus K. Porter gave this picture of a new era slowly getting under way:

Things are beginning to look up in this long-decaying town . . . the town is full of life and bustle and reminding one of our palmy days . . . the new road to Yuma . . . will be the great highway of traffic between this coast and Fort Yuma, Arizona, New Mexico, etc.

Six months later, after San Diego had dug itself out of the mud of a March storm that had dropped five and a half inches of rain and wiped out roads and bridges, the town was aroused once again by fresh reports that the Southern Pacific at last was about to break ground in San Diego. The next turn of fortune for San Diego, however, would not be the decision of a railroad corporation but that of an obscure individual who had never seen the town and wasn't too sure just where it was.

In San Francisco, Alonzo Erastus Horton, who owned and operated a furniture store, was informed of a lecture on the subject of the ports of the Pacific Coast and was persuaded to attend. Years later he told what happened.

So I went, and the speaker commenced at Seattle and said it was going to be a big city; and then he came down to San Francisco, which he said would be one of the biggest cities in California. Then he kept going down along the coast to San Diego, and he said that San Diego was one of the healthiest places in the world; that it had one of the best harbors in the world; that there was no better harbor.

This was the queen city of San Francisco which Alonzo Horton deserted to establish a town he thought would crown the West.

Horton could not sleep that night for thinking about San Diego. He was fifty-four years of age. His thoughts drifted back over an already full life that had brought him alternate periods of plenty and poverty. But the big prizes so far had escaped him. He was a descendant of an impoverished family of English ancestry that first arrived in this country with the Puritans in about 1630. His grandfather, the Rev. Ezra Horton, went to Union, Connecticut, from New York, as a pastor in 1759. This was ten years before Fr. Serra arrived in California to found the first of the twenty-one Franciscan missions in the area where Alonzo Horton would leave a city.

Alonzo Horton was born in Union, on October 24, 1813, one of seven children of Erastus Horton and Tryphena Burleigh. Within two years the family had removed to Madison County, New York, and then, after four years, to the cold and damp shores of Lake

Ontario, near Oswego, which had seen its first white settlers only eighteen years before. The family lived in a log cabin as did their neighbors. The people along Lake Ontario were known as the "hunters" who organized into secret lodges and took part in the "patriot war" in the Canadian rebellion against British power.

When his father became temporarily blind, Alonzo, though a frail boy, worked as basketmaker at night while going to school in the day. Evidently his father in time recovered his sight, as Alonzo as a young man was able to purchase the remainder of his minority, a period of six months, from his father for $50, as was the custom, and went to work as a lumberjack and grocer. He saved enough money to purchase a small lake boat with which he traded in wheat between Oswego and Canada. He gave this up to become a cooper, or a manufacturer of flour barrels, served a short while as constable at Scriba, and then turned to dealing in land.

In this raw pioneering land he became familiar with the plank roads which connected the towns of eastern and upper New York. Many years later, residents of San Diego were to make a desperate effort to break their isolation by laying a similar plank roadway across a desert.

Alonzo E. Horton as a young man

In 1836, he was warned that he had developed consumption and was advised to go West. "West" was the newly-opened and primitive country of Wisconsin, and for the next fifteen years, with the exception of a period of several years in the East, Horton engaged in speculating in land and trading in cattle, mostly in the booming area of Milwaukee.

He married Sally Millington Wright in 1841, but she died five years later. In 1847, at the close of the war with Mexico, Horton, the speculator, went to St. Louis and purchased land warrants from discharged soldiers and came into possession of 1500 acres of land in east central Wisconsin in the Rock River country. They had cost him 70 cents an acre. He established a steamer landing, a saw mill for lumber for sleds and ox carts, and then a year later founded his own town, which he named Hortonville, a few miles north of Lake Winnebago and south of Green Bay. He gave away lots to attract settlers, helped to finance the homes they built with his lumber, and in many cases provided them with jobs.

In 1964, Hortonville still was mostly a one-street, red-brick town and the memory of Alonzo Horton was as alive there as it was in Southern California. Fields are wrapped in mist on a damp and cloudy day. It is a land rich in water and woods, but locked up in snow in winter.

While immigrants were settling in his own little town and buying his land, Horton was receiving exciting letters from two brothers who had joined the Gold Rush to California, and finally after two years he succumbed to the temptation of easy riches, sold his holdings for about $7000, and made the long sea journey to a new frontier.

The gold fields were a disappointment. He invested his money in shares in a mining company which failed, and went into the fields himself. But the easily accessible gold had been taken out and mining was becoming big business. Horton turned back to what he knew best, and opened a store in the little mining town of Pilot Hill in El Dorado County, subsequently constructing a ditch to bring a supply of water to the settlement, cutting and selling mountain lake ice, and buying gold dust at the mines and selling it in the larger towns. By 1854 his profits sometimes were as high as $1000 a month. By the standards of the times, he accumulated a comfortable stake. It was time to go home, to the Wisconsin where he had established his parents.

In March of the next year he boarded the steamer *Cortez* for Panama from where he expected to cross the Isthmus to the Atlantic seaboard as had hundreds of thousands of persons going and coming from the mines of California. A native riot, however, engulfed most of the passengers who had come on the *Cortez*, and Horton took command of a resistance in which several of the natives were slain, and led the passengers back on board the ship. But the bag in which he had carried $10,000 in gold dust was lost. All he had left was the $5000 which he carried in a money belt. Many other passengers also lost their possessions and Horton was delegated to represent them in Washington in pressing claims through the government of the United States. All had their money returned, except Horton. He was held responsible for the deaths of several natives and the government of New Granada, now known as Colombia, of which Panama then was a province, insisted that if Horton's claim had to be paid, no claim would be settled. Horton said he voluntarily waived his rights.

In Wisconsin, with the Civil War rushing upon the nation, and fortune still eluding him, and with the attractions of California still in his memory, he married Sarah Wilson Babe in 1861 and soon departed for San Francisco, arriving in the autumn of 1862. Another venture into mining in British Columbia ended in failure. He returned to San Francisco, penniless and discouraged. All the dreams faded.

He opened a furniture store and settled down. That is, until he listened to the lecture on the ports of California and the prospects

San Francisco represented the height of sophistication at the time Alonzo Horton left its "lunch and bar" to gamble for wealth.

of San Diego. The newspapers were filled with the news of immigrant trains a hundred wagons long crossing the mountains into California, and of the transcontinental trains which soon would be bringing hundreds of thousands of settlers for the millions of acres of land waiting for them in the public domain. Then it all came back, the high moments of success and the bitter hours of defeat, of a town founded and now almost forgotten, and of the emotional and mental stimulus of creating and building.

At 2 o'clock in the morning of that same night, unable to sleep, he got out of bed and studied a map showing the location of San Diego.

In the morning I said to my wife: "I am going to sell my goods and go to San Diego and build a city." She said I talked like a wild man, that I could not dispose of my goods in six months. But I commenced that morning and made a large sale that day. The second day it was the same and I had to hire two more helpers. By the third day I had five men hired and in these three days I had sold out all my stock. It was not an auction sale but just a run of business which seemed providential. Then my wife said she would not oppose me any longer, for she had always noticed when it was right for me to do anything, it always went right in my favor, and as this had gone that way, she believed it was right for me to do so.

On April 15, 1867, Alonzo Erastus Horton clambered out of a small boat from the paddle-wheel steamer *Pacific* and stepped ashore at San Diego. He was rather stocky of build, his health having improved over the years, and was about five feet, ten inches tall. Stately in appearance, he had a flowing beard typical of the times and liked to wear a frock coat and a high silk hat. He neither smoked nor drank.

The place of landing was at about the foot of Market Street. The town of San Diego was three miles away to the north, at the mouth of Mission Valley and on the edge of a sandy plain through which the San Diego River in the wet seasons spread out into the bay, pushing its silt in front of it and slowly leaving the town farther and farther away from deep water.

With several hours to wait for the arrival of a wagon to take him into what is now known as Old Town, he strolled across the broad flattish land that slowly rises back from the bay onto a wide mesa that stretches out to the foothills of the coastal mountains. There were only a few buildings in sight. They were all that remained of a town that had been laid out at the height of the Gold Rush, and had died with its end. Originally established as New San Diego, it had become known as Graytown or as Davis' Folly, after two of its principal promoters, Andrew B. Gray, who had come to San Diego as an engineer with the United States Boundary Commission, and William Heath Davis, an enterprising sea captain, trader and merchant. The wharf they had built out into the bay had been torn up to provide fuel for soldiers stationed at the now deserted Army barracks. The only residents were Matthew Sherman and his bride, Augusta Jane Barrett, who had come to Old Town from San Francisco in 1866 to become a teacher. La Playa, across the bay on the shore of Point Loma, once the center of the hide trade with Boston in the Spanish and Mexican periods, also had boomed during the Gold Rush, when it was the stopping place for San Francisco-bound vessels, and then too had dwindled away.

Alonzo E. Horton at middleage

Horton walked through the brush-covered area, which in time became the business heart of San Diego, and from a high point where the land begins to lift into the Hillcrest district, he could look back upon the long curving bay, one of the world's finest natural harbors. To the west was the long protecting arm of Point Loma, a familiar landmark for navigators for three centuries. Below were the two bare sandy islands which were tied together and then to the mainland by the narrow Silver Strand, to close the port from the south. His eye could follow the coastline into Mexico, where Table Mountain was etched against the sky. On the horizon, off the Mexican coast, arose the majestic Coronado Islands. To the east the blue mountains loomed as sentinels watching over a land still awaiting the arrival of those who would see its beauty and appreciate its softness.

14

This was a land different from the hardness of the shores of Lake Ontario and the marshy countryside of Wisconsin. There wasn't a tree or a stream, but the air of spring was fresh, the grass and brush were green, and as the morning overcast rolled away, the sea and the bay sparkled under a warming sun. It was a land of pastel distances and vivid foregrounds. Carpets of wild yellow poppies and blue lupine were scattered across the mesas to the edge of the pink and blue hills. In size it dwarfed the state in which he had been born. San Diego County then was three times as large as Connecticut. Though nostalgia may have sweetened the memory over the years, he later said:

I thought San Diego must be heaven-on-earth, if it was all as fine as that. It seemed to be the best spot for building a city I ever saw.

Old Town itself must have been a disappointment to Horton, for he realized that its location precluded its growth into a major city. On the trip down the coast with him had been an agent of Wells, Fargo & Company, who continually extolled the advantages of San Diego. He now asked Horton what he thought of the town. Horton replied:

I would not give you five dollars for a deed to the whole of it. I would not take it as a gift. It doesn't lie right. Never in the world can you have a city here.

Listening to the conversation was Ephraim Morse, the merchant, and he asked Horton where he thought the city should be situated, and was told it must be in the same area where so many had failed.

How to get possession of the land was the problem. The pueblo of San Diego was governed by a Board of Trustees with limited powers and responsible to the State Legislature. Nobody had thought to call an election for two years, and there was a question as to the legal authority of the holdover trustees to dispose of any more land. But the town decided it was in need of tax revenue, and with an eager and most certainly misguided customer waiting to purchase a lot of wasteland, an election was quickly arranged when Horton gave the county clerk, George A. Pendleton, $10 to cover the costs. All this had happened on his first day in San Diego.

A ten-day notice had to be given for an election, and in the meantime, Horton and Morse, who had become imbued with Horton's enthusiasm, spent long hours driving over the site of the present city of San Diego. Where Horton, upon leaving San Francisco, had hoped to be able to acquire perhaps forty acres, enough to begin a town, he now realized the little value that San

This was San Diego when Alonzo Horton arrived. It was no San Francisco. He left it to wither and laid out a new site with room to grow.

Joseph S. Mannasse

Diegans placed on the area, and became aware of the possibility of a much greater gamble than any he had yet experienced in his life. In their minds they laid out streets and planned buildings, and in the evening the western sky turned to a molten gold that seemed an omen of things to come.

Five dollars in silver in the collection plate of the town's only Catholic Church aroused the interest of Fr. Antonio Ubach and he promised to assist in making sure of the election of such cooperative residents as Joseph S. Mannasse, a merchant and money-

At a Sale of City Lands held at the Court House on Friday May 10th 1867 the following Lots were Sold

Lot	Purchaser	Price
1146 1147 1156	A. E. Horton	150.00
1145	A. E. Horton	40.00
Fractional lot lying between 1156 & 1157	Edd Hewh	9.50
1134	A. E. Horton	20.00
1173	John Murray	20.50
1133	A. E. Horton	55.00
		$295.00

Jas. M. Coy
Sheriff and
Ex Officio Auctioneer
by E. W. Morse
(Deputy)

Purchased by A. E. Horton 960 acres.
Price — $265.50
average about 27½ cents per acre

This memorandum records how Alonzo Horton bought 960 acres at auction for $265, partly with borrowed money. It became New San Diego.

lender who had come into possession of ranch lands formerly held by the languid and improvident natives, and Thomas H. Bush, a Pennsylvania bookbinder who had tried his luck in gold exploration in Lower California, Mexico, and now kept a store in Old Town.

The election was held on April 27, with Morse and the other two candidates chosen unanimously with thirty-two votes being cast. The new board was organized on April 30, with Mannasse elected as president, Bush as secretary and Morse as treasurer, and they adopted a resolution for the sale "of certain farming lands."

The sale was conducted on May 10, with Morse, in the absence of Sheriff James McCoy, as the auctioneer. With the help of $123 advanced by Morse, Horton acquired 960 acres in 160-acre lots and some fractional parcels, to the amusement of the citizens, for which he paid $265 or an average price of 27½ cents an acre. He had paid 70 cents an acre for land that had to be cleared of timber in the wilderness of central Wisconsin.

On one parcel he was outbid $5 by D. A. Hollister, a district judge, and told him he could have it. The alarmed and penniless judge, who had merely tried to run up the price on behalf of the taxpayers, pleaded with Horton to come to his rescue, which he did, by raising the bid 25 cents. Two other persons also acquired some acreage.

Horton's purchases lay to the east of Davis' Folly and the Middletown subdivision. Middletown had been laid out on former pueblo lands along the upper bay between New San Diego and Old Town, during the same Gold Rush boom, but had never materialized. The southern portion of Horton's land included most of what is now all of the commercial center of San Diego lying between Front Street and Fifteenth Street, and from A Street south to Commercial Street. This took in all of the bay front from Eighth Avenue to Front Street. The northern portion was a long stretch beginning above A Street and including all the land now lying between Balboa Park and Union Street.

Horton had the land and the problem now was to find buyers. His name had received only casual mention in news reports from San Diego published in San Francisco newspapers, and the contemporary correspondence of San Diegans contains only a few references to him. As the principal immigrant trails still led to San Francisco, Horton returned there, wound up his business affairs, and opened a land sales office on Montgomery Street. San Diego, he proclaimed, was sure to be the city of the future.

MOVE OVER, SAN FRANCISCO...

CHAPTER II

Dreams of greatness were being born of visionary railroads. Gen. John C. Frémont, who had been court-martialed after the conquest of California, and subsequently pardoned, and was now a millionaire as a result of his holdings in the California gold country, was the principal promoter of the proposed second transcontinental railroad.

In the East he purchased the franchise and rights of the Kansas Pacific Railroad, picked up an interest in the Memphis and Little Rock, and convinced the Legislature of Texas to grant additional land for the Memphis and El Paso. Frémont would put these together in a great consolidated line running from Norfolk in Virginia on the Atlantic to San Diego in California on the Pacific.

In San Francisco, near where Horton began offering lots in San Diego, Gen. William S. Rosecrans, an organizer of the Southern Pacific Railroad, brooded over a harsh change in fortune. At one time commander of the second largest Union Army, but short-tempered and argumentative, he had been shunted aside near the end of the Civil War, and subsequently had resigned and come to California in the hope of striking it rich. Now, as one of the two men to whom San Diego looked for its transcontinental rail connections, he found himself outwitted in an age of exploitation and

21

speculative financing. An assessment had been levied on the line's stock and a notice published in an obscure newspaper. When Rosecrans failed to pay it, his stock was secretly auctioned off. Then, to counter any legal action he might take against them, his enemies sent squatters onto his property to harass him. He saved his land but lost his stock.

A correspondent from *The New York Times* reported an encounter with Gen. Rosecrans, whom he had known during the Civil War:

> When I last saw him he had his martial cloak about him and was in the zenith of his glory and popularity. No man who ever saw him upon the field of action can forget him, his dash, his excited manner, and his great personal intrepidity. Now he looked sad and careworn, dismal and unfriendly. His clothes were clean but old and rusty, and his hair and whiskers looked uncombed and shaggy.

Still interested in railroads, he became acquainted with Horton and returned with him to look over San Diego and its prospects. There were no 100-gun salutes this time. But he reasoned, if a railroad could be built over the mountains and across the desert, the lands held by Horton would be invaluable. They went by steamer to San Diego, and in two wagons, one for passengers and one for provisions, started east from San Diego. With them were Ephraim Morse and Joseph Mannasse and several other persons.

Rails were being driven across the country, as shown in this Currier & Ives print, and the rush to the West would become a torrent.

Horton tells the story:

> We went first down to Tijuana and from there about a hundred miles east to Jacumba Pass, where we could see out across the desert. General Rosecrans said to me: "Horton, this is the best route for a railroad through the mountains that I have ever seen in California." He said he had been all over the state and he was now satisfied that my property was well worth a million dollars.

They had taken the natural route through a series of gently

rising valleys below the international border and which connected the ranchos of old Spanish families at Tijuana and Tecate in Lower California. The problem with this route was that it lay largely through foreign territory.

At Jacumba Pass they looked down upon the desert, as had Morse a year before. Both Morse and Horton were well aware, however, that as early as 1852 Army Engineers had rejected Jacumba as a railroad pass. The same surveys reported the route from Yuma through the desert Carrizo Corridor and up the San Felipe Valley was passable, but the rest of the road from Warner's to San Diego was impracticable.

Gen. William S. Rosecrans

This had been a serious blow to the hopes of San Diego. The recommended routes into Southern California lay through the San Gorgonio and Cajon Passes. San Gorgonio Pass lies in that portion of Riverside County which at that time was part of San Diego County. Cajon Pass is in San Bernardino County, which originally had been part of San Diego County until it was cut away by the State Legislature in 1851. San Gorgonio and Cajon Passes have long sloping approaches in contrast to Jacumba Pass which requires a climb of 2000 feet in five miles. The highest point of San Gorgonio Pass is only 2000 feet. Although Cajon reaches 4000 feet, the climb from Barstow, at 2000 feet, to the crest of the pass is up over fifty miles of easy terrain. Both Cajon and San Gorgonio Passes point directly to Los Angeles, 125 miles north of San Diego, a factor that was to play a deciding role in shaping the future of both towns.

Undaunted, San Diegans in 1854 had organized the San Diego & Gila, Southern Pacific & Atlantic Railroad, voted the company 8850 acres of public land, and boldly announced plans to construct their own railroad across the mountains to meet any line coming westward. An engineer was hired to make a survey of the San Diego River route to Warner's and, contrary to the judgment of Army engineers, he said he had found it passable and acceptable. The Civil War brought that scheme to an end.

After the war, and when the first transcontinental railroad was under construction, a second route, along either the 35th or the 32nd parallel, was inevitable, though as far as San Diego was concerned disappointment followed disappointment.

Gen. W. J. Palmer, in the "Report of Surveys Across the Continent on the 35th and 32nd Parallels," 1867-68, also made an adverse recommendation. While he acknowledged in correspondence that the port of San Diego must certainly become an important one in the Pacific trade, it was impossible to forecast the time when this would come about, and it would be more practical to terminate a transcontinental line along the 35th parallel at San Francisco, where commerce already existed, and extend a branch line to San Diego.

Rosecrans, however, persisted in his belief that a railroad along the 32nd parallel, with San Diego as a terminus, was natural and practical. He insisted that the new route which he had explored between San Diego and Yuma was more favorable and less in distance than the one by way of Warner's Ranch.

But, in a letter to Rosecrans, Palmer wrote that though he had found excellent gradients for a route along the Rio Grande River to the Tia Juana River, there was "no timber, no settlements, too much desert, and bad climate."

In a letter to Rosecrans expressing his disappointment, Morse wrote:

> You blame the San Diego people for not doing anything. This is very true. Nothing has been done, literally nothing. The reason with most of us is we are too poor to experiment...

Despite the report by Gen. Palmer, the Southern route across the United States gained support in Congress and from Eastern financial interests, and Rosecrans diverted his interest to the Frémont enterprise. The hopes of a San Diego already imbued with the enthusiasm of Horton had begun to rise once again.

By what route the proposed Memphis and El Paso was expected to enter San Diego, in view of the record of adverse governmental reports, was not known. As a transcontinental railroad it was still a "paper" line existing only in the minds of the promoters. It was thought engineers might arrive in San Diego at any time, to begin their own survey.

After he had resumed his sales campaign in San Francisco, Horton was approached by Rosecrans and introduced to two men who offered to buy all of his land for $100,000. But the crafty Horton hesitated and the bid was raised to $200,000 and then to $250,000. He wasn't convinced they had that kind of money, and anyway, if the land was worth that much he might as well proceed with building his city and keep all of the future profits to himself. It was a surprise and a disappointment to Rosecrans. The men did have the money and he had thought Horton would choose to sell and at last be able to live in comfort the rest of his life.

The acreage which Horton purchased had been in the 160-acre tracts marked out by United States surveyors after the war with Mexico, and while it was being resurveyed into lots, with corners marked by little flags as has been done by land speculators ever since, he pressed his promotion campaign, but the year dragged on with sales totaling only $3000.

Settlers were arriving but not in large numbers, though on October 29 the advance group of a huge wagon train from Texas rolled into San Diego. The train had 200 yoke of oxen and had negotiated the Jacumba Pass without difficulty. Most of them were Southerners still carrying the scars of bitterness, and many announced their intention of remaining in San Diego. Horton had arrived in San Diego as a Republican and soon learned that he had established himself in a town largely settled by Southerners

To the early-day cartoonists, there were two roads to California, to ruin or to happiness. To many, the first proved to be more exciting.

and which during the Civil War had been described as the "worst copperhead hole" in California. In the election of 1867 the state Democratic ticket led by Henry H. Haight for governor swept San Diego by a large majority, and, as the news reports had it, "many guns were fired and much strychnine whisky consumed by the faithful." With rising prosperity Horton soon got the newcomers on the right track by announcing that he would employ only Republicans, and for the next century with only occasional lapses from grace, San Diego voted Republican. In his correspondence for the *San Francisco Bulletin* for that period, Porter wrote:

> Old San Diego is full of people, many of whom are newcomers, and I think they are here in preference to New Town on account of better accommodations. The fact is New San Diego is not up to the mark in the matter of hotels. There are some good ones, but too small and crowded — not comfortable for families. Mr. Horton will have to take care of that matter himself or I fear it will not be done . . . we have a barber's shop, new restaurant, etc. . .

Many settlers had unceremoniously moved onto Davis' Folly, adjoining Horton's new subdivision, and its buildings, evidently including the Pantoja House across from a block marked out as a central plaza, were being occupied. Horton himself proceeded to purchase from William Heath Davis, one of the founders, a lot and building at State and F Streets for $100, and then sold it to Capt. S. S. Dunnells for $1000, for conversion into a hotel. In payment for papering the building, before its sale to Dunnells, Horton gave a corner lot in his own New San Diego to John Allyn. It was at the southeast corner of what in time became the principal busi-

This old newspaper sketch shows immigrant wagons rolling into San Diego. Even then it was expected to become a great railroad terminus.

SAN DIEGO, SOUTHERN CALIFORNIA

ness intersection on San Diego's Fifth Avenue and Broadway.

The heart of Horton's subdivision was Fifth Street, and the first building was his own office in the 300 block on Sixth Street. Free land was offered to those who would put up buildings. The dividing lines between Davis' Folly and Horton's development fused and disappeared and all of it became known generally as New San Diego.

On June 3, 900 additional acres of pueblo lands were sold at auction for subdivision for a total of $262. A few days later seven of the 160-acre lots were sold for $341. Matthew Sherman purchased two lots for $160 and A. Wilson bought two for only $22.

By the end of the year land was changing hands swiftly. Rancho Bernardo, once the 20,000-acre domain of a former English sea captain, Joseph Snook, who had had the good judgment to marry into a Spanish family, was auctioned off for $4020 and soon passed into the possession of Sheriff James McCoy. Lying across what is now Highway 395, it contained some of the best grazing land in the county and an abundance of water and wood. Three quarters of El Cajon Rancho, or El Cajon Valley, were purchased from the heirs of Don Miguel de Pedrorena for $35,000 by a group of investors who announced they would divide the valley into small farms. O. S. Witherby sold El Rincón del Diablo, now the site of Escondido.

Many of the newcomers were pioneers from other sections of the country where land was to be had for the taking, and they

Capt. S. S. Dunnells

OF THE SOUTHERN PACIFIC RAILWAY.

Dunnells' Hotel

Marcus Schiller

were frustrated or angered to find much of the rich acreage of Southern California already in other hands, and by the legal confusion surrounding titles coming down from Spain and Mexico, many of which were not to be cleared up for years. Government surveys did not always coincide with the rough *diseños* or maps of the original Spanish and Mexican grants.

In El Cajon Valley there was a question over the line of a survey, and as Porter noted in the *San Francisco Bulletin:*

> About fifty squatters have taken possession of as many quarter sections of land in that portion of the Cajon Valley not embraced in Jack Hays' survey, and, as many of them have some means, they intend to fight it out on that line. Maj. Chase (Levi Chase), as one of the owners, and also as agent for the rest or part of them, has prosecuted one or more of said squatters, who have even embraced his cultivated land in their claims. The prospect is that there will be lively times thereabouts before very long. Whether the squatters prevail or not, it is pretty certain that a large amount of the valley land in the Cajon will be cultivated speedily.

The strategic location of San Diego, at the southwest corner of the United States, with an open frontier and conditions still unsettled, was recognized by the federal government and the City Trustees were asked to formally convey to the government the southern portion of Point Loma, even though the military had claimed possession since 1852, for the building of fortifications and establishing a naval depot and a "harbor of refuge" for naval and commercial vessels, and permission from the Legislature to transfer the land was requested. As a consequence hopes rose that San Diego also would become an important military post, even though it had to fight the ambitions and maneuvers of its northern neighbor, Los Angeles. Los Angeles already had succeeded in having the mail for Tucson, Arizona, diverted to the route through San Bernardino and the San Gorgonio Pass, instead of through San Diego and Jacumba as authorized by the Post Office Department.

Porter reported to the *San Francisco Bulletin:*

> The Los Angeles folks do not look with favor at anything tending to promote the prosperity of this town, anyway, so the San Diegans must fight their own battles and expect no favors from our neighbors in Los Angeles.

The indefatigable Horton was busy lobbying in the state capitol at Sacramento for a franchise to build a wharf and though the Legislature did grant one to Horton and Morse, as partners, a similar franchise also was awarded to Stephen S. Culverwell. So San Diego would have two piers, one at Davis' New Town and the other at Horton's subdivision. Financing was another matter. Promises of aid were withdrawn when out-of-town backers learned that the financial centers of the state were not as enthusiastic as Horton about the future of San Diego, and he finally had to start his wharf with his own funds.

By the beginning of 1868, San Diego was feeling the first flush of a boom, and Porter reported to the *San Francisco Bulletin:*

For the first time in the history of San Diego a drug store is opened and in running order, as is also a jewelry store . . . Great improvement has been made during the past year in the aspect of the town generally. The unsightly old adobe house standing so long on the Plaza has been torn down and the rubbish removed. Dwelling houses are very scarce and difficult to obtain at any price by newcomers, but it is no great hardship to camp out in such a climate as this.

The adobe ruins in the Plaza were those of the Town Hall dating back to Spanish times. The Plaza had served as a town park during the late 1820's when the Spaniards had begun moving out of the crumbling walled presidio on the hill and erecting their adobe homes on the flats below. The principal public events held there were bullfights. It was Ephraim Morse, the New Englander, who first suggested that some of the town's 40,000 acres be set aside for a public park and on February 15, 1868, he presented a resolution to the Board of Trustees that two of the 160-acre tracts be selected and held for park purposes. It was adopted and Morse and Bush were chosen to select the land. Morse soon realized that

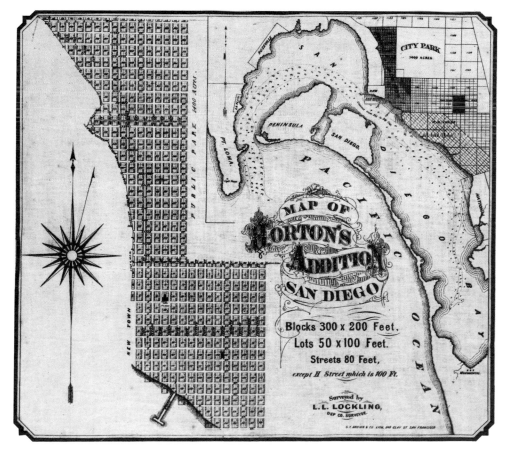

Horton's Addition, carved out of Spanish pueblo lands, soon was laid out in lots and streets and an era of booms and busts was born.

29

*Frank A. Kimball
as a young man*

Warren C. Kimball

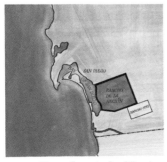

Rancho de la Nacion

in view of the tremendous acreage available to the city a much larger area could be set aside, and in later years he recalled that he and Horton selected the actual site of what became world-famous Balboa Park. They selected nine lots for a total acreage of 1440. The selection report was signed by Morse and Bush and the land set aside by the next Board of Trustees composed of Joshua Sloane, Marcus Schiller and José Estudillo. Though there was a surreptitious effort made in the State Legislature to slip in a clause permitting the sale of 480 acres, to the high indignation of San Diegans, the action of the trustees finally was ratified on February 4, 1870, though in the meantime forty acres had been disposed of.

It was the climate that brought three Kimball brothers to San Diego, and their influence on the area in its early days was to become almost as great as that of Horton. Frank A., Warren C. and Levi W. Kimball had resided in San Francisco and Oakland since leaving their home in Contoocook, a quiet and peaceful village in New Hampshire, in 1861. It was an old family that had been in the region since the mid-1700's, though their name appears in the records generally as Kimble. The brothers were successful carpenters and builders, as had been their father, but when the health of Frank, only thirty-six years old and the youngest of the three brothers, began to decline, they looked about for a more congenial climate. They searched the length of California, at one time taking an option on 48,000 acres near Los Angeles, and on another occasion, on 6000 acres on which Pasadena now stands. But they were not satisfied. Then in May of 1868, Frank Kimball, on a visit to the United States District Court and the General Land Office in San Francisco, found what he was looking for. On May 25 he noted in his diary that he was "getting ready to go to San Diego."

On June 1, 1868, he arrived at San Diego by stage coach and the next morning began a tour of the land surrounding the bay. On the following day he visited the old Spanish land grant, Rancho de la Nación, which embraced the present sites of National City and Chula Vista. It was owned by a financial firm in San Francisco. On June 15, Frank Kimball met with Francois Pioche in San Francisco and on behalf of himself and his two brothers agreed to buy the 26,632 acres of Rancho de la Nación with its six miles of waterfront for $30,000, of which $10,000 was paid in coin and $20,000 was to be paid in three annual payments at eight percent. The going price for open land in San Diego County was only little more than $1 an acre. This was up considerably, however, from the 27½ cents an acre which Horton had paid.

Two weeks later, on July 1, the three brothers knocked together a small dwelling on their ranch, and soon after completed arrangements for a survey to determine the exact boundaries of their forty-two square miles of land. With the experience of Horton before them, and convinced of the coming of a railroad and of the future of the port, they, too, would build a city. They cleared and laid out a thoroughfare 100 feet wide and six miles long through the entire ranch, and chose the northwest corner as the site for the first building development. Streets were cleared and lots marked off. They named their town National City.

Not to be outdone, Louis Rose, who had come to San Diego over the Gila Trail from Texas in 1850, hoped for the revival of La Playa, where he had invested heavily many years before in the expectation that the first transcontinental railroad would naturally terminate at the historic ship anchorage behind Ballast Point.

As Porter reported to the *San Francisco Bulletin:*

Our old friend and fellow citizen, Louis Rose, . . . is soon to receive some cargoes of lumber for building purposes, and I doubt not (will) have it landed at the Playa where he intends founding the real San Diego. I hear he intends to erect a tenement thereon, expecting in this manner to start quite a village immediately. Success to him, I say, for his perseverance and faith deserve it. He is already quite an old gentleman, but he firmly believes that he shall live to see his pet city one of the wonders of the coast.

The name of Rose lives on, in Roseville, on Point Loma, and in Rose Canyon.

The promotional activities of Horton were producing results at last, and many persons were picking up their belongings and deserting the colder northern counties for the gentler climate of San Diego. In September of 1868 Porter was able to report to the *San Francisco Bulletin:*

Louis Rose

New Town is going onward with its new houses, and Mr. Horton's wharf has a very city-like appearance, being built substantially. I think some 200 feet are already finished, and the work seems to be progressing rapidly. Mr. Culverwell has a wharf for his lighters, which will facilitate the discharge of cargoes very much . . . As matters now stand, it is almost impossible for a man to get a hold of a piece of Government land within 20 miles of this place which is not claimed by someone . . . there seems to be no way left for a poor honest man to get hold of any land for himself but to purchase of speculators.

Culverwell's wharf projected due west from what is now the intersection of Pacific Highway and F Street, while Horton's extended southwest from what is now the intersection of Harbor Drive and Fourth Avenue.

A great deal of the land in the immediate vicinity of San Diego was tied up in the claims involving the Mexican grant of the lands

Joseph Nash

William Jeff Gatewood

(Foldout opposite page) This is a facsimile of the first edition of The San Diego Union, *published on October 10, 1868. A weekly, it became a daily in 1871.*

of the San Diego Mission to the family of the old Don, Santiago Arguello. Another election that year had released more of the town's pueblo lands and they were being sold in competition with Horton's lots in New San Diego and the lots privately owned in Davis' Folly. But the tide of development began to swing in Horton's favor when construction of a two-story hotel, The Bay View, and a large one in relation to Dunnells' and the Franklin House in Old Town, was started at Twelfth Avenue and I Street by R. D. Case.

Horton was successful in persuading a young Englishman who had accumulated a considerable stake in Australia and New Zealand, and whom he had met in San Francisco, to open a general store. He was Joseph Nash. At that time there were only twenty-three residents in New Town. Nash's first store was at State and G Streets, but he soon moved it to Horton's Addition, at Fifth Avenue and J Street.

Matthew Sherman, who had served in both the Navy and Army in the Mexican and Civil Wars, and had married the town's only school teacher and brought education to another of its periodic halts, jumped in and carved out a little subdivision of his own, Sherman's Addition, which adjoined Horton's on the southeast. Others quickly followed suit. In October, the Rev. Sidney Wilbur arrived and began clearing out the deserted owl roost which had once been the Army barracks, preparatory to conducting Episcopal services.

San Diego had been without a newspaper for eight years, since the suspension of the weekly *San Diego Herald* in 1860. In the spring of 1868 Philip Crosthwaite, who had been an otter fur hunter in Lower California when war with Mexico began, and now laid claim to much of the Mission Valley lands, visited his sister in San Andreas, a gold town in Calaveras County, in northern California, where her husband, William Jeff Gatewood, an attorney, published the local newspaper, the *Register*. Crosthwaite was so enthusiastic about the future of San Diego that Col. Gatewood, as he was known, decided to take a look for himself. He did, was impressed, and returned to San Andreas, suspended the *Register* and prepared to move.

The heavily-bearded colonel, though a native of Kentucky, was straight out of the sentimental and romantic age that had begun just before the Civil War. In obeying the code of personal honor he had shot and killed one of his friends in a duel arising out of a political squabble. The story is told in the *San Andreas Independent* for September 17, 1859:

For several days past, we have heard suspicions rumored about town that a duel was in contemplation between two gentlemen residents here, but nothing was known publicly, as whatever arrangements were being made were kept secret. On Thursday night, however, it was pretty generally suspected that a meeting was arranged for the next morning between William J. Gatewood, Esq., and Dr. P. Goodwyn...

Early yesterday morning, four or five carriages containing the principals, seconds, surgeons and a few friends left town... coming to a halt on the flat near Foreman's. Here they alighted and proceeded to measure off the ground. The agreement was to fight with rifles, distance 40 yards...

The principals are reported to have appeared cool and to have exchanged courtesies at the moment of taking positions assigned by the seconds. The word was given thus: "Are you ready? Fire, one, two, three."

At the moment three was about to be articulated, both sprung the triggers of their rifles. Dr. Goodwyn's hung fire and he lost his shot. Mr. Gatewood's shot struck Goodwyn in the abdomen, ranging obliquely and downward, passing out at the hip.

The San Diego Union's first home in 1868

Immediately upon Dr. Goodwyn's fall, Mr. Gatewood advanced toward him, extending his hand and remarking: "Doctor, I am very sorry that this affair has terminated this way, so very sorry, indeed." To which the doctor replied: "I am glad to know that you acted like a gentleman." Gatewood thanked him for his kind remark and left the field with his surgeon.

Dr. Goodwyn lived only a few hours. No blame attached to Gatewood. He had acted out the drama as the times and conditions demanded.

The hand press and printing equipment of the *Register* were brought to San Diego by steamer and installed in a small frame building in Old Town which had been built by the Pedrorena family. Don Miguel de Pedrorena had married a daughter of José Antonio Estudillo, a grand Don of the Spanish and Mexican days whose great adobe casa in later years became known as Ramona's Marriage Place. The frame building, still standing in 1964, was situated just behind the Estudillo House and evidently was rented to Gatewood.

E. W. Bushyhead

The first issue of *The San Diego Union* came off the press on October 10, 1868. Associated with Gatewood in the venture was Edward W. Bushyhead, though for a time the publisher was listed as J. N. Briseño, who is believed to have been a printer. In an editorial, Gatewood told San Diego that its newspaper would be neutral politically, and that:

The *Union* will be a faithful mirror, reflecting from its pages times of distress as well as of prosperity—hopes and fears, gloom and gayety and smiles and tears. A faithful chronicler of today, and a future reliable historian of the past. Along its columns shall grow the daily record of works, enterprises and improvements, that will linger upon the earth long after we and our dreams and hopes shall have been laid quietly beneath the sod...

We only pray that our lives may be spared to see the waters of our bay fretting beneath the burdens of a heavy commerce—to hear the shrill whistle of the iron horse as it spurns the sand of the desert—toils over the mountains and shoots through the valleys in its flight from the Atlantic to meet in our harbor the rich cargoes from the Orient—to see our bay surrounded by mammoth manufacturing and mercantile houses, princely residences, domes and spires of churches and schools of learning—the streets teeming with a prosperous and industrious people, and our lovely valleys lifting to our genial skies flowers and fruits, in tints as varied and gorgeous as our incomparable sunsets.

The editors of *The San Diego Union* made a survey of New Town and reported there were twenty houses under construction. Horton offered to whitewash the south and west sides to improve their appearance for visitors arriving by steamer. Thomas Whaley, the merchant, wrote to his wife that "there is no mistake about San Diego. The county is rapidly settling up and soon all the land will be taken up." The editors, however, were upset by an article in a national magazine which said that San Francisco was the only port on the Pacific Coast. *The San Diego Union* dismissed the author as a swindler.

Even though Point Loma was considered within the pueblo and the State Legislature had not granted the city authority, as requested, to transfer any lands to the federal government for military purposes, in the closing months of the year the United States government moved to take 750 to 1000 acres of Point Loma for a military reservation. The steamer *Oriflamme* joined the *Orizaba* on a regular schedule to San Diego, a number of immigrant trains arrived from Texas, and, as in Mexican days, bull fights continued in the Plaza to the general disgust of the newcomers. Many wells were sunk in New Town though water was sold at 10 cents a bucket from casks on a water wagon, that is, until the salesman lost both of his legs as a result of gunshot, according to the *memoirs* of Daniel Cleveland, pioneer attorney. San Diego also was convinced of its future as a silk producing area and Ephraim Morse imported 65,000 mulberry trees and 105,000 cuttings, to grow silk worms, and thousands of them were planted in the Sweetwater River Valley. The Whaley House in Old Town was taken over by the Board of Supervisors for county offices and a courtroom, and the second story was converted into a theater, and traveling companies of actors brought a brush of culture. A number of the new Texas families settled in the Jacumba Valley and soon reported the discovery of three or four leads of silver in the nearby hills and *The San Diego Union* said it was the opinion of the settlers that gold and silver abounded in the mountains.

Daniel Cleveland

THE TRAIN THAT
NEVER CAME

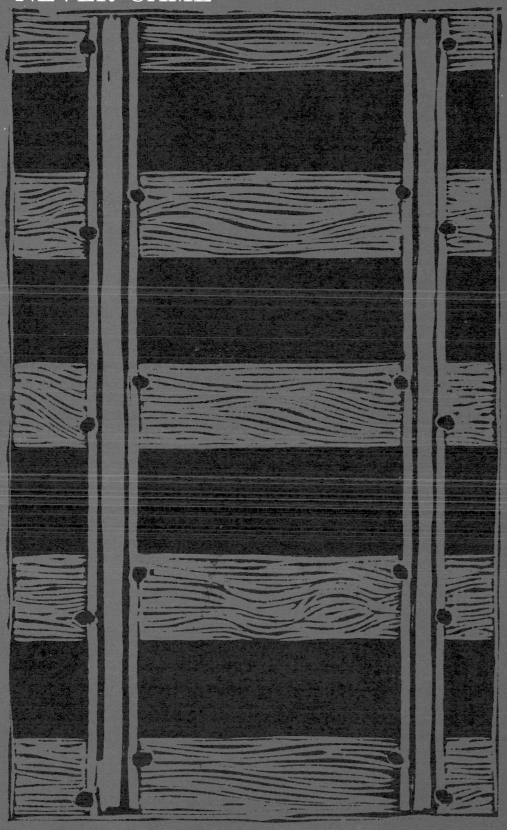

CHAPTER III

A visitor returned to San Diego after the absence of a year and
couldn't believe his eyes. It was a city, as the Poet of the Sierra,
Joaquin Miller, wrote, "as suddenly born as if shot from a gun."
Horton had his salesmen everywhere, even as far as Fort Yuma
at the crossing of the Colorado River, where they told the weary
immigrants looking out over the bleak wastes of the desert basin,
all about "the land of the sundown sea" that lay just over the
horizon of the mountains.

The visitor in a letter to *The San Diego Union*, wrote:

It is true that when I was here Horton had a town on paper—that everybody
was ready to make an affidavit that Horton was insane and should be sent
to Stockton—but today that paper town is a live city, full of active, energetic
householders, who have built good houses and are now busy in the development
of and beautifying of their homes. The same men who were then ready to swear
that Horton was crazy, are now scratching their heads anxiously, inquiring
of their nearest relatives if anyone accuses them of belonging to the "dam
phule family."

In the spring *The San Diego Union* was able to report that 120
houses had been erected and completed in New Town since July 4,
and that "the music of plane and hammer can be heard in every
direction," and that the streets were filled with teams carrying
freight from San Diego to Fort Yuma. Horton was selling $600

to $1000 worth of lots every day. On one occasion they rose to
$6000 and settlers and speculators had to stand in line to hand
over their money.

The personal success of Horton and the rapid rise of New Town
aroused the animosity of many residents of Old Town and a number of law suits were instituted seeking to set aside the deeds by
which Horton had obtained his lands. Charles DeWolf filed suit

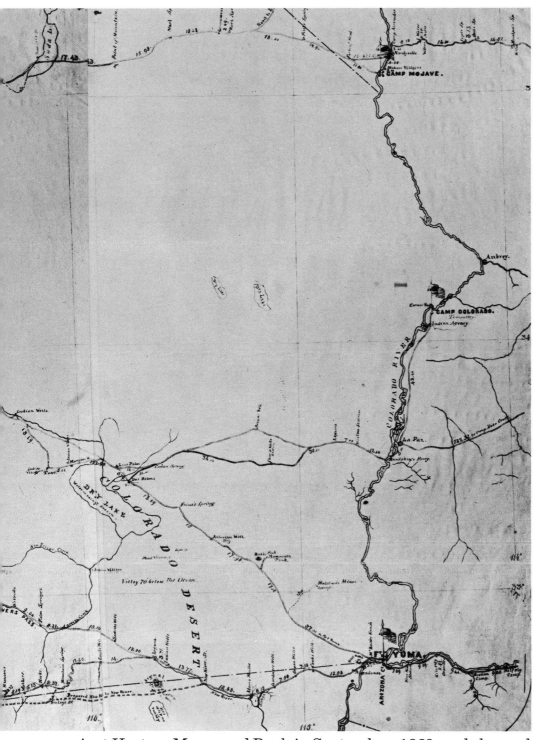

Roads to Southern California were mostly trails between Army Posts, mountain passes and the coast as shown in this Army sketch of 1869.

against Horton, Morse and Bush in September, 1869, and charged that the City Trustees had illegally disposed of the pueblo lands, because the city had not been in debt as stipulated by law, that there had been collusion between them and Horton, that Morse profited as a trustee and as a purchaser with Horton.

The suits touched off a wave of landjumping. Newcomers rushed onto Horton's lands and began fencing them off and claiming squatter's rights. But the owners fought back, and as in one case cited by *The San Diego Union* of December 16:

A would-be smart alec by the name of Stapleton, hailing from San Francisco, took it into his head on Thursday last to appropriate a block of land in Horton's Addition by fencing the same without leave or license of the owner, Mr. Frank M. Pixley, of San Francisco. He dug the post holes, put in the posts, and was in the act of putting on the boards when about 200 of the best people in New Town turned out in mass, took up the posts, piled up the lumber on top of the posts, sprinkled a little kerosene oil on the whole and applied a match and then, Ye Gods, there was a bonfire that would have done credit to all the politicians in the United States. It was huge. It was fine. It was glorious, and we hope the light that went up from that fire will open the eyes of the rest of the would-be smarties that come here filled with unholy desire to gobble up other people's property. Jumping property that you have no claim to won't pay in this locality, gentlemen. . .

In time Horton won in court. His title was upheld. The sale of more pueblo lands followed and the foundations were beginning to be laid for the city that was to come and the agriculture that was to turn a semi-arid land into an empire.

The lower Otay and Tia Juana River Valleys were opened as public lands, under the laws of the United States, and settlers rushed onto the fertile bottom country that had been enriched by a winter of heavy rains. The descendants of Don Santiago Arguello fought them off, as squatters. The Arguellos contended that all the land from La Punta, their home at the foot of the bay, to the border, was included in Rancho Milíjo, a Mexican grant. But the United States Land Commission had rejected the Arguello claim and now rejected it for the second time.

By May, Gatewood, who had dedicated *The San Diego Union* to a lifelong fight for civic morality and progress, sold his interest to Charles P. Taggart. Gatewood had been elected president of the reorganized San Diego & Gila Railroad, which held public lands for rights of way and the terminal for any line that might come in, and was sent to Memphis to represent San Diego at a national railroad convention. When he returned, he resumed the practice of law.

A few days after he had left for the railroad conference, the Atlantic and Pacific coasts were linked by rail for the first time. The Central and Union Pacific lines came together at Promontory Point, fifty-three miles west of Ogden, Utah, on May 10, 1869.

What this meant to the people of the United States is best described by Frederick B. Goddard in the book, *Where to Emigrate, and Why,* which was published in that same year. Goddard wrote:

The people of the Pacific Coast experience a just feeling of pride in the Central Pacific Road, and have rejoiced in its completion as the dawn of a brilliant future for that entire region. Already every branch of commercial industry on the coast has begun to glow with new life, in anticipation of the impulse which a finished railway communication across the continent will give to trade and enterprise. Eastern Asia and Japan, the innumerable islands of the Pacific, and farther India, will all contribute to the wonderful traffic which will mingle in a common current and float to the western terminus of the Pacific Railroad...

During the last two years more than six hundred thousand sturdy immigrants have landed upon our shores, and there is no ebb to the flowing tide. Our land is ringing with the din of her internal improvements; cottages are springing up far away to the west upon sunny acres where, but yesterday, roamed the Indian and the buffalo. Grand lines of railroad are stretching out across the continent—iron monsters resting upon either ocean, swallowing the values of one hemisphere to void them upon the other—revealing what our first Great Emigrant, Columbus, vainly sought to manifest in the gloom of earlier ages—that the shortest way to the Indies was *via* America.

John Charles Frémont

Though he had visited San Diego in July, Gen. Morton C. Hunter, representing Gen. Frémont and the Memphis and El Paso railroad, returned in September with an official party which included Thomas S. Sedgwick, the chief engineer; Gen. Rosecrans; William H. Seward, who as Secretary of State in 1867 had negotiated the purchase of Alaska; and several congressmen. They arrived from San Francisco on the *Orizaba* at 7:30 on the morning of September 22, and landed at Horton's wharf. Several hundred persons were on hand, the Town Band played, and *The San Diego Union* commented that "those who had just arrived rushed ashore to invest in real estate, so as to have a good excuse for being enthusiastic."

Champagne corks popped at a reception in the Franklin House in Old Town and that evening, to be impartial, the proceedings were moved to New Town, in Gregg's Hall, with 500 persons crowded inside and 1000 outside. Engineer Sedgwick said he was there to begin building the railroad to San Diego and to break the monopoly of the Central Pacific. San Diego promptly offered $500,000 in land and rights that had been held by the San Diego & Gila in exchange for railroad stock. The next month some survey work was undertaken between the town and the mountain crossing.

Frank and Warren Kimball's wagon, 1868

However, Frank Kimball had secretly visited Gen. Hunter and offered him 500 acres if he would see that the railroad terminated on the bay in National City, and 500 blocks additional if the terminal, shops and depot were also located on his lands. The offer was accepted, and the Kimball brothers had stolen the proposed terminal from New Town and Old Town without the knowledge of Horton or the rest of San Diego. That San Diego had a future as a great trading center, with a transcontinental railroad terminating somewhere along its splendid harbor opening to the commerce of the Pacific, seemed more assured than ever

(Next page)
In this painting the last spike is driven to link transcontinental railroads. From then on, it was "California here we come..."

41

when word was received that Congress had passed the bill designating San Diego as a port of entry.

A survey party for the Memphis and El Paso gave assurance that the railroad could be built, that the descent to the desert through Carrizo Gorge could be accomplished by a grade of less than eighty feet per mile. The route chosen was from the bay up a branch of Otay Valley and by way of Jamul to Milquatay Valley, thence to Summit Pass in Walker Canyon and into Carrizo Gorge at the northern end of Jacumba Valley. The highest elevation was 3850 feet.

A second newspaper made its appearance, Republican in policy and apparently encouraged and financed by Horton and Morse, in New or South San Diego, in opposition to *The San Diego Union* whose loyalty was attached to Old Town. The *San Diego Weekly Bulletin* began publishing on August 21, 1869, with William H. Gould as editor and publisher. It wasn't long before the two publications were battling for subscribers, and *The San Diego Union* was forced to take formal public notice of its competitor, though not perhaps in the spirit expressed in Gatewood's original editorial dedication. *The San Diego Union* stated:

> From the date of its first appearance, it has been the special organ of Mr. A. E. Horton, and has been noteworthy only for the publication of some two columns per week of the most remarkable ungrammatical sentences under which typers have ever writhed . . . its circulation is trifling at home, and fortunately for the reputation of the place, but few copies have ever gone abroad.

Frank Kimball was selling land at $17 an acre for which he paid a little more than $1, and though wells were providing an adequate supply for residential purposes, farming depended on a variable weather with an average rainfall of ten inches a year, and the Kimball brothers were among the first to realize that irrigation would prove to be necessary. They formed a water company to obtain and hold the water rights to the Sweetwater River. San Bernardo Rancho which had been purchased by Sheriff McCoy for $4000 was sold for $35,000 to a group of northern California investors. These sales, and the crops being raised, refuted the contention that San Diego had little agricultural potential. The J. W. Gale & Company reported it had sold 2500 pounds of seed corn for planting and had ordered 2000 pounds more. It sold 2000 orange trees and 400 walnut trees to be planted in the Sweetwater Valley, and also had sold several hundred dollars worth of apple, lime and lemon trees, "all of which goes in the virgin soil of San Diego County." Lee Utt, of San Luis Rey, and Charles P. Taggart, the new co-owner of *The San Diego Union*, were planting 2000 orange trees on land adjoining Horton's. Grain and barley crops crept across El Cajon, San Luis Rey and Tia Juana Valleys. Cattle were still the mainstay of the ranchos remaining in private hands, and Cave J. Couts of Rancho Guajome started 600 head toward the northern markets and large herds were being assembled at Rancho Santa Margarita for other drives, as had been done since the days of the Gold Rush.

The editor of *The San Diego Union* paid a first visit to La Jolla, or La Joya, as it was then spelled, and was entranced:

> We had the pleasure of a ride to this noted place on Sunday last. Every person having any poetry in his soul, or an eye for the beautiful and the grand in nature, should take a pilgrimage to La Joya. The deep caverns in the rocks and the roar of the wild waves, the sea mosses to be gathered, all go to make this one of the most desirable places to visit about San Diego. There is a beautiful valley leading back from the beach that is being settled by Mr. Butler and Mr. Fredley, each having eighty acres of land. The soil is very rich and the vegetation rank. The mustard is from 10 to 15 feet high. Mr. B. is sinking a well. He is down forty-five feet, but no water yet. Mr. F. has just commenced his well . . . The Sizer brothers are east of La Joya, about two miles and have a very promising place. They have good fresh water at a depth of 14 feet and plenty of it. Their vineyard of 5,000 vines is doing well. The vegetable garden is doing fine. We expect to eat watermelon at this place on the Fourth of July. Vegetables will not grow in San Diego! "Oh, no?"

These were the first settlers in La Jolla, as far as is known. The Sizer brothers, Samuel and Daniel, in 1869 bought two pueblo lots of eighty acres each for $1.25 an acre. The land lay between La Jolla Boulevard and Fay Street and Palomar and Marine Streets. John Butler purchased another pueblo lot for the same price in the little valley through which winds the Torrey Pines road. F. Fredley followed him by purchasing the pueblo lands lying just behind the present La Jolla Beach and Tennis Club.

The incoming tide of people pushed against others, and the law struggled to bring about protection of life and property. Chinese were coming into California in swiftly increasing numbers, most

The mountain barrier was a challenge to settlers and even as late as 1880 wagons had to pick their way through wild areas of rock and heat.

of them unmarried and bent to labor by which they hoped some day to return to their homeland, either to be with their families or to be at last buried. The railroad over the High Sierra could not have been built without them. Others found a livelihood in menial work spurned by white men in an era of exploitation and speculation. In San Diego the Chinese began to erect small shacks along the waterfront, between the Horton and Culverwell wharves, and with their odd junks were bringing fish to local markets and beginning an industry that was still an important one a century later. But with unemployment appearing in the north, the first pangs of racial trouble were being experienced. One night a fire was set underneath a Chinese laundry at the foot of K Street, where a number of people were asleep, though the reports of the incident failed to state whether anyone was burned.

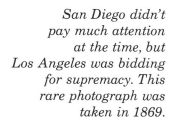

San Diego didn't pay much attention at the time, but Los Angeles was bidding for supremacy. This rare photograph was taken in 1869.

Stage service was irregular, with many new lines springing up from time to time. It was an era of free but rough competition, and, though the records are few, a network linking the areas of San Diego County, and San Diego to other communities, was gradually formed. Two stage companies competed for business between Old and New San Diego, the C. North Stage Line and A. C. Tedford's Pioneer Stage, early in 1869. Late in 1869 the Carpenter Line of Los Angeles installed a Concord coach running from Old Town to New Town several times daily, but it wasn't until December that William Tweed put on a daily stage from New Town to Kimball's development, or National City.

In Old Town, Alfred L. Seeley operated the 130-mile San Diego-Los Angeles Stage Line, using his remodeled Franklin Hotel as a depot. Passenger and mail stages bound for Los Angeles left San

Diego at 5 a.m. on Monday, Wednesday and Friday. The trip required twenty-four hours with an overnight stop at San Juan Capistrano. Way stations for changing horses were generally eighteen to twenty miles apart, but the main depot stations on the Los Angeles route were San Dieguito, Encinitas, San Luis Rey, Las Flores, San Juan Capistrano, Anaheim, Los Nietos and Los Angeles, in that order.

In October of 1868 a published schedule showed at that time that mail arrived at San Diego from Fort Yuma on Monday and Thursday and departed on Sunday and Wednesday, but the evidence indicates that J. J. Tomlinson had given up and the mail was being carried over the Jacumba Pass to Fort Yuma and Tucson in local buckboards. Dunnells' New San Diego Hotel served as the depot in New Town.

In November of 1868 Seeley announced that he would begin

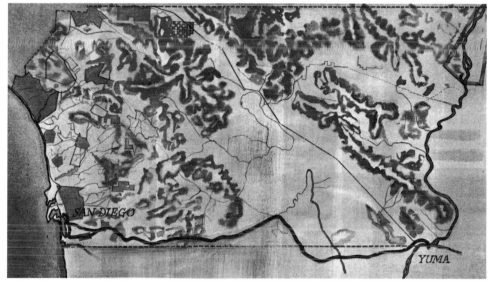

A stage route to Yuma was San Diego's first achievement. It ran partly through Mexico and gave rise to hopes for a railroad route.

operation of the San Diego and Fort Yuma Stage Company, using Concord coaches. However, on December 19 *The San Diego Union* complained that there was no stage service to Yuma, and that at least one stage should run on a weekly service.

A new route again was taken up and money raised among local citizens under the leadership of stageman John Capron. As a result, the first San Diego-Yuma route to run all within United States territory was laid out by the county surveyor, James Pascoe, early in 1869. It was twenty-five miles shorter than the old wagon trail through Warner's Pass to Yuma, and it had fifty-five miles less of desert travel. Pascoe's route turned up the Otay River course at La Punta, thirteen miles south of San Diego. It followed the river to the Otay Lake basin, passing through Otay, Janal and Jamul Ranchos, then traced the course of Dulzura Creek easterly through the valleys, climbing into the summit country of San Diego's eastern mountain barrier along the course followed by the present State Route 94 through Potrero and Campo. It crossed the high rolling country by way of Milquatay Valley, twelve miles from Campo to Jacumba, then passed ten miles from Jacumba eastward and down the steep grade at Mountain Springs. It was eighty-six miles from San Diego to the head of the desert. From there it was 110 miles across the desert to Yuma.

Low wooden structures made New San Diego look like any rough town of the Old West. This is a view down lower Fifth Street in 1871.

Seeley & Wright made Bandini House a hotel, 1870

The long hoped-for commercial connections with the inland area of San Bernardino were beginning to materialize, and Miller and Schaffer Company stages to San Bernardino were running over the 165-mile route so heavily loaded that on one trip one of them carried twenty-five passengers. Settlements were growing up at Ballena, fifty miles into the backcountry, and at Warner's, seventy-five miles away by wagon, and Samuel Warnock, a rancher who had carried the first military mail from San Diego to Fort Yuma in 1854, announced on March 17, 1869, that he and three partners were starting the Ballena to San Diego Stage Company. Marre & Company started a regular San Diego-Santo Tomas, Lower California, line in mid-November of 1869.

With an expanding passenger business, Seeley required a larger hotel as a depot and on May 1, 1869, he purchased the crumbling casa of the late Don Juan Bandini, once the finest residence in Old Town and host to all the famed personalities of the conquest, and added a second story and converted it into a hotel and stage terminal. New Town got its first Post Office on April 8, 1869, in the drug store of Dr. Jacob Allen on Fifth below F Street. It was designated "South San Diego" and Old Town was listed as "San Diego." The conversion of the Bandini House into a large hotel and depot posed a problem for Horton and his plans for New San Diego. He offered Seeley a block of land between Fourth and Fifth Avenus and E and F Streets if he would desert Old Town. Seeley replied, according to the *memoirs* of Daniel Cleveland, a lawyer:

Old Town is *the* town, the real San Diego; your mushroom town . . . will soon peter out, and all the people who want to travel will have to come to Old Town to take the stage.

Capron apparently failed to carry the mail to Yuma and Tucson over the new route on the promised schedule of three times a week and the contract was shifted to Seeley who already was running the mail to San Diego from Los Angeles. He took a partner, Charles Wright, and while their Concord coaches were leaving for Los Angeles from his new Cosmopolitan Hotel they evidently used only buckboards on the run to Yuma. Service was no better than that of their predecessors.

The citizens were enraged at the indifference to schedules and the continuing reluctance of contractors to deliver the Tucson mail by way of San Diego, despite all promises to the contrary. Seeley was accused of "coming to the first drinking place out of the city of the Angels and then hurrying back the next day." Before the end of the year Capron was back on the Yuma run, but was avoiding the difficult Mountain Springs grade by driving his buckboards through Mexican territory.

The roads were difficult enough just to negotiate by coach or wagon without the added hazard of armed robbery. The stage from Los Angeles was held up and robbed and then the same four bandits, stripped to the buff, or waist, held up the Yuma stage sixteen miles out from the fort. They were after the Wells, Fargo & Company treasure box. As far as San Diego was concerned, Wells, Fargo & Company was a forwarding company which used local stages for shipments of valuables. When the command to halt was ignored, they shot one of the horses, the off-wheeler, but the six passengers were in possession of a shotgun and three revolvers and fired back. One of the bandits received a charge of buckshot in the stomach and the others fled under fire. The three survivors were later captured with the aid of Indian trackers and sentenced to prison.

The stage was here and the railroad, despite the surveys that had been made, and they were casual at best, still seemed as far away as ever. Only three miles of track had been laid in Texas and only six locomotives purchased. Then came disquieting reports out of France. The agents of Gen. Frémont had gone to the financial center of Paris to sell their railroad bonds, and though

John G. Capron

John Capron's mail stages ran to Yuma and then to Tucson

William Tweed

there had been an initial rush to buy them, it soon became known that the representations made by his agents, that the United States government had offered huge land grant subsidies and had guaranteed the bonds and the interest, were false. Buyers rushed to unload the bonds and a panic developed.

San Diegans also began to realize that the Southern Pacific Railroad was merely a creature of the Central Pacific and the "Big Four," Collis P. Huntington, Mark Hopkins, Leland Stanford and Charles Crocker, and they intended to monopolize the rail business in California, and that its line was not coming down the coast to San Diego. The Southern Pacific had shifted inland and was going down the Central Valleys, and at the Tehachapi it intended to run a branch eastward to block any line seeking to enter California.

Investors in the financial centers of California became wary of the situation in San Diego and the boom began to wear a bit thin. Joseph Nash, his shelves stocked to overflowing, cut his prices twenty-five percent below cost. In Old Town Thomas Whaley and Philip Crosthwaite, partners in a general store, were selling cheap for cash, as was Joseph Mannasse.

For weeks fires had raged across the mesas and the mountain slopes. They evidently had been started by squatters burning off grass and brush, and once out of control had ringed San Diego with flames and spread a haze of apprehension. It had been trying enough to learn that the planting seasons in Southern California were the reverse of what they had experienced elsewhere, and that summer meant no or little rain, and now came a dry winter and some of the newcomers' enthusiasm for Southern California turned to fright. The grass was gone and crops failed to sprout on the hard waterless mesas. Cattlemen sent their stock into the higher mountain pastures.

In this period of doubt and distress *The San Diego Union* reported there were several gentlemen prospecting in the mountains and they had sent samples of rock to San Francisco for assaying. Placer gold was washed out of sands in Peñasquitos Canyon and along the San Bernardo, or San Dieguito River, and near San Ysidro. Six silver strikes were located by a man named Walker in the Jacumba Mountains. By the first of the year the town was thrown into an uproar when a Mexican came into the McDonald and Gale lumber and building supply establishment near Horton's wharf and deposited 100 pounds of gold and silver amalgam which he had dug up about sixty miles south of the border. *The San Diego Union* cautioned people not to get excited.

William Tweed's stage line serviced Julian Gold Rush, 1870

THE MOUNTAIN THAT SPOUTED GOLD

The discovery of gold sent thousands into Cuyamaca Mountains. Artist Marjorie Reed Creese depicts ore being ground on stone arrastras.

CHAPTER IV

In the dry winter of 1869-70 Fred Coleman, a rancher who resided with an Indian family in a high little valley north of the Cuyamacas and west of the huge bulk that comprises Volcan Mountain, was riding his horse along a creek and, halting to let it drink, glanced down and saw some small yellow particles. The story persists that Coleman, whose real name was A. H. Coleman, was a Negro who had fled the South for the gold fields of northern California, and then had drifted down into the mountainous region of San Diego County. He was sure that he knew gold when he saw it. He dismounted and using a pan from his pack, washed out a few nuggets.

The creek is now known as Coleman Creek and it flows down from the mountains southwest of the town of Julian through Spencer Valley on its way to the head of the San Diego River. Gnarled oaks grow out of split granite boulders in the exposed bed of a creek which during the winter rushes toward the sea carrying the melted snows of the Cuyamacas. Spencer Valley is a mere stop on the road lifting into the mountains, but it has a settlement named Wynola and is known for its fine apples.

Its elevation of about 3600 feet puts it 700 feet above the wide fertile plain of Santa Ysabel Valley two and a half miles below. It is 500 feet below Julian, which is about four miles farther up into the wooded mountains so often shrouded in winter clouds. State Highways 78 and 79 follow Coleman Creek from just below Julian and into Spencer Valley, crossing it twice on the route to Santa Ysabel, where Highway 79 turns north along the base of the mountain mass to the Warner Springs while Highway 78 proceeds west along the historical route of Gen. Stephen Watts Kearny who crossed the Santa Ysabel Valley on the way to Ramona and to the Battle of San Pasqual in the conquest of California.

Coleman's discovery of placer gold occurred some time in late January or early February of 1870, and he was quick to spread the word, "gold!" Other casual prospectors and homesteaders began panning the waters of Coleman Creek and gold in significant amounts, enough to return at least $2 and $3 a day, was being taken out. In a short time scores of men were wading the creek and following its twisting course and that of other streams up into the hills and into the pine and cedar forests of Volcan Mountain and the Cuyamacas. The hills were described as alive with excited men.

Mining authorities placed little faith in the finding of placer gold, as it had long been found throughout the region, and the skeptical *San Francisco Bulletin* reported on February 12 that the excitement in San Diego resulting from the gold brought up from Lower California already had died out:

The stories of rich diggings in Lower California, just over the line, appear to have been put in circulation by a few persons with a design of getting rid, temporarily, of several hundred people who can find no employment in the city... San Diego has been injured by this disreputable trick. One of the newspapers, *The Weekly Bulletin*, has shown no wisdom in giving currency to wild statements . . . *The San Diego Union* on the other hand has discouraged the excitement and expressed a total lack of confidence in the stories that were told. What San Diego wants just now is what is ably advocated by the latter paper—namely a good wagon road to Fort Yuma.

The San Diego Union lost some of its assurance when in finally acknowledging the Coleman discovery, it reported on March 10 that:

On Thursday last, a load of some 1500 pounds of rich gold-bearing quartz as we have ever seen came in from the Cuyamaca Country and a specimen weighing perhaps ten pounds, and containing at least $100 in gold, was left at our office . . .

Of course the arrival of so large a quantity of rich gold-bearing quartz created intense excitement in town. A stampede immediately ensued and the road has now for several days been lined with teams of every description and men mounted and on foot enroute to the mines. From persons who returned yesterday we learned that there are now on the ground not less than 600 persons and the number is daily increasing.

The gold quartz was brought to San Diego from the first real strike made by H. C. Bickers on February 20. A prospector who had worked fields in California and Idaho, he had answered the latest call of placer gold in San Diego County, and one morning while following the tracks of a bear he wandered up a ravine through the pine trees above the site of the present town of Julian, and saw a bunch of quartz rocks. An examination revealed the presence of free gold.

He hurried back to his companions, George Gower, a surveyor, and J. Bruen Wells, a preacher, at their mountain camp, but as it was Sunday and Wells would not even look at the rocks, they put off any action until the following day.

As Bickers later told the story:

> On the following morning I took tools and started for the spot, inviting Gower to accompany me . . . On Tuesday, the 22nd, the news got around, and men began to show themselves, looking for the extensions. So, in a highly excited state of mind, Gower wrote a note commencing with my name, then Gower, then Wells, then my son, then his son, then Wells spoke of some brother in New York, Gower more sons, and Bickers more sons, until 21 names had been set down, covering a space from New York to San Francisco and also covering the ledge for the space of 4,200 feet.

Mining claims were limited to 200 feet of ground for each person, or partner. As the day was George Washington's Birthday, they named their mine the George Washington and their nearby camp in the Julian Valley, Mount Vernon. Except for the presence

Among the legends of the discovery of gold is that of the Gorman boy who found gold-bearing quartz on the hill above present Julian.

Horace Fenton Wilcox

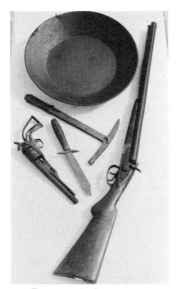

Prospector's equipment

Mike Julian

of trees, the site of the first mine can be seen from the highway entering the town of Julian on Washington Street. The mine lies beyond the end of Washington Street, up a curving tree-shaded ravine.

Another version of the discovery of gold-bearing quartz rock has been left by Horace F. Wilcox, who resided in Julian for half a century, and he said it had been told to him by Drury Bailey. There were only six families living in the north Cuyamacas and in the vicinity of Volcan Mountain, and one of them, the Gormans, with their four children were camped in the Julian area. The eldest boy, Billy, thirteen years of age, had been sent out for firewood and hiking up the same ravine on the side of "Gold Hill" found white rocks with yellow veins and took them to his father, who recognized them for what they were. But the Gorman family, if it existed, quickly faded into the legends of Julian.

The three men who did file on the George Washington claim dug out more than a ton of ore, packed it and loaded it onto the backs of mules, and Bickers and Gowers delivered it to San Diego. After leaving it on display for a time in Dunham's store on lower Fifth Avenue and losing some of it to souvenir hunters, Gower shipped the ore by steamer to San Francisco where he sold it for $532.87. He spent the money on a celebration and returned to his companions empty-handed.

If that wasn't enough to excite interest in San Francisco, a letter written by J. W. Gale, the San Diego merchant, to his brother-in-law was published in the *Alta California* and it stated:

We have just found the best quartz ledge ever discovered in the State of California . . . have seen rich quartz before, but never rich specimens in such quantities . . . I am now satisfied we have the richest mining county in the State.

When the steamer *Oriflamme* returned to San Diego it was jammed with 150 gold hunters who rushed to join the hundreds already in the Julian hills. The excitement touched Los Angeles, and as most of the prospectors were coming overland through Los Angeles and by way of Temecula and Warner's to Julian, the *Los Angeles News* stated:

There will be an immense crowd of gold seekers. They must naturally be skinned. Fellow citizens, let us prepare to do the skinning.

While *The San Diego Union* rebuked Gale for his letter, and still sought to calm the situation, it did at last publish a detailed report from the scene on March 17, as follows, in part:

The fact is that here the excitement is so intense that one scarcely knows whether he is on head or heels. Imagine 800 men turned out loose on the mountains, with little sense and as much "friskyness" as so many horses. The people here are positively wild. Such a thing as sober thought is unknown. The rumor comes that "Tom, Dick or Harry" has "struck it" and forthwith the whole camp rushes pell mell for the new diggings. People don't sleep here at all (or if they do, they are more lucky than I). All night long, the ferocious prospectors make the hills resound with their stories of the day's adventures. Talk of Babel! Let a fellow try camping out in the mountains hereabouts and he will realize the force of the quotation: "Confusion worse confounded."

James O. Bailey

The most important discovery following that of the George Washington mine and the nearby Van Wert, belonging to Mike Julian and Caliway Putnam, was the Hayden, discovered on March 4 by Paul Hayden. The ledge was opened in three different places and according to the correspondent of *The San Diego Union*, the rock was yielding $1 to the pound. Three days later George W. Swain and a Capt. Mitler discovered another ledge a half mile north of the George Washington and the vein was reported to be two feet thick.

San Diego was half-deserted, as were San Juan Capistrano and San Bernardino, and the scene at Julian was remindful of the days of the Gold Rush in the Sierra Nevada. It was winter and storms were adding to the hazards. *The San Diego Union's* report continued:

> The flush times of California seem to be revived for a season here. As in days of yore, men sleep upon the ground and eat around their campfires. But few tents comparatively speaking, have yet been put up. In "Julian City" there are two log cabins and some 20-odd tents, and at "Coleman City" three miles west, there are a dozen tents. Probably 800 people encamped in the Julian District, and about 150 at Coleman City. A townsite has been layed off on a flat near the "Washington" mine, and the locators have gone to your city to sell lots. But in spite of the lack of habitations, men congregate in knots and talk excitedly over the "prospects." We have two "rum-mills" in full blast which are well patronized and our grocery store is likewise doing a thriving business. People are flocking in daily from Los Angeles and San Bernardino counties, besides the throngs from San Diego and we have now at the mines an aggregate population of not far from 1,000. There has been considerable suffering from the recent cold weather. The night of Thursday, March 10, was terrible. A very large proportion of the people were without shelter and the driving storm came upon them with full force.

Frank Bailey

In the Julian country at the time of the gold fever were the Bailey and Julian brothers, cousins and all hailing from Georgia. There were Drury, James and Frank Bailey and Mike and Webb Julian. After serving in the Confederate Army they had returned to their homes to find nothing but poverty. Frank Bailey was the first to leave, for a new life in the West. One by one the brothers followed the sun and were reunited in Utah, from where they made their way into Arizona, and then hearing of the proposed new transcontinental railroad, they decided to make their home in San Diego. Upon reaching the mountains they spent the winter

(Next page)
A stage rolls into the gold rush town of Julian in this painting by Marjorie Reed Creese. Thousands tore at the hills, gambled at night.

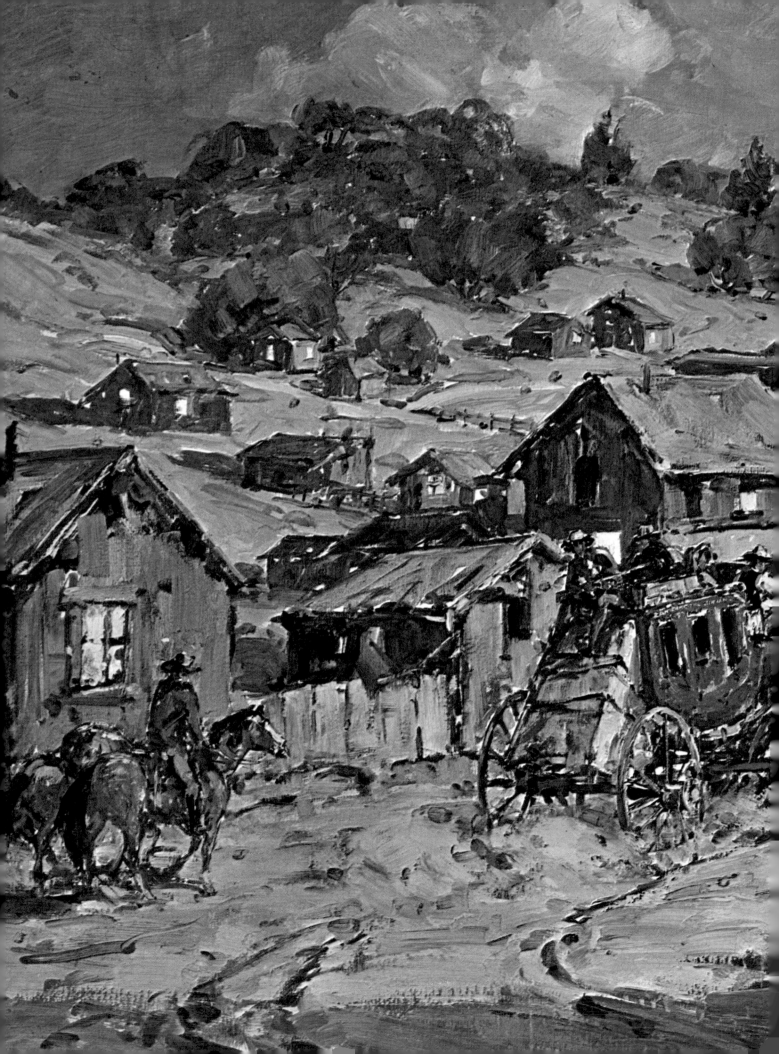

Drury D. Bailey, 1875

months prospecting, as a number of other Southerners were doing. Drury in particular was captivated by the scenic beauty of the little Julian Valley, and wanted to make his home there and persuaded the others to help him build a log cabin. However, they joined the gold hunt along Coleman Creek, after the discovery made by Fred Coleman, and in fact located the first gold quartz claim, which they named the Warrior's Rest, but it petered out within a few days.

The land on which most of the gold hunters were camping belonged to Drury under the homestead laws, and he promptly began laying out lots and offering them, as had Horton, free to anyone who would immediately erect a structure. He set aside land for a school and churches and named his town Julian City in honor of his cousin, Mike. By the end of March Julian had acquired three or four stores and a dozen saloons, all evidently established at first in tents, log cabins or shacks, and lots were selling at prices of $50 to $150. Soon 300 persons were tented or living in the immediate area and there were at least 1000 more in the surrounding hills and canyons.

The Julians and Baileys were instrumental in organizing the first Julian mining district on February 15 and Mike Julian was designated as district recorder. The boundaries were described as "beginning one thousand yards west of Harrall's store and running north five miles and south five miles and four miles west in width." Harrall's store was in a large adobe house a mile north of Julian.

In a month's time at least forty claims had been filed. The largest rich strike of all occurred in late March, seven miles south of Julian, outside of the Julian mining district on the south shore of Cuyamaca Lake. Conflicting stories are told as to its discovery, though the weight of evidence indicates that it was found by William Skidmore, who had brought his family to San Diego County in a mule wagon train from Texas. The dry winter had caused him to take his mules into the mountains for grazing. He named his mine the Stonewall Jackson for the Southern general, but is believed to have dropped the "Jackson" because of the strong anti-Southern feeling still running with many of the incoming gold hunters. Other reports credit the discovery to a Charles Hensley, on March 22. Within ten hours there were 500 persons in Cuyamaca Valley. Whatever the truth about its discovery, the claim soon had a number of partners, including S. S. Culverwell, builder of the wharf in San Diego, who organized the Hensley Mining District with Skidmore as recorder. Eventually the mine yielded more than $2,000,000 in gold.

A town sprouted up near the Stonewall mine and became known as Cuyamaca City. Julian soon had a rival, Branson City, which was founded by Lewis A. Branson a mile west of Julian. It quickly acquired the indispensable saloon, a boarding house and a dance hall. Joseph Stancliff, who had packed hay down from the mountain valleys for the Butterfield Stage station at Vallecito in the late 1850's, laid out another settlement a mile east of Julian and offered lots for sale.

The Julian district was dotted with openings and hundreds of prospectors were still clawing away at the hills. The claims that had been filed bore such formal names as the Mount Vernon, Lincoln, Owens, Kelly, Hayden, The Monroe, General McClelland,

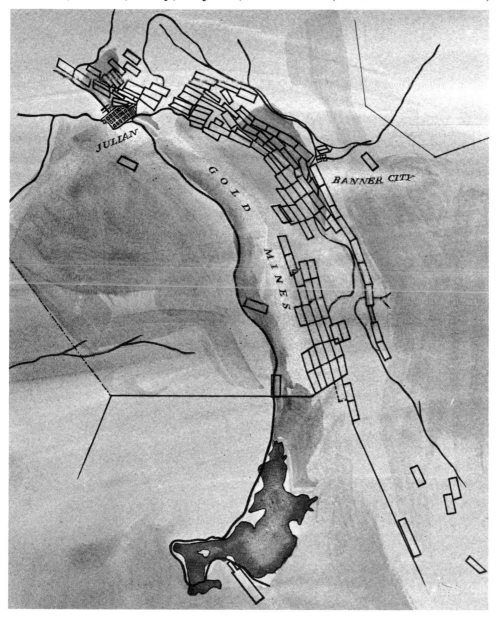

The extent of the mines in the Julian-Banner area is shown in this map. The gold belt was not large and the ore difficult to reach.

Atlas and the U.S. Grant, while others bore odd names such as Mamouth, Cleopatra, Yellow Jacket, Shoo Fly, Charmer, You Bet, April Fool, Fino and Warpath. The *San Diego Bulletin* contended that 300 claims had been located but that only eight or ten ledges as yet had been found profitable.

Original Stonewall Jackson Mine

Apparently with the aid of Indian labor, Coleman carved out a wagon road up the sharp mountain trail from Santa Ysabel to Spencer or Coleman Valley as it was then known. North & Knight, who were running stages between Old Town and New Town, put in a stage service to Julian by way of Poway and Ramona. The opportunity for business attracted Chester Gunn, who had come to California in 1851 and had met with indifferent success as a machinist and miner. He negotiated for a pony express mail service from the mines to San Diego to connect with the steamers from San Francisco and Los Angeles, and opened an office in a store established by a native of Poland who always referred to himself as "Count" Dwarkowski. His San Diego depots were listed as H. H. Bancroft's News Depot in New Town and Charles E. Judd's office in Old Town. Mining conditions were difficult, with a lack of machinery and continuing cold weather to contend with. Capital was lacking and miners built stone *arrastras* and ground the ore by mule and horse power. Grazing cattle owned by settlers were captured and killed for food and Chinese workers released with the completion of the Central Pacific Railroad invaded the mining area and met with resistance, a number being killed in fights of one kind or another. Julian is in the snow country and the winds can wail through the mountain passes with the ferocity of a tornado. On April 3, *The San Diego Union's* correspondent reported:

Chester Gunn

Julian City (what is left of it) April 3 . . . I am in great tribulation. I did live in Julian City, but that city is very much scattered just now and it bothers me to know where to find the old camping ground. Saturday afternoon, the north wind and the south wind and the east wind and the west wind came together and after the passage of appropriate resolutions, proceeded to demolish the town. The gale culminated at midnight, when its fury was beyond anything yet known by the dwellers of this section of the county. Every tent was swept away; the Count's store was swept off and Gunn's express matter was distributed among the hills and gulches gratis. The Count loses at least $200 by this little blow and Gunn is about $10 out on illustrated papers.

Justice began to exert its pressure and an aged man named Robert Crawford was accused of stealing a saddle and hauled off to a nearby tree by a vigilantes committee and a rope placed around his neck. He was hauled up and down a couple of times until he confessed to being a member of a ring of horse thieves.

He was allowed to go free on condition he left the territory. The committee then voted to hang the first murderer and adjourned.

Who owned the land being mined became an angry issue for more than a year. The Cuyamaca Valley was within an old Mexican grant which had been purchased a year before by Robert Allison, Juan Luco, Isaac Hartman and John Treat for timber, but they suddenly "floated" the boundaries of the grant northward to cover the entire mining district. They assured the miners they had no intention of rejecting them, but expected a royalty on each ton of ore mined, and the schedule of rates was handed to them on May 25, at a mass meeting of 500 miners in the town of Julian. *The San Diego Union's* correspondent was indignant about the "grab" and said that had no mines been discovered nothing would have been heard about the Cuyamaca Grant. His words echoed those being heard throughout the state as labor troubles began to mount and socialism which had been brought across the Atlantic, became an issue of public debate and controversy:

> The grabbers are, forsooth, willing to let the hardworking miners give their time, labor and means toward the development of mineral wealth, and then not having expended a dollar on their own part, these gentlemen of virtue of a pretended grant will graciously accept a fat percentage of the profits of the miners' toil. A single one of the hardy prospectors who bravely push their way into the wilderness, toiling painfully over the mountains, sleeping on the ground, encountering the privations of hunger and thirst, giving way against bloodthirsty savages and periling life continually to open new stores of wealth for the enrichment of the state, is worth to the Commonwealth more than a thousand of the greedy capitalists who leave their lands unimproved and lie in wait for the profit of the labor and enterprise of honest men. (This, Mister editor, is simply the way the thing looks to me; if the digression seems out of place, you need not print it.)

As Spring died away the crude *arrastras* used to crush the quartz gave way to machinery. The stamp mill of the Rincón del Diablo Rancho & Escondido Mining Company, which had been used in working the gold mine just west of the old Escondido ranch house, was moved to Julian, and a two-stamp mill was brought down on the *Oriflamme* from San Francisco. In September a third mill was erected at the Stonewall mine. A saw mill was cutting lumber for stores and houses and especially for saloons. Wells, Fargo & Company opened an office with Chester Gunn as agent. Charles Yale and Louis Redman opened an assay shop. By summer, gold production was a business, and in August the first 105½ ounces from Julian City arrived in San Diego and were trans-shipped to San Francisco. During August and September Wells, Fargo & Company shipments totaled $20,000 in value, though it was believed that a much larger amount was being shipped north

Gold stamp mill, Chariot Canyon

by other means.

It was in August that a new and rich field was discovered and it was not within the disputed Cuyamaca land grant. Louis Redman, the assayer at Julian, tripped over quartz rock in a canyon about six miles and 1500 feet below Julian and almost on the edge of the desert country. He marked his find with a small American flag, and the name "Banner" became attached to the settlement which promptly sprang up with miners and prospectors who emptied Julian almost overnight. The Redman mine was in a canyon opening to the right of the present State Highway 78 at the foot of Banner grade, which is named Chariot Canyon. Banner Canyon arises out of San Felipe Valley and enters Volcan Mountain and circles "gold hill" above Julian. The Ready Relief and the North Hubbard mines were claimed soon after the Redman. Prospectors worked up the sylvan-like little canyon and through a narrow gorge and onto a higher valley where rich finds awaited them. Tents and shacks began to appear on the narrow flat land that parallels the highway about a half mile below the entrance to Chariot Canyon.

The financiers and mining men who came down from San Francisco to inspect the mines returned home with adverse reports. As a result mining in the Julian-Banner area never developed large enterprises with the possible exception of the Stonewall.

The schist deposit in which the gold was being found is about twelve miles long and about four miles wide, running northwest

Louis Redman

Huge freight wagon trains hauled supplies to the mines and to other settlements in the backcountry, despite floods and rough roads.

from the Laguna Mountains and Pine Valley through the Cuya-macas and Julian and dying out about a mile north of Julian. Quality was erratic and the extent always uncertain. Ore generally assayed from $10 to $2000 the ton, though one sample from the Ready Relief Mine in Chariot Canyon was assayed by county officials at $250,000 to the ton.

Ready Relief Mine

San Diego's deposits differed from the Mother Lode of the Sierra Nevada. Where the Mother Lode was formed as a mesothermal deposit of great masses of gold-bearing rock moved into position under relatively low pressures, San Diego's deposits were of hypo-thermal origin of small amounts of mineral-bearing rock forced into tiny cracks under extreme pressures.

When the sea floor of a cooling earth's crust buckled upward to form the mountain barrier of eastern San Diego County, it carried with it a great patch of sedimentary deposit that was then several miles underground in the gigantic accordion pleats that were mountains. The slow cooling and shrinking through millions of years cracked the solidifying schist layers and great pressures forced molten gold-bearing material up into the tiny fissures, where it slowly cooled and hardened and became quartz. Meanwhile, erosion ate away the thousands of feet of surface material and exposed the white quartz streaks with their threads and flecks of yellow metal. But unfortunately for the miners, a deep "crinkling" action in the rock caused the layers to slip and slide sometimes as much as two miles from their original position, and

Inside Ready Relief Mine

65

One of the rich mines of the Julian gold belt was the North Hubbard in Chariot Canyon. It penetrated about 800 feet into the mountain.

great fault lines split the formation. The largest, the Elsinore Fault, runs through Pala up the bed of the San Luis Rey River, across Mesa Grande, Santa Ysabel, through Julian and down Banner Canyon into the desert. Another is the Agua Tibia Fault, running northeast of Volcan Mountain, through Warner's Basin, Agua Caliente, Jacumba and into Baja California, bubbling up hot sulphur springs along the way. As a result of these multiple actions, the schistose rock and the thin, rich quartz veins are so split and displaced that the miners were never certain from one day to the next whether the veins would peter out against a blank wall that was formed when a mountain heaved and tossed in the violence of nature. The exception was the Stonewall mine, a huge and consistent pocket of ore.

Long years after the sweating miners had realized a few sporadic fortunes and many bitter disappointments in the elusive and unpredictable gold ore veins of the Julian schist belt, geologists began to learn more of the character of the formation and to realize that while a fabulous wealth in gold was there, most of it would remain forever locked in its rock vaults.

THE PANIC THAT
BROKE THE BUBBLE

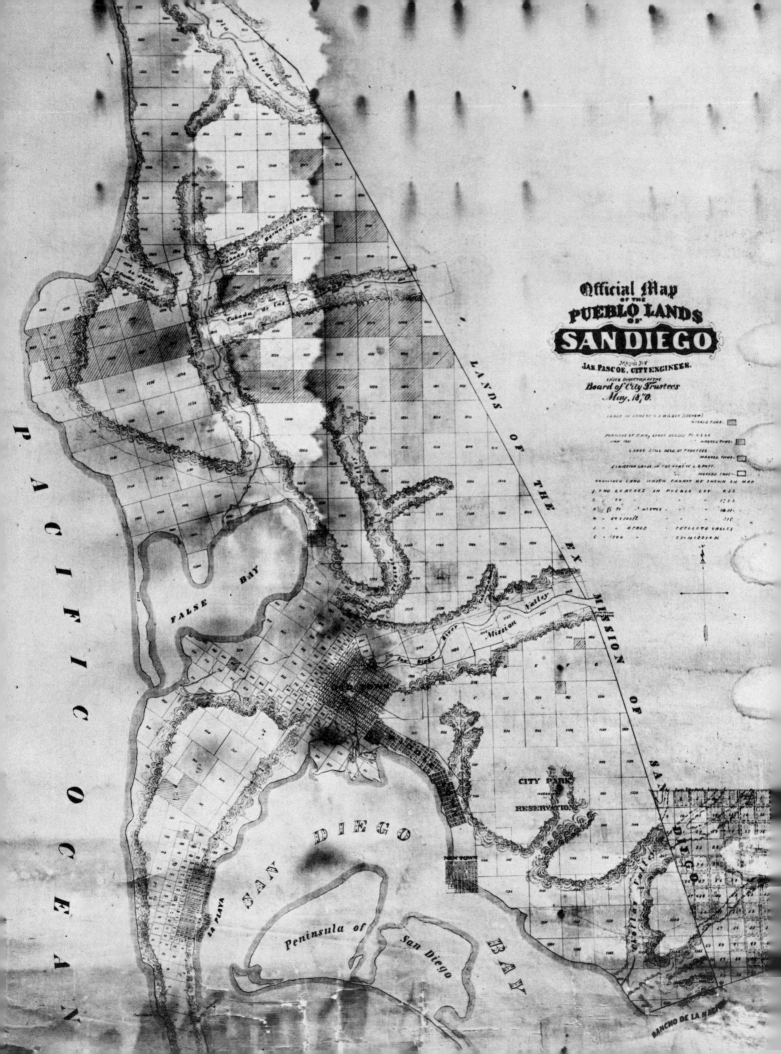

PACIFIC OCEAN

LANDS OF THE EX MISSION OF SAN DIEGO

Official Map
OF THE
PUEBLO LANDS
OF
SAN DIEGO

Drawn by
JAS. PASCOE, CITY ENGINEER.

UNDER DIRECTION OF THE
Board of City Trustees
May, 1870.

FALSE BAY

SAN DIEGO BAY

Peninsula of San Diego

LA PLAYA

NEW TOWN

CITY PARK RESERVATION

Mission Valley

San Diego River

RANCHO DE LA NACION

*This official pueblo map of 1870 shows
the settled areas, the designation of pueblo
lots and the mission lands still unavailable.*

CHAPTER V

In San Diego, Horton was lord of all he surveyed. He was now fifty-seven years of age and, after three years of strenuous but exhilarating endeavor, he was at last a wealthy man, at least on paper. The gold in Julian had caused everyone to minimize the warning signs of trouble and the indefatigable Horton went ahead with the building of a major hotel. He had turned the first spadeful of dirt on January 1, 1870, at a site uptown from the center of activity near the bay. It was on D Street, later Broadway, between Third and Fourth Streets.

Rufus K. Porter, the San Diego correspondent of the *San Francisco Bulletin*, wrote:

> Business in Old and New San Diego is pretty much at a standstill, very little improvement in the way of building being discernible. Horton is going ahead with his mammoth hotel, which tops over all the surrounding country. His faith in the country and in his town does not diminish.

The Episcopalians, Methodists and Baptists erected churches on lots granted by Horton. The Presbyterians would do likewise. The tall white New England steeple of the Baptist Church held the first church bells in New Town, and they had been donated by Horton. Porter commented that "the music of the church-going bells, heard here for the first time, is pleasant to the ears of every lover of his old home."

69

Aaron Pauly

Horton Hall, a two-story brick building, with stores on the first floor and an auditorium on the second, was completed at Sixth and F Streets. He began the building of another brick structure at Third and D Streets, to house railroad offices.

School classes which were begun in the old Army barracks were moved to rented storerooms, then moved back to the barracks, but at last 1870 saw the construction of a school, again on land donated by Horton at Sixth and B Streets, and the three little clapboard structures, known as the "Pink Schools," soon had more than 200 students.

Merchants began to desert Old Town. The addition of Whaley & Crosthwaite and J. S. Mannasse & Company raised the number of general merchandising stores in New Town to ten. The others were Joseph Nash, A. Pauly & Sons, Bush & Hinds, Lowenstein & Company, J. Connell, Steiner & Klauber, A. B. McKean & Company, and McCormick & McLellan. When Frederick A. Taylor arrived from San Francisco he purchased the interest of Charles P. Taggart in *The San Diego Union,* on January 1, 1870, and *The Union* began to take a more kindly attitude toward Horton, Republicans and New Town in general and to consider moving from Old Town. Porter reported to the *San Francisco Bulletin:*

> The firm of Whaley & Crosthwaite have given up business in Old San Diego, and are fitting up the first floor of Horton's Hall, where they will hang out in the future. "One by one the leaves are falling" from Old Town, and the old place begins to look desolate. Nothing will be left there in a short time but a few saloons and lawyers...

The dry winter also had taken its toll and Porter wrote that crops were pretty much out of the question for the year "and something must be done for the poor squatters."

Efforts were made in the State Legislature and in Washington to force the Southern Pacific company to adhere to its original franchise for a line down the coast to San Diego, even though it already was proceeding down the Central Valleys of California at the rate of 100 miles a year in an effort to reach the Colorado River at The Needles before any rival could reach there from the east along the 35th parallel. The effort was unsuccessful and the federal government then withdrew 7,500,000 acres of public lands along the line, in alternate sections, to be granted to the Southern Pacific as a subsidy.

Abraham Klauber

Not to be left without a connection along the coast, in event of becoming the terminus of a transcontinental railroad, San Diegans in March of 1870 organized the San Diego and Los Angeles

Railroad Company, and proposed to construct their own line to Los Angeles, with a branch to San Bernardino, to meet the Southern Pacific.

Economic conditions were bad across the entire country, and the *Bulletin* in an editorial pointed out that despite that fact, and the distress brought about by the drought and the disappointment over the lack of progress in the railroad project, San Diegans should consider themselves fairly fortunate:

It would be worse than folly for anyone in Southern California to deny that "times are hard" and "money is scarce" in this section of the country at the present time. The citizens of San Diego may well point to the number of elegant buildings now in course of construction; to the fact that there is not a vacant dwelling house or tenement in our city; and to intelligent countenances, the bloom of health, the hopeful, confident expression met with everywhere upon our streets and in our public gatherings as evidencing the prosperity, health and happiness of our people; yet it cannot be denied that the extremely dry season now prevailing bears heavily upon many of our best and most enterprising men, causing distress in some instances among the poorer class; that has put their little all into a home, depending on the product of their gardens and fields for the means of sustenance for themselves and their families.

Mechanics that have come here from all parts of the country, having been thrown out of employment at home by the "hard times" that prevail everywhere in the United States, are unable to procure steady work, and particularly feel the "hard times;" and in some instances, become dissatisfied—and it is not to be wondered at—the wonder is that so few of our people have become disheartened or think of looking elsewhere to better their condition.

By May, the Memphis and El Paso railroad company was bankrupt. Gen. Frémont was personally financially ruined by the disaster arising from the bond-selling deception in Paris, though he himself had been unaware of it, and for the rest of his life he was dependent on the generosity of friends. A railroad for San Diego faded farther into the future, but the *New York Tribune* commented editorially on the advantages of a railroad along the 32nd parallel and said "it is just a question of time."

There was another transcontinental railroad bill before Congress, called the Texas & Pacific, and it had significant backing in Washington as well as New York. The "Big Four" of California had no intention of allowing another line to enter California, if they could help it. The Southern Pacific shifted again and won permission to extend eastward through the San Gorgonio Pass to Yuma, the gateway of the proposed 32nd parallel railroad, but only on condition that the proposed Texas & Pacific had not already entered California.

Considerable unemployment followed the end of San Diego's second railroad boom. Frank Kimball was borrowing in San Francisco to keep his development going. The need for supplies and equipment for the mines in Julian was a boon to San Diego at this time. The Army, too, was using San Diego as a depot, and heavy freight wagons were moving out over the hills and down Mountain Springs grade to posts throughout the Southwest. A turnpike company was organized to further improve the road and lower the grade.

The $40,000 with which Horton had started the construction of his hotel had been used up, and many workmen were laid off or promised their pay in lots. W. W. Bowers, who designed the hotel for Horton and later became a state senator, went to San Francisco in the hope of finding a lessee who would complete and furnish the hotel and operate it without charge for the first three years. He failed in that but was able to obtain furniture on credit, on assurances that once the hotel opened, it would cause a resumption of San Diego's boom times. By the time the furniture arrived, all work on the hotel had stopped. It was quickly resumed, with the extension of more credit from New Town merchants.

San Diego had the land, the climate, and the country was growing, and there was the waiting port. The railroad surely must be built. The Chamber of Commerce, which had been organized in January at the instigation of Horton and Morse, published a bro-

River boats made the Yuma crossing of the Colorado River one of the most important points of Southern California in days of stages.

chure in May. Its glowing words gave heart to its own citizens, if not to the world:

> San Diego is the natural commercial center of a vast scope of country, rich in mineral and agricultural wealth, embracing all of Southern California, Southern Nevada, Arizona, New Mexico, and Northern Mexico . . . On the completion of the 32nd parallel railway, the bulk of the traffic between the States east of the Mississippi and the Asiatic ports, must of necessity pass through San Diego, and make this the Pacific Coast port of trans-shipment.

Horton's Hall

The San Diego Union tried to cheer its readers with a steady run of editorials pointing out that the bill was sure to pass in the next session of Congress and even republished an optimistic editorial from its arch enemy, the *Bulletin,* saying that everyone should hang on and continue the projects begun in anticipation of the railroad.

The Rev. Sydney Wilbur wrote to the Worcester, Massachusetts, *Gazette:*

> . . . the crops have been all but a perfect failure. The country around here was settling up rapidly, previous to this severe drouth, but immigration is now stopped to a great extent, at least for some months.

The building which Horton erected to house railroad offices was converted into a bank upon organization of the San Diego Bank,

the city's first, with Horton as president. Horton, however, continued using a San Francisco bank and issuing his own certificates which were as good as cash in San Diego. He soon resigned, and it was the opinion of Morse, as expressed in his correspondence, that he was piqued because he had not received sufficient recognition. A theater was opened in Horton's Hall, but the public library, which had been organized as the Horton Library Association upon the promise of Horton that he would donate 600 books he had obtained from Hubert Howe Bancroft, the historian, in exchange for lots, became nothing more than a reading room. Newspaper files indicate that Horton later asked for $1000 in $100 library memberships and when this was refused, he withdrew his offer of the books. William H. Perry brought in equipment to begin the first gas company but the venture failed. Agents of the Western Union Telegraph Company promised to install a telegraph line to Los Angeles if San Diegans underwrote it to the amount of $8000. A good part of the money was quickly subscribed, though in the end Horton had to put up $5000 — but he asked and obtained half of the profits for three years. The first message, greetings to San Francisco, was sent by Horton on August 20.

The San Diego Union saw that the tide had irrevocably turned against Old Town. Frederick Taylor sold his interest to William S. Dodge, and when he was promised all of Horton's advertising, he announced on June 23 that *The San Diego Union* was moving to Horton's Addition. Seven days later it began publishing from a two-story wood building at Fourth and D Streets, near where Horton's Hotel was being erected. Four months later Dodge retired and was succeeded by Douglas Gunn, a cousin of Chester Gunn, who had opened the Wells, Fargo office in Julian. Gunn became a partner of E. W. Bushyhead and served as printer, reporter and editor.

New public buildings were needed and where they were to be erected was the issue that brought the clash between Old and New San Diego to a climax. The supporters of New Town were determined that they were to be in Horton's Addition. On July 9 a majority of the Board of Supervisors, upon petition of residents of New San Diego, ordered the removal of all county records from Whaley's Building in Old Town to the Express Building in New San Diego, and designated Horton's Hall as the temporary place for the court. In retaliation, Judge Murray Morrison of the District Court in Los Angeles and Judge Thomas Bush of the County

Home of The San Diego Union *when it became a daily newspaper in 1871.*

Court immediately ordered all writs from their courts returnable at Old Town.

The reaction of the merchants and residents of Old Town to the action of the Supervisors was immediate and vigorous. County Judge Thomas Bush on July 17 ordered the sheriff to use force if necessary to prevent the removal of the records. A posse was organized to aid the sheriff and a cannon was placed in front of the city and a guard mounted over the records. *The San Diego Union* was delighted:

Old Town Plaza, 1874

> Old Town has seceded . . . They have nailed their flag to the staff in the Plaza . . . The indomitable Bush commands the artillery, and the watchword is, "Old Town—Now and Forever, One and Inseparable."

In September the defenders of Old Town successfully carried their fight to the District Court in Los Angeles and Judge Morrison issued an order removing three of the five supervisors, Joseph C. Riley, E. D. French and G. W. B. McDonald, from office and fining them each $500, presumably for their effrontery in ordering the establishment of a new county seat. Disregarding state law, which called for the election of supervisors, County Judge Bush promptly appointed Charles Thomas, Joseph Mannasse and William E. Flynn to succeed those who had been removed. Suit was brought immediately to prevent their assuming office. The fight dragged on, but Old Town's day was done. For a full century it had been the San Diego known to padres, the Spanish Dons and the American conquerors. The ruins of the original Royal Spanish Presidio on the hill above the town were grim reminders of the passage of time and the fate of towns as well as empires.

Only ruins marked Presidio

The Horton House was ready to open. It was built of brick and was 200 feet long and two and a half stories in height, and crowned by an observatory with a view of the bay which *The San Diego Union* described as "the most magnificent in Christendom." The *Bulletin* was even more ecstatic and wrote:

> What the Grand Hotel is to Paris; Langham's to London; The Astor, Fifth Avenue and St. Nicholas to New York; the Continental to Philadelphia; the Tremont and Parker's to Boston; Barnum's to Baltimore; St. Charles to New Orleans and the Galt to Louisville; the Southern to St. Louis; the Sherman and Trenton to Chicago; the Grand Lick, Occidental and Cosmopolitan to San Francisco; the Pico to Los Angeles, the Horton House is to San Diego. It is by far the most elaborate, attractive and spacious hotel outside San Francisco; and everything taken into consideration, it is the most (if not, indeed the most) complete and agreeable edifice of entertainment upon the Pacific Coast, and this is the loftiest praise, for all travelers pronounce San Francisco hotels the finest in the world.

Indeed it was a magnificent structure for a town the size of San Diego and had cost $150,000. Rooms were heated and pipes car-

The first Southern California boom was about to end when Alonzo Horton completed the Horton Hotel, a grand structure in a raw land.

ried both hot and cold water, a luxury in those times. The hotel provided its own gas for lighting and had its own well capable of producing 2000 gallons of water an hour. The main floor had a reading room, a bar and billiard room with a dais for observers circling the entire room, and a ladies' parlor. There was a lavishly furnished and decorated bridal suite and thick carpeting and marble-topped furniture. Twenty rooms were fitted out for the invalids who came to San Diego to rest in its healthful climate.

The opening ceremonies on October 17, 1870, were attended by visitors from Mexico and as far north as San Francisco. Among them were Commodore William Rogers Taylor, commanding the Pacific Squadron, United States Navy, and a score of other military officers, both Navy and Army, foreshadowing, as it were, the town's coming role as a military city. Across the street, Horton set aside a half block as a plaza, to provide a place for his visitors to bask in the sun.

While economic prospects may not have been attractive at the time, the climate drew the ill in health and someday it would bring the tourists and the pleasure-seekers from all over the world. A visitor to California and subsequently San Diego in late 1869 and early 1870 was George Phillips Marston, a pioneer farmer and merchant of Fort Atkinson on the Rock River in lower Wisconsin, a state which had been settled largely by Scandinavians and Germans, though he had migrated from New England and was of English descent.

He suffered from asthma and in two letters to members of his family, one from San Jose, near San Francisco, and the other from the mountain town of Grass Valley, he wrote:

I like the climate of San Diego very much. The night air here (San Jose) is very chilly and damp, but in San Diego it is soft and delightful . . . my health has been so much better here than in Wisconsin that you need not be surprised if I should feel it to be my duty to move here one of these days . . . I have been to San Diego, a nice little spot in the corner of the United States where the climate is delightful and Oranges, Lemons, Figs, Olives, and all Semi-tropical productions flourish. . .

In early October of 1870 George P. Marston and his son, George White Marston, started by train for a new home in San Diego, with the rest of the family to follow them later. At San Francisco they boarded a steamer and on October 24, two days after young George had passed his twentieth birthday, they arrived at San Diego.

The same day he got a job as a clerk at the Horton House. One of his duties was to dust off the travelers who arrived by stage from Yuma. In his reminiscences, he recalled:

This experience of six months in the old Horton House was the most picturesque period of my life. There was a large Spanish and Mexican element in town at that time and our guests included travelers from every part of the world, soldiers from the Indian wars in Arizona, mining men from Lower California, and adventurers from everywhere.

Though many persons were leaving, more were arriving, and by the end of the year when the census was taken the city of San Diego, which included both Old and New Town and La Playa, had a population of 2300 and the county, which still covered 14,969 square miles, 4951. In ten years the town had grown by more than 1500 residents and had 915 occupied buildings, though the county as a whole had increased only by about 600 persons. The growth was enough to bring about daily mail service to Los Angeles.

George W. Marston in 1875

Holliday & Company, which operated the *Orizaba* on the San Francisco to San Diego run, was charging $15 a ton for freight and $60 for a round trip for passengers. Horton went to San Francisco and requested William W. Wright to put the steamer *William Taber* on the run as competition and promised him a large share of San Diego's business, at $9 a ton for freight and $30 a round trip for passengers. He did, and for two months Horton diverted cargo to the *William Taber,* sometimes by withholding business from reluctant firms and threatening to destroy them, until Holliday & Company agreed to meet the lower rates and paid Wright $100,000 to withdraw the *William Taber.*

San Diego sent representatives to Washington to press for passage of the new railroad bill and to engage in the honored practice

Capt. Matthew Sherman

In the memory of coastal residents trips on the steamer Orizaba were sweet with nostalgia. She brought railroad barons and miners.

of the day of assuring directors and promoters of the proposed railroad of gifts of land that certainly would turn up small fortunes for themselves in the event San Diego became the western terminus.

Donations of land were taken and the deeds deposited in the San Diego Bank. Ephraim Morse, who was in charge of raising the gifts, reported to Matthew Sherman, who was in Washington, that he had asked Joseph Mannasse and Marcus Schiller to canvass Old Town for subscriptions, but that the residents there were suspicious of the whole deal and suspected Sherman wanted the land for himself or was being humbugged by Washington sharpsters:

> Witherby (Oliver Witherby) of course, says he can live without the railroad ... It is terribly dry here and all over California, and we all fear another year of drouth ... Should the bill fail to pass and the drouth together would ruin many of our merchants and be almost a deathblow to San Diego.

The rains finally came but Morse wrote that already many had left the country, "cursing it for a desert."

By the end of January of 1871 they had subscribed 848 lots and 558 acres. The lots were valued at $126,000 and the acres at $56,000. Morse said he thought these were fair estimates but:

> Horton abused the committee shamefully for putting so low an estimate upon it ... I never saw Horton more mad than he was with us. He swore he would never give another cent, and he was sorry he had given this, would never work with us again, etc., etc., that we were making d--n fools of ourselves and doing more harm than good as he wanted to call it a *million*.

A few days later Morse reported that nearly all the deeds had been signed and delivered to the bank but Horton was among those who had refused to sign. The *San Francisco Chronicle* reported the bill was sure to pass, and Morse wrote:

> Horton is going around denouncing Sherman and his scheme of getting lands as a swindle to benefit himself in buying into some fat situations, etc., etc. ... there are plenty of people here to invest if the bill passes ... I wish I could look

78

Lonely Army posts of the Southwestern frontier held little for soldiers and even the desert wild flower could recall a better life.

into the future—I am offered half price for some lots, and I think I shall take it for fear of accidents, though I know they would be worth four times as much a week after the passage of the bill.

Horton was finally listed as giving twenty blocks and Louis Rose 153 blocks in Roseville and 80 acres.

San Diego still had two rival Boards of Supervisors, each claiming political jurisdiction and each planning to build its own courthouse, as a result of the feud between New San Diego and Old Town, and in January Morse wrote:

> The Bogus Board of Supervisors have finally located the Court House at Old Town... and the bonds are being printed. If the courts are not too slow they may be stopped before they go much farther.

The court fight which would settle the issue between Old Town and New San Diego came to a conclusion on January 27, 1871, when the Supreme Court of California ruled that the Board of Supervisors did have the authority to remove the county records

The Mexican influence lingered in California, as reflected in this old photograph of the stage station in the San Luis Rey Valley.

to Horton's Addition and that Judge Morrison had no power to remove three of the Supervisors from office. In a letter Morse commented:

> The decision of the Supreme Court on the Court House question was a terrible blow to Old Town and a scathing rebuke to Judge Morrison. I don't think they will fight any longer, but they may, and if they do they will be crowded without mercy.

Chalmers Scott

The old Board was still in power, and with the subsequent death of County Clerk George A. Pendleton, a champion of Old Town, the Supervisors appointed Chalmers Scott as clerk. On March 29 Judge Morrison ordered the sheriff and Board of Supervisors to provide a courtroom in South San Diego for the April term of the court, and on the following night the new clerk and a few friends went into the Whaley House in Old Town, carried the records out to waiting express wagons, and removed them to New San Diego, where they were temporarily placed in the Express Building on the northwest corner of Sixth and G Streets.

With the champions of Old Town routed, the residents of New San Diego fell to quarreling among themselves over the building of a permanent courthouse and jail. The Board of Supervisors was accused of wasting the taxpayers' money in proposing to spend $45,000 for a new building, when the county already was $90,000 in debt, and at a gathering of citizens it was decided that an existing building should be purchased for $10,000 and the rest of the money expended on roads.

The wily Horton stepped in and offered Horton's Hall for $10,000 or a free site on Cedar Street, between Third and Fourth, far uptown on the portion of Horton's Addition lying west of Balboa Park. Things had been moving rather slowly up there.

In the end, neither Horton nor the citizens' group won out. The Supervisors were going to have their new building and Horton was forced to capitulate with a site on D Street, between Front and First Streets, on which it was to stand for ninety years. It was a significant political defeat for Horton in the town he had founded only four years earlier.

The cornerstone was laid on August 12, 1871, and perhaps symbolically, a box referred to as a casket was carried by four men through the streets with due ceremony, filled with historic and timely documents, and while Martin's Band played, sealed into the wall. Dr. E. D. French, president of the Board of Supervisors, made "some very neat and appropriate remarks hoping that all the ill feelings that have existed between Old and New San Diego might be buried in the stone."

THE GREAT TIDELANDS ROBBERY

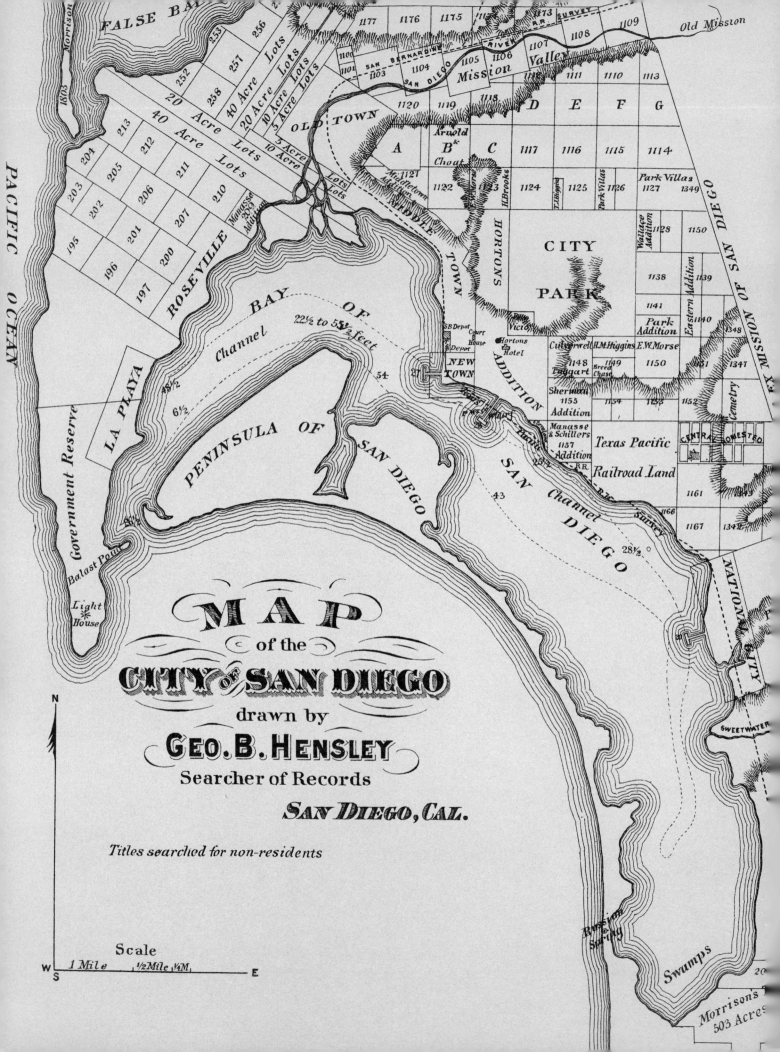

MAP
of the
CITY of SAN DIEGO
drawn by
GEO. B. HENSLEY
Searcher of Records

SAN DIEGO, CAL.

Titles searched for non-residents

Scale
1 Mile   ½ Mile   ¼ M.

Horton's Addition was becoming a town,
additional subdivisions were springing
up, and large areas were set aside as
railroad lands.

CHAPTER VI

It was in March of 1871 that the great news came to San Diego. The sky was again tinted with the promise of a future unmatched on the Pacific Coast. On March 3 the Congress chartered the Texas and Pacific Railroad Company, with former Sen. John S. Harris of Louisiana as director and Thomas A. Scott as president. It was backed by the power and resources of the Pennsylvania Railroad, of which Scott was president. Five days before the railroad bill was actually passed, *The San Diego Union* printed a free extra on a dispatch that the bill was moving and would be passed. In its regular edition next day it said:

> There was a sensation in town when the *Union* extras came out yesterday morning. The news was almost too good to be true; but in a few minutes the boom of anvil salutes in various parts of town, the scream of steam whistles, and the rattle of Chinese bombs showed that in spite of the driving storm the enthusiasm of the people must have vent.

On March 3 there was a crowd of 300 persons jammed in front of the telegraph office all day waiting for the final news. They waited in suspense until 7:30 that night before the telegraph began clicking out the dispatches. *The San Diego Union* was printing and giving away free extras as the news came in, a total of 4900 from Friday night to Monday night. A jubilee committee

This early etching depicts a Texas & Pacific train arriving at San Diego. It never happened. But all hopes rode with visionary railroads.

declared the next Friday, March 10, a local holiday. The jubilee started at 3 o'clock in the afternoon with speeches in front of the Horton House. The cannon from the steamer *California* was moved up to the Plaza to fire a 100-gun salute as fireworks were shot from the Horton House balcony. Martin's Brass Band led a torchlight parade of 400 persons through a city with every lamp lit and the marchers firing rockets as they went along. The parade paused in front of *The San Diego Union* office to give three cheers for the extras it had furnished, and finished the evening with a grand ball in Horton's Hall. On March 20 the weekly *San Diego Union* was converted into a daily newspaper with 400 subscribers.

Though their own town had only about 250 residents, Frank and Warren Kimball were not to be outsmarted by developments and made a trip to New York in early April to participate in an organizational meeting of the Texas and Pacific Railroad Company, to which they had been invited by their powerful friend, Sen. Harris. At the meeting, they were assured by Col. T. S. Sedgwick, who formerly had been associated with the Frémont enterprise, that the new company would carry out all the commitments that had been made to the Kimballs and that the railroad would come to National City. San Diego as yet had no assurance that the line would even reach to this area. However, a rivalry would once again pit Frank Kimball against Horton and National City against San Diego.

Horton began moving tenantless houses in his addition closer to the Horton House, as he was determined to build up that section, and Morse wrote that it "looks rather ridiculous to see those

old houses travelling through the streets to locate around the hotel, but Horton is a strange genius   "

In two months land sales had reached $100,000, and Morse wrote:

Horton has sold about $80,000. He is erecting several buildings near his hotel. Buildings are going up all over town, but business is not as brisk as we all had expected, and I think I was very moderate in my expectations too . . . Old Rose (Louis Rose) is being cursed by the Old Town folks for not showing a little of Horton's energy in building up Roseville and La Playa. Old Town is nearly deserted.

The remaining pueblo lands and the tidelands were coveted by those who expected to grow rich with a new tide of immigrants, and they sought ways by which they could seize unappropriated lands or challenge the titles of lands already granted.

San Diego had never received a final patent to its pueblo lands from the United States government, and even the original Spanish grant and its boundaries, particularly as to shore lines and as to whether the town's political jurisdiction extended across the bay to include Coronado and North Island, were in dispute. The first map of the pueblo made by Capt. Henry Fitch after the American conquest had included North Island, Coronado, Point Loma and the waters of both San Diego and Mission bays, but a survey made by J. C. Hays, a surveyor for the United States in 1858, who evidently worked along the generally accepted line that tidelands belonged to the states, left out the bays as well as Coronado and North Island, but included all of Point Loma.

A suit was filed which challenged the concept of the pueblo

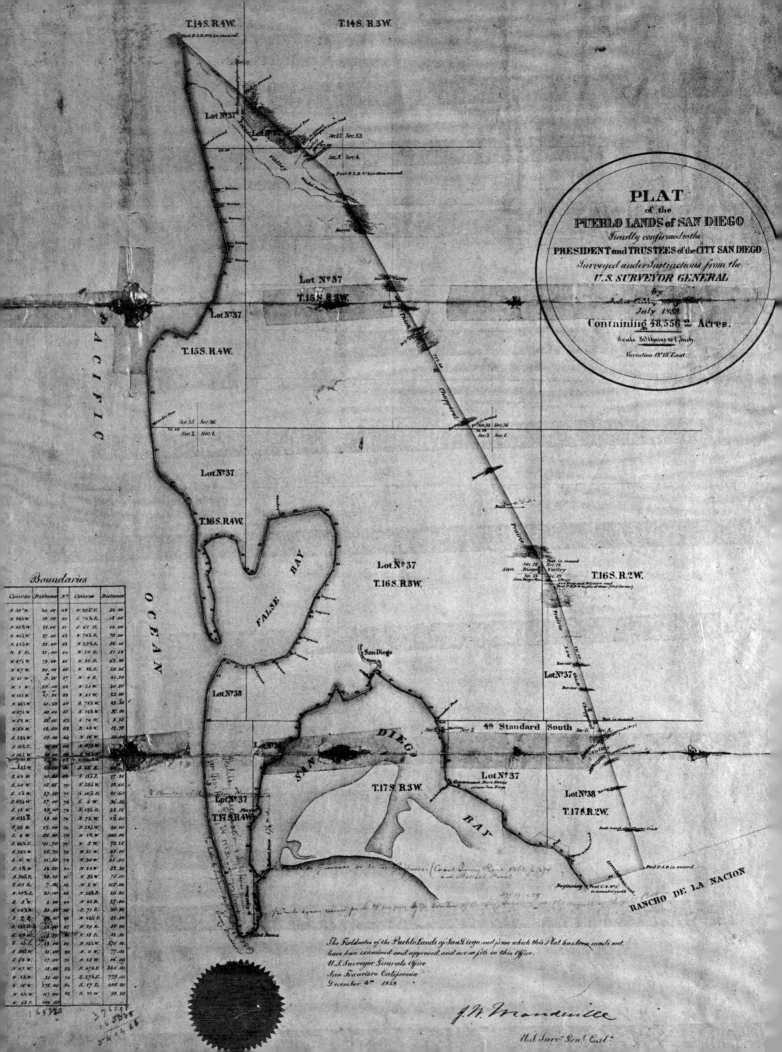

grant as being composed of eleven leagues of land, on the grounds that Spanish law had stipulated that all pueblos in the New World were to be four square leagues, as was the case with San Francisco. This suit was brought by the same parties who had purchased the Cuyamaca grant and had tried to inflate the boundaries to include the Julian gold fields.

There had been considerable dispute in California as to whether the original Spanish ordinance establishing pueblos in the new territories called for four square leagues or four common leagues from the center of the presidio square, or two leagues in each direction. In the case of San Diego, the suit contended that anything above four square leagues had been the property of the San Diego Mission and therefore now was private land by right of the grant of the mission properties to the Arguello family by the last of the Mexican governors, Pio Pico, and the trustees had had no legal authority to sell any of it. The Fitch map, however, which was based on the testimony of Don Santiago Arguello, a former *alcalde*, and other witnesses from the Spanish and Mexican periods, had been accepted by the United States Land Commission as showing the true and accepted boundaries.

In 1868 the State Legislature passed an act which permitted the sale of certain "swamp and tidelands" and Horton and Morse had moved quickly to locate under state law all of the remaining tidelands within the pueblo limits, or eighteen miles of waterfront, and they contended they were acting in the public interest to prevent their falling into the hands of speculators who might try to blackmail any railroad company entering San Diego.

The City Board of Trustees, however, challenged the state's title to the tidelands, insisting they always had been the property of the pueblo, regardless of what the Hays' survey showed, and voted to convey to the city attorney, C. P. Taggart, and a Los Angeles attorney and railroad promoter, Volney E. Howard, five miles of tidelands lying between National City and New San Diego, if they were successful in defending the suit brought to reduce the pueblo to four square leagues and in pressing the city's claims to the tidelands.

The trustees proceeded to hand out large tracts of dry lands as well, to their friends at low prices and without public auctions as required by law. At a public meeting called by the trustees it was resolved by those attending that the city should proceed with the disposition of tidelands in small lots of equal size and at a uniform price to all citizens who should apply. In retaliation Horton and Morse hurried to perfect a vested interest in the eighteen miles

(Opposite page)
This is the original Hays map which reduced the size of the pueblo and led to a century of legal difficulties over titles and tidelands.

of tidelands by filing their locators fees with the state, and they were accepted by the Surveyor General upon the advice of the Attorney General.

Horton set out to destroy what was known as the "Taggart clique" and he and Morse were successful in unseating Taggart as Republican "boss." When *The San Diego Union* abandoned Horton and sided with Taggart, on the contention that local citizens and not the state should decide the fate of tidelands fronting the town, Morse and other citizens purchased the *Bulletin* and eventually converted it into a daily and the two newspapers launched into an editorial war by lambasting each other with the bombast typical of the times.

The San Diego Union and the Taggart group accused Morse, Horton and their friends of having privately acquired large sections of waterfront and tidelands through old grants, Horton alone holding more than 400 acres, and now were attempting to "grab" the remainder and this might force the railroad to go around the Silver Strand or bridge the lower bay to terminate at Coronado where it also owned land.

Horton became Republican candidate for the State Senate to carry the tidelands issue into the State Legislature. His opponent was Democrat James McCoy, the former sheriff and a member of the Board of Trustees. In the voting of September 1871 Horton won in San Diego, but only by fifty votes, and lost out in San Bernardino which then was included in the one senatorial district. There was a total of 1110 votes for McCoy and 965 for Horton. McCoy went to the Legislature determined to see that

James McCoy

the tidelands were declared within the jurisdiction of the city and that their granting had been legal. He did submit a measure to formally convey to San Diego all tidelands lying within the boundaries of the city, and all land covered by water in the bay of San Diego from the high water mark to a depth of twelve feet at low tide.

The Legislature approved the sales of pueblo lands without the requirement of public auctions but refused to act on confirming any grants of tidelands. The fight gathered intensity and Morse wrote to Sherman, who was in Washington, on February 25, 1872, regarding the approaching election of a new Board of Trustees which would have the power to review the tidelands issue as well as the disposition of other lands that might or might not be held to be outside the pueblo boundaries:

> I hope you will get here before the city election comes off. We shall need every vote and I fear defeat. McCoy-Taggart & Company are buying up a great many votes with promises of land by often unflinching bribery. At a plaza public meeting last Thursday night, they actually said in their speeches, now is your time to get cheap lands, the last chance to make a fortune, elect these old trustees and you can get your piece of land free.
>
> Truman (B. C. Truman, editor of the *Bulletin*) gives them some hard knocks in today's *Bulletin*. He has canvassed the town and taken down names and says we will beat them yet. Taggart walked into the Horton House this morning when G. A. Johnson sat reading a paper, and securing him by the throat, called him everything bad till they were parted.
>
> A stranger at the Horton House said he would not settle or buy land in a place where such profane and obscene vulgar speeches could be made at a public meeting as Taggart . . . made last Thursday night.

In defense of the "tidelanders," and also claiming virtue as its cause, *The San Diego Union* stated editorially:

Maj. Ben C. Truman

A fixture of every civic celebration in Southern California was the decorated fire wagon. Here is a pioneer Hook & Ladder of 1871.

Harpies and tricksters have within the last three years squandered away 40,000 acres of pueblo land and 2000 acres of tidelands, and brought our city to the verge of bankruptcy ... we believe there is more honest manhood in the little finger of C. P. Taggart than in the aggregated bodies of the hypocritical pack of lying land thieves that bark at his heels ... he has detected and exposed their frauds and therefore they hate him.

We don't advocate Taggart & Company's claim to the tidelands because we don't want to see the water front go into the hands of *any* private individual. We think it should be held by the city for the use and benefit of the city. But when the State Tide Landers abuse the trustees for making that bargain with Taggart and denounce Taggart for making as good a bargain as he could with the trustees, we can't help expressing our disgust at the contemptible hypocrisy of the creatures. Why, these very fellows deeded away half of their interest to non-resident lobby agents and other parties to help them to get away with their grab. It is all *right* according to these men, to give away half the city water front in order to secure the other half for themselves; but it is all *wrong* for the trustees to deed a small part of the water front to attorneys to save all the rest, and thirty thousand acres of dry lands besides, for the city.

The election of a new Board of Trustees took place on May 9 under a reorganization act passed by the Legislature which had reincorporated the city of San Diego and provided for five instead of three trustees. The candidates backed by Taggart won. It was another severe political defeat for Horton as well as Morse. Taggart and Howard offered to return their lands to the city, for a fair cash settlement, if Horton and Morse would do likewise, but things had gone too far for compromise and a long series of court actions followed.

The sincerity of Taggart and Howard might be questioned as they immediately attempted another "grab," this time of the lands set aside for a public park at the urging of Morse and Horton. Senator McCoy introduced a bill in the State Legislature to repeal the grant of 1400 acres and return the land to disposition by the trustees. It was met with a storm of protest, and a petition opposing repeal was signed by more than 400 persons. In his correspondence Morse said that the trustees had already given to their friends deeds to portions of the park and to the 200-acre public cemetery, Mount Hope, which had been laid aside in 1871, and that if they won out a vigilante committee surely would hang all concerned:

McCoy and Taggart are at work for themselves at Sacramento in the most scandalous manner trying to induce the state to pass a law to put fortunes (in land) in their pockets by swindling the city. Two years ago the state passed a law setting aside 1400 acres of land as a public park forever. McCoy has just introduced a bill to cede back this park to the city, probably because they have already divided it up among their ring. They have stolen and given away all the other city lands dry and wet, even to ships channel, and one-half the Island (given to Taggart) which belongs to Peachy, Billings & Aspinwall ... Some 15 or 20 of us ... decided to circulate petitions against cutting down the park or cemetery or distributing them in any way. We districted the town and got started with about 10 or 12 canvassers who in about an hour got about 400 signers.

The "island" to which Morse referred was composed of North Island and Coronado which in 1869 had been obtained from the family of Pedro C. Carrillo by Archibald C. Peachey, Frederick Billings and William H. Aspinwall. The effort to repeal the park grant was defeated. Though the land would remain unused for two more decades, it was the richest heritage left by the settlers of New San Diego.

After lengthy litigation and numerous court actions, the State Supreme Court ruled that the act which had authorized the sale of marsh lands did not apply to the ocean shore, that the tidelands belonged to the State, and that the City Trustees had no authority to grant them to individuals. Thus the tidelands were left for public use and development.

As the size of the pueblo also had been questioned, Morse warned that most of the property titles in San Diego would be worthless, and there was a possibility of violence and bloodshed, should the pueblo grant be reduced from eleven to four leagues. The disputes over the titles of lands even within the pueblo, and of the legality of sales made by the trustees, set off another wave of landjumping, and Morse wrote regarding "landjumpers:"

Of course they have no money and have only built little "shanties" just to hold the lot or block that they have jumped, and no capitalist or person with money would buy from them in order to put up a good building, and then to get them off by the rightful owner takes a long time, perhaps 3 or 4 years, by law...

A group laying out a new addition or subdivision evidently included some of the land owned by Morse and J. R. Bleeker, and they were erecting fences, and making repossession difficult without repayment of costs, and Morse wrote:

My wagon load of fighting men and fire arms did you a good service in saving your two blocks. The second lot east of yours was mine and the same parties who were fencing up a portion of yours were also taking mine into a large tract... I went to them and they said they did not claim my lot, I could have possession whenever I wished... but a few months afterward, when I proposed to take possession, they ignored all their promises and I only got possession... by a compromise, paying them... some $400.

The names of the scamps are John Treat, S. S. Culverwell and H. W. Whitcomb. These parties have some money and are well practiced in this kind of land stealing, having made money at it in San Francisco.

Riding shotgun

Morse went to Washington and received assurances from the Secretary of Interior that the government would recognize the eleven leagues. Even though the federal survey of 1858 had indicated that Point Loma was within the pueblo's boundaries, the

War Department had claimed possession of the southern portion on the contention that as it had been used for military purposes by both the Spanish and Mexican governments it therefore was not city land but properly the property of the United States government. The city, which once had offered Point Loma land for fortifications, challenged the contention and went as far as to sell two lots within the jurisdiction claimed by the Army. But it was to no avail. A new federal survey in 1872 eliminated the southern portion of Point Loma, or 1233 acres. Point Loma was destined to form the base for the future of San Diego as a military center.

San Diego, however, did not receive the final patent to its pueblo lands until April 10, 1874.

Meanwhile it had been discovered that the lands which Horton had donated for influencing the passing of the railroad bill, and to assure the building of the line, were of questionable value, and Morse wrote to Gen. Rosecrans, who was still involved in railroad promotions and had helped in organizing the campaign for the bill:

> I greatly regret this for it was the intention of the Committee and I think of Mr. Horton also that three of the best blocks of all the land donated should be deeded to you. We have urged Mr. Horton, who still has an immense amount of property, to exchange these blocks for some as good as he then represented these to be, but he positively refuses. They are situated on the sides of a deep ravine, and I am ashamed to write to you of what little value they are...

The speculations and expectations did not, however, sustain the rate of business growth that had been foreseen. A large party of excursionists organized by Eastern real estate promoters arrived in San Diego, but all of them refused to buy any land, and they said they would wait for the railroad. Employment once again began to level off and public tax revenues fell to a point where the school had to be temporarily closed. A roller skating craze was sweeping the country and San Diego acquired two skating rinks, one on the lower floor of Horton's Hall and the other in a building on Second Street, between D, or Broadway, and E Streets. By the end of 1871 a total of fifty-one new buildings had been erected and the number of business structures had risen to sixty nine. There were twenty-five citizens whose property assessments were $10,000 or higher. Horton's property was assessed at $124,971, that of the Kimball brothers $52,849, and that of Juan Forster, who owned the huge Santa Margarita Rancho, the largest grant in San Diego County, $87,681.

THE DAY THE TOWN
WENT WILD

It was a proud day when the town
opened its new Courthouse in 1872. Ornate,
it was typical of a town struggling
for civic distinction.

CHAPTER VII

The southern counties of California had long been known as the "cow counties." From the days of the Silver Dons they had been mostly vast cattle ranges, as the light rainfall had discouraged extensive development of agriculture. Settlements generally were along the coastal plateau in the same pattern that had characterized the mission period. Money as well as water was lacking, and both were needed in large quantities.

A traveler through Southern California and the other semiarid portions of the Southwest, Stephen Powers, wrote:

California is not *now* a good home for small men. More than any other State I know of, it is a theatre for pioneer operations in the large, and is no place for patches. Rich men must occupy the dry lands, and dig costly wells, and cut long trenches, and then give liberal terms to tenants, or small purchasers...

Nature is obstinate here and must be broken with steam and with steel. Until strong men take hold of the State this way and break it in — I speak of Southern California which I have seen — its agriculture will be the merest clod whacking...

The climate was attractive but the state gained a poor reputation for agriculture as it overturned all the habits and ideas of Eastern farmers. Charles Nordhoff wrote in his famed book, *California: A Book for Travellers and Settlers*, that:

Our people came to the State, and attempted to plant and sow in May or

June, when the rains were over, and, of course, they got no more return than if they had planted corn in Illinois in August. Then, getting no crop from their planting, they beheld the whole great plain in June turn brown and sere, the grass dry up, the clover utterly disappear, and of course they were ready to give up the country as a desert. They did not then know that the grass lies on the plain fine naturally cured hay; that the clover-seed, by a curious provision of nature, is preserved in a little bur, on which the cattle and sheep actually fatten, when to the careless eye the ground seems to be bare; and that the wild oat also holds a nutritious seed all the season; so that these brown pastures are perhaps the sweetest and best support for cattle and sheep in the world.

Even in the mission days agriculture had been secondary to cattle raising and crop growing had been restricted to the usually narrow valleys of the rivers which normally ran above ground only in the wet seasons. The mission lands and the ranchos—and most of the ranchos were carved out of mission property when the missions were secularized—straddled the rivers and creeks or lay in the high pastures of the hill and mountain country. Of the thirty original Spanish and Mexican ranchos comprising more than a half million acres, only El Cajon and Rancho de la Nación, or National City, had been opened to settlement, with the exception of the lands which had comprised the Milíjo grant from the southern borders of the bay to the Mexican border and which had been rejected by the United States Land Commission. Beyond the old pueblo boundaries of the town of San Diego usable available land was scarce.

Settlers and ranchers fought each other over water rights and the wet belts along the flow of rivers and creeks. For a century cattle had roamed at will, and after the American conquest a "trespass" law was placed on the books to protect the cattle owners. Barbed wire had not been invented and it was impossible to enclose the great ranges. Then, with settlers trying to put in crops or grow feed for their own animals, and with newcomers in political ascendancy, cultivated lands in and near the pueblo were placed "out of bounds" to cattle. Finally, an act was pushed through the State Legislature, on February 14, 1872, "to protect agriculture, and to prevent trespassing of animals upon private property in the County of Los Angeles, and the County of San Diego, and parts of Monterey County."

It was called the "no-fence" law. The burden of protecting agriculture from grazing cattle was placed on the rancher, not on the farmer. The day of the cattle baron was drawing to an end.

Porter reported on the working of the law as it applied to the settled areas of San Diego, to his newspaper, the *San Francisco Bulletin:*

The new no-fence law is working beautifully in this agricultural part of San Diego county. What little stock there is within thirty miles of the coast is getting a precarious living on last year's grass; but would even do that, and live along till winter, if allowed to by the squatters who are scattered all over the country. Nearly all of the latter have something green, if only a few potato vines, and now that the law protects his potato patch without any fence, owners of stock must look out lest their hungry animals covet a mouthful of green stuff owned by a squatter. The recent Act of the Legislature, though well understood here does not prevent unprincipled men from killing and maiming stock. Instead of shutting the offending animals in a corral and letting the owner know where he can find his property and redeem it, shooting is the order of the day, or rather night, for the shooters are too mean and cowardly to shoot cattle or other stock in daytime. In the famous "Cajon Valley" where there are only two farms out of more than fifty which will even raise hay, shooting is resorted to all the time, and the wretches who do it, shoot with rifles and pistols, on purpose to kill, and are no respecters of persons.

Luiseño Indian

Even at that the cattle were better off than the Indians. The Indians, now generally referred to as the Mission Indians though they represented a number of large groupings, long ago had been driven from their lands, and, released from the protection and guardianship of the Franciscan missionaries, had declined morally and physically. Enough of them were allowed in the immediate area of the town to undertake labor nobody else wanted to do. There was an encampment in Switzer Canyon, in the southern portion of what is now Balboa Park. The others were removed to the Pala area on the San Luis Rey River and to San Pasqual Valley, on the San Dieguito River system, but they were unable to hold their lands from the pressure of white settlers who found it easier to dislodge the helpless and dispirited Indian than to challenge the big land holders. The records of the times are filled with the cruel and cynical actions taken against the Indians. In 1873 the chief of the Capitan tribe was ordered to keep his thieving Indians out of town and he in turn protested that the citizens had been putting out poisoned meat for stray dogs and killing his men.

They were not without their friends and protectors, however, and Fr. Ubach, of the Catholic Church in Old Town, the "last of the padres," took to the missionary trails as much as possible, visiting their *rancherias* from San Diego to the Colorado Desert, baptizing the children born of Christianized Indians and administering the last sacraments to those who once had owned lands as far as their eyes could see. White settlers would find him living off the country, or sleeping on the ground beside a campfire, even as had Fr. Junípero Serra in his pilgrimages from mission to mission along California's El Camino Real.

The Indians and their problems were of small concern in the

Fr. Antonio Ubach

struggles for land among those who had inherited the West. All of the land lying immediately east of the pueblo of San Diego, from Miramar to the National Ranch and east to El Cajon Valley, was still unavailable to settlers. This was the principal land of the San Diego Mission and consisted of more than 58,000 acres. Here Indians had raised corn and wheat and tended and watered cattle to support the mission population. It had been hurriedly granted to Don Santiago Arguello for unspecified services to the government at the close of the Mexican period, and upon his death descendants had been selling out their interest from time to time for paltry sums. The grant was not confirmed by the United States government until 1876. Included in this large tract were parts of the Kearny and Miramar Mesas, the modern districts of East San Diego, Normal Heights, Kensington Heights, Talmadge Park, the San Diego State College, La Mesa, Encanto, and Lemon Grove.

There were continuing challenges to the size and boundaries of the grant, and even to its validity. There were many envious eyes to see that when New Town had been developed, the future lay to the east, on the broad dry mesas and intervening valleys which

reached back to the low foothills. As Porter wrote to the *San Francisco Bulletin:*

People are still flocking hither by water and by land, and branching out into the country in search of farms, chance to work etc. I am sorry to say that farms on Government land anywhere near this town are very scarce; in fact there are none. The famous "Mission grant" has just been surveyed and swallowed up about a dozen leagues of land. It does not seem possible that they can ever get the survey confirmed, for it seems too huge a grab, particularly at this time, when so many poor men are hunting homes in this vicinity. The Surveyors only did their duty, and as far as I know, the administrator of the estate of the deceased has done nothing contrary to law through his attorney. The great trouble, or swindle, or mistake, was when the grant was confirmed . . . in 1858. The testimony of the witnesses was very vague, and it seems to me, contradictory. J. J. Warner *believed* the Mission Lands commenced at Jamacha, thence north to the Cajon, thence west to a certain *cañada,* thence south to a pool of water thence back to the starting point. The Surveyors have followed his belief and taken in thirteen, instead of three leagues. . .

Porter commented that San Diego could never go ahead as long as speculators owned all the land within the vicinity and kept up the prices. He wrote:

Many a man has gone away disgusted from this place on ascertaining the prices of land near the town. The City Trustees have seemed disposed to be

This is how San Diego looked to an artist from across the bay in 1873. Shown are Culverwell's wharf, center, and Horton's Wharf.

liberal, but their favorites come in for the tit-bits generally, and a poor fellow had to be thankful for almost anything. In order to obtain deeds for lands ceded to them by the Board of Trustees whose term of office expired March 1st, many persons hurriedly put up a shanty costing from $75 to $100, made it appear to the old Board that they had complied with the ordinance which compelled every owner of 40 acres to put up $250 of improvements, got their deeds of the old Board before March 2nd, and are now all hunk. With about half a dozen exceptions not a man has put up a house worth a $150, on any of the ceded lands, though most of them have deeds of the land. How these things are managed I don't know, as I don't reside in the heart of the city, and am not posted.

The real rush to California had not yet begun and Charles Nordhoff in 1872 in his book, *California: A Book for Travellers and Settlers*, commented that California to Eastern people was still a land of big beets and pumpkins, of rough miners, of pistols, bowie knives, abundant fruit, queer wines, high prices — full of discomforts and abounding in dangers to the peaceful traveler:

A New Yorker, inefficient except in his own business, looking to the government, municipal, State, or Federal, for almost every thing except his daily dollars; overridden by a semi-barbarous foreign population; troubled with incapable servants, private as well as public; subject to daily rudeness from cab-drivers and others who ought to be civil; rolled helplessly and tediously down town to his business in a lumbering omnibus; exposed to inconveniences, to dirty streets, bad gas, beggars, loss of time through improper conveyances; to high taxes, theft, and all kinds of public wrong, year in and year out — this New Yorker fondly imagines himself to be living at the centre of civilization, and pities the unlucky friend who is "going to California."

But, Nordhoff wrote, the New Yorker was mistaken. There were no dangers to travelers on the beaten track in California, there were no inconveniences which a child or a tenderly-reared woman would not laugh at and they dined in San Francisco rather better, and with quite as much form and more elegant service than in New York; the San Francisco hotels were the best and cheapest in the world; the noble art of cooking was better understood in California than anywhere else, and the cost of living was less. As a matter of fact, he considered New York more of a frontier than California.

As for San Diego, Nordhoff found:

San Diego seems to me to possess the mildest and sunniest climate on the coast. It has the advantage of a large and excellent hotel, and very good shops, and the disadvantage of an almost entire absence of shade and trees. It has pleasant society, and within thirty miles very fine and varied scenery. If I were spending a winter in California for my health, I think I should go first to San Diego, and stay there the months of December and January. It is the most southern town in the state, and presumably warmer than either Santa Barbara or San Bernardino, though the difference is but slight. It affords some simple amusements, in fishing, shell-hunting, and boat-sailing; and here, as all over Southern California, horses are cheap; and to those who are fond of driving or riding, very fair roads are open. There is less rain here than in any other part of the State; and as the so-called winter in this State is a rainy season, San Diego has the advantage over other places of less mud in December and January. In fact, I doubt if it is ever muddy there.

People made land valuable, and all of San Diego waited upon the railroad. While many poor settlers had arrived to seek new homes and a piece of friendly earth, and hundreds of others had come in the search for health, all were certain that capital, industry and commerce would follow a railroad, and with them, people in numbers perhaps undreamed of. Water could be brought to the dry mesas, the fear of drought lifted forever, and the baked ground broken to the plow and made to yield the riches that seemed to escape so many.

San Diego did not intend to take any chances of being outsmarted in the struggle for the railroad, and in late March appointed a Committee of Forty, with Thomas L. Nesmith as chairman, and Horton was sent to Washington to cooperate with Congressman S. O. Houghton and Col. Sedgwick. San Diego insisted the charter granted by Congress should be amended to specify that the line should be started from both ends simultaneously, that work should commence within a year, and that a minimum mileage should be constructed each year.

Thomas L. Nesmith

Ephraim Morse, in a letter to his father wrote:

People are in a state of suspense in respect to the railroad matter. Scott, the president of the Texas and Pacific Railroad, applied to Congress to be allowed to build the road . . . from the eastern end, but we made such a fight against him, getting the whole Pacific delegation in Congress to oppose him, that he has agreed to compromise by making a commitment of work on this end within the year and building not less than ten miles next year — and he promises to have the whole road done in three years. Expect to sell 20 or 30 acres of land, but times very dull . . . no sale of real estate at any price . . . a lot of gold bars came in from the mines yesterday valued at $10,000.

The people went about their business, and waited. Seeley & Wright were operating stages daily to Los Angeles, except on Sunday. William Tweed's stages left the Horton House three times a week for Julian City, and John Capron was running his stages to Yuma also three times a week. The whaling industry continued on Ballast Point, and 55,000 gallons of whale oil were taken in the 1871-72 season. The *Bulletin,* which had been converted into a daily by Morse and others during the tidelands fight, was sold to W. Jeff Gatewood, the lawyer who had helped to found *The San Diego Union.* He changed the name to the *Daily World* and made it Democratic in policy. The population of San Diego County was estimated to be 7359.

On April 20, 1872, a large section of Old Town burned. It was the final humiliation in the decline of California's first settle-

Old Town, in the area where civilization began on the West Coast, faded with time and a fire left it a final loser to New San Diego.

ment. The fire started in the old courthouse, or office of the mayor, on San Diego Avenue near the intersection of Mason Street. It had been built by members of the Mormon Battalion during the military occupation of California, and at the time was being used as a store by Marcus Schiller. The fire spread to the adjoining buildings, the Colorado House, the Franklin House, and other structures. The buildings were on the west side of the Plaza. The sparks fell on the tile roof of the Estudillo House, or Ramona's Marriage Place, across the street on the south side of the Plaza, and the tiles alone saved it from catching fire and threatening the Seeley House, the former home of Juan Bandini which had been converted into a hotel. Losses approached $20,000. Old Town slipped into history and was virtually forgotten.

On May 2 against powerful opposition from Northern California, Congress authorized the Texas and Pacific Railroad Company to build and equip a railroad from the Mississippi River to the Pacific Coast. Scott acquired the rights of the ill-fated Memphis and El Paso and with federal land grants calculated to be worth $68,000,000, he announced he was ready to begin building the long-desired railroad along the 32nd parallel, from Marshall, Texas, to San Diego. Engineers arrived to begin making the necessary surveys along three possible routes, by way of Campo and Jacumba, by way of San Felipe Pass and Warner's Ranch, and by way of the San Gorgonio Pass and then southwest to San Diego. This last should have raised a flag of warning, but San Diego was too happy and too enthused over the prospective visit of Tom Scott himself.

102

A settlement became a town. At the left can be seen the Horton House and to the right the courthouse looms up against the bright bay.

As Morse wrote to his father on August 21:

This is the critical period in the history of San Diego. A few days will decide whether we are to be one of the great cities of the United States within the next ten years, or whether that time is still in the distant future . . . Tom Scott, the greatest railroad man in the world, president of half a dozen great railroads, and director of a dozen more, will be here in San Diego if no accident happens next Monday, and he says for the purpose of fixing the terminus of the Texas and Pacific Railway, locating sites for shops. He is now in San Francisco with a party of 20 capitalists and financiers of the road . . . our enemies still say he does not intend to build the road to San Diego and they give a thousand reasons for this say-so . . . But the great influence of San Francisco and the Central Pacific Railroad, and in fact the whole of California, will be brought to bear on Tom Scott, to induce him to deflect at Fort Yuma on the Colorado River and run to Los Angeles and San Francisco, so leaving San Diego out in the cold . . . fortunately for us, Tom Scott is immensely wealthy, money can't tempt him . . . he wants the honor of building and controlling a through line from the Pacific to the Atlantic, and to carry the Asiatic commerce from Asia to Europe in his own steamers and on his own railway . . . so I think we are safe, but the crisis is so tremendous I dare not leave.

The day came. A long procession of buggies was lined up at Horton's wharf as the steamer *California* warped up to the dock at 10 o'clock in the morning of August 26, 1872, bringing Tom Scott, the railroad king, and his party of seventeen officials and aides. Waiting on the pier was a huge crowd of San Diegans cheering and applauding Scott's party which waved back at them from the steamer's upper deck.

Thomas L. Nesmith, chairman of San Diego's Committee of Forty, made the introductions at the gangway for San Diego's civic leadership. Among those with Scott were Gen. G. M. Dodge, chief engineer for the Texas and Pacific; W. T. Walters, a Baltimore capitalist; Col. John W. Forney, a Texas and Pacific director and former secretary of the United States Senate; John McManus, a Pennsylvania manufacturer; John S. Harris, the former United States Senator; Gov. J. W. Throckmorton, of Texas; Col. George Williamson, a Louisiana capitalist; Sen. John Sherman, of Ohio, brother of Gen. Tecumseh Sherman; and Gov. Richard C. McCormick, congressional delegate from Arizona. They were quartered at the Horton House.

On the first afternoon the party took a buggy trip through the railroad lands of San Diego, rode out to view the Old Mission and returned for a reception at the Horton House. By 7 o'clock, an hour before a mass meeting was scheduled to begin, more than a thousand San Diegans were waiting in a slow drizzle outside the Horton House. Because of the rain, the meeting was moved to the skating rink across the Plaza, where Scott's party was greeted with more cheers as it entered. Scott's speech was short and to the point:

Thomas Scott

> I say to you now, that we are ready to commence work here at your town, but we expect you to do your share in the enterprise and help us all you can.

He told the happy though rain-spattered San Diegans that arrangements already were completed for laying 500 miles of track through Texas, and that more engineers would be sent to San Diego at once so construction could begin at the western end within four months. He said he saw no reason why the entire project could not be finished within five years:

> Your harbor . . . is more than capacious enough to accommodate the immense amount of trade that will gather at the gateway for the East to be distributed throughout the United States by the trains of the Texas and Pacific Railroad. You have neighbors who will expect to divide this work with you. Among these is San Francisco.

Then, Col. Williamson, Sen. Sherman, Gov. McCormick, Sen. Harris and Col. Forney added promises that painted a golden future for San Diego. They said the Texas and Pacific would result in a San Diego of churches, temples, factories, hotels, schools and thousands of dwelling residences even before the railroad was finished—or at the latest, a few years afterward. Arizona would open up and support hundreds of thousands of head of cattle, and her mines would ship fortunes to the world through San Diego. Texas alone would produce 15,000,000 bales of cotton for export.

The San Diego Union said in its editorial column the next day:

> The people of San Diego, every man, woman and child, welcome to the city the distinguished men whose coming is the signal for the commencement of that great railroad for which we have so long hoped and waited . . . Hard times come again no more. In San Diego henceforth, our course is onward without check or hindrance.

That morning Scott, Throckmorton and McManus took a buggy trip with their hosts to the Border Monument, from where *The San Diego Union's* reporter commented:

The unanimous opinion of the different members of the party was that it was a mere question of time, not only concerning the cession of Lower California to the United States, but also the entire northern portion of Old Mexico.

Returning, the party had lunch at National City as guests of Warren and Frank Kimball, then moved on to the ranch of Col. George Stone and Chalmers Scott where they were toasted with champagne punch by another group of San Diegans, then returned to town in a long procession of buggies. That afternoon Scott's group and the city trustees met in the San Diego Bank. C. P. Taggart spoke for the San Diegans and told Scott that, "We have willing hearts and strong shoulders, but our pockets are empty." San Diego's conditions were that the terminus and depot were to be placed so as to best serve the public, though within the city, and that the line was to be built due east from San Diego.

Scott agreed to the location of the terminus and depot, but reserved judgment on whether the line would run directly east, pending the opinion of his engineers. Scott then presented his conditions. They were that while he would not ask San Diego for bonds or cash subsidies, they wanted title to all the lands of the San Diego & Gila Railroad which the company valued at $1,000,000 but Scott at $5,000,000, and a right of way through the city and county 100 feet wide; a lot 1500 feet in length and 600 feet wide adjoining the waterfront; and 100 acres of tidelands acceptable to the company. To the relief of the San Diegans, the conditions seemed reasonable. They adjourned the meeting to discuss them. At 4 o'clock they met again in the Horton House parlor and agreed on all of the conditions. Announcement of the news was met with applause from a crowd outside the Horton House.

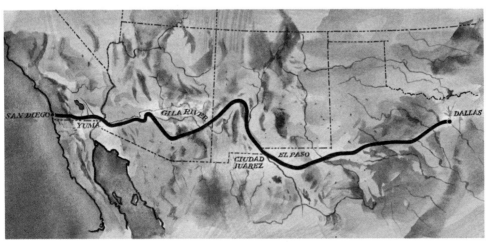

The projected route of the Texas & Pacific Railroad led to San Diego. But a financial panic dashed the town's great hopes for the future.

San Diegans were satisfied that the line would enter San Diego County through the Jacumba Pass, or, at the worst, by way of Warner's Ranch.

That night, while the railroad king and his party feasted at a lavish banquet with the San Diegans at the Horton House, other San Diegans celebrated outside in the Plaza by firing off explosions in salute to Scott and the railroad. After dinner, a procession of San Diegans, light-headed with golden promises, followed Scott and his party back to the *California,* where they gave three rousing cheers as the steamer put out into the stream.

When the *California* sailed at midnight, one of the passengers was Frank Kimball. He had conferred privately with Scott and noted in his diary that they had come to a general understanding. At San Francisco, Kimball agreed to convey half of the National Ranch, or 11,000 acres in alternate portions, including all of the town site not yet deeded to others, and the wharf and franchise, in exchange for $40,000 in gold, and on condition that the railroad line cross the ranch eastward. The agreement of sale was made out in the name of John P. Green, private secretary to Scott. The Kimballs were certain they had slipped the depot away from San Diego.

The land and home building boom began all over again. In September Frank Kimball met with James A. Evans, chief engineer of the California division for the Texas and Pacific, and privately received the disturbing information that engineering studies made it advisable to select the northernmost route through San Gorgonio Pass. He assured Kimball, however, that from there the line would turn southwest to San Diego and that the commitments to him on National City would be fulfilled.

In the early months of 1873, San Diegans began to get restless. The route had not been formally announced and no construction had been undertaken. On February 12 *The San Diego Union* commented that the people were manifesting some anxiety lest the railroad should reach San Diego from the north instead of the east:

> We have heard a lot of foolish talk about the consequences of such an event ...it is a matter of little moment whether the road comes directly from Fort Yuma directly west, along the boundary line, or by way of San Gorgonio Pass. Indeed by the latter route the immediate interests of the city would be advantaged because it would open up at an early day connections with the rich San Bernardino Valley.

But the fears were not calmed. The congressional deadline for starting work was May 2, 1873. A letter from Scott gave assurance that the delay was due only to the necessity of a thorough survey through San Diego County. At last, in April, and with only a few days advance notice, Texas and Pacific officials arrived to begin the long-promised work.

On April 21 a ground-breaking ceremony was held at a point on the bay near the southeast corner of Horton's Addition and near the railroad lands originally granted by the people to the San Diego and Gila company. These lands lay to the east of Horton's Addition along the waterfront from New San Diego to National City. These were the tidelands which Taggart and Howard had sought to appropriate for themselves.

Horton turned over the first spadeful of earth. It was an emotional moment for him and "the greatest honor that the Pacific Coast could possibly confer on me." Forgiveness was the spirit of the occasion. Taggart reminded San Diegans that Horton had commenced the city and that it had gone ahead more rapidly than any other on the coast. As for Horton's turning the first spadeful of dirt, Taggart said:

I do not say this to flatter Mr. Horton, because he don't like me and I don't like him . . . but . . . I conceive his selection as the most appropriate thing.

Confident that he had secured the terminus for his land, Frank Kimball dismissed the proceedings as "disgraceful."

Several weeks later, on May 7, San Diego received a telegram

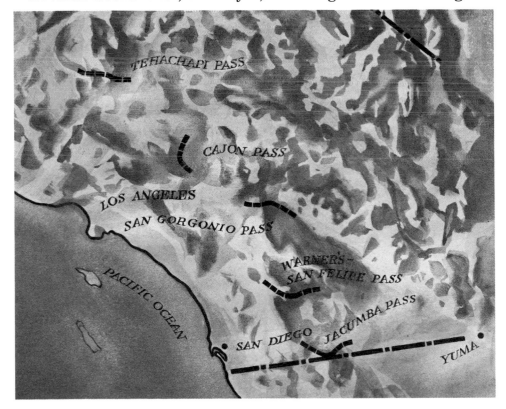

These were the mountain passes into Southern California—and the best ones led to Los Angeles. Because of them, San Diego took a back seat.

from Scott confirming the selection of the San Gorgonio Pass as the best and cheapest route to San Diego. The line was to run from San Diego up the coast to the entrance to the San Luis Rey River Valley, up the valley and then across the Santa Margarita Ranch through Temecula Canyon and then to San Gorgonio and from there to the Yuma gateway. The terminal and depot and shops would be located in San Diego. It was a blow to Frank Kimball. Most of his hopes for National City died with that telegram. Hundreds of persons who had invested in his lands saw the fortunes they had anticipated vanish overnight. But San Diego spun gaily on.

D. M. Berry, who represented a colonization scheme that later established the city of Pasadena, looked over El Cajon Valley and said it was the most beautiful place he had seen in California but doubted any colonists would bore through granite to reach water. He commented in a letter:

> The people are all in the real estate business, and will not dig wells and irrigate the land and develop the country . . . even the ice they use is made in a factory in Los Angeles, and the hay and fruit come from here . . . The "meanest" place of 20 acres you would think was in paradise from the newspapers. But the thing will ruin the owners . . . the lying of the San Diego papers is something awful to think of . . . Horton asked $5000 for a bare city lot in the center of San Diego.

It was a glorious year. The town outgrew its 150 wells and twenty-six windmills, many of which supplied groups of houses by systems of pipes, though, unfortunately, most of them tapped a streak of salt water that coursed diagonally under the town. The San Diego Water Company was formed and drilled in Pound Canyon, where stray horses and cattle were being impounded under the no-fence law. This was in the canyon in the southwest part of Balboa Park where the Cabrillo Freeway was later constructed. A strong subterranean stream and cavern were tapped at 300 feet, with a capacity of 54,000 gallons per hour. Two concrete tank reservoirs of 70,000 and 100,000 gallon capacities were constructed on opposite mesas above the canyon. Plans were developed to lay mains and deliver water by gravity flow to the new homes rising so fast on the waterfront mesas. A second bank, the Commercial Bank, opened for business. The assessor listed 825,263 acres of agricultural land—though a half million of that was still tied up in the large ranchos and mostly devoted to cattle and sheep raising—valued at $1,263,542, or about $1.50 an acre. Horton himself had built a wharf and ten major structures. The city had a population of 4000 and 1000 homes, but Horton urged everybody to build still more houses.

WHY NOT SELL
THE CLIMATE?

This is how Stonewall mine appeared at its height in the late 1800's. Heavy snows in the Cuyamacas often closed down mining operations.

CHAPTER VIII

In California 1873 was a year of frenzied speculation. The Comstock silver lode in Nevada was pouring new riches into the pockets of San Francisco stock syndicates. Everyone, no matter how poor, speculated in mining shares. No rumor was too wild to be believed. Even some of San Francisco's shrewdest financiers, including the presumably infallible William C. Ralston, president of the Bank of California, succumbed to the promotion of a fictitious diamond field in which uncut diamonds were "salted" over the ground in the Rocky Mountains. They were saved from being swindled only by the belated discovery of a geological report.

Millions of acres in the Central Valleys of California, some of it from old Spanish and Mexican grants but mostly former government lands, had passed into the hands of the railroads and large companies which began to introduce grain growing on a gigantic scale, and as W. H. Bishop, a visitor to the state wrote in 1872, "A man will plough but a single furrow a day on his farm, but this may be twenty miles long."

On September 13, 1873, the bottom fell out of the stock market in New York. It was "Black Friday."

Tom Scott, the president of the Texas and Pacific Railroad, was in Europe. He had made arrangements with the leading financial houses of Paris to market $54,000,000 worth of railroad bonds, and while waiting for the negotiations to be completed, he had gone to London to enjoy the city's entertainment. Not knowing he had left for London, the French brokers tried in vain to reach him to complete the deal and accept the bonds. By the time Scott had returned to Paris, the American economy on the Eastern seaboard was in wild disorder, and the French financiers were no longer interested.

For more than a month after "Black Friday" San Diegans went on believing that Tom Scott and the Texas and Pacific had survived the financial disaster. *The San Diego Union's* telegraph stories told of Scott's success in placing the Texas and Pacific bonds in Europe. Then on November 6, after Scott had returned to New York, came the news that the bonds had not been placed, though there was no reason for alarm because Scott was sure to receive a government subsidy to complete the railroad.

In San Diego, the roadbed construction crew continued grading as if nothing had happened, laying the roadbed across the San Diego River and northward along the shore of Mission Bay. Twenty thousand railroad ties and 1,670,000 feet of lumber had arrived and a locomotive water tank was under construction at the depot site. *The San Diego Union* noted that new settlers were continuing to arrive in town and "San Diego today is the liveliest town on the coast and her future prospects are as bright as ever."

In Julian in early December the miners held a jubilee and torchlight procession to celebrate the favorable court decision in the Cuyamaca Grant case. United States Land Commissioner Willis Drummond ruled that the Cuyamaca Grant was limited to the boundaries obvious on the original Mexican *diseño*, or map, and not to the lines of later surveys, and that the northern boundary was marked by Cuyamaca peak, or Iguai; the Laguna Seca, or

This neat etching shows progress in appearance of Western building. It was made in 1873 and looks south from Third and D Streets.

lake; and the Cuyamaca Indian *rancheria,* all of which were some five miles south of the Julian mining district.

The San Diego horse racing season opened at the track in Mission Valley with the largest crowd in history. Ranchers and whalers had had a good year, producing 599,756 pounds of wool, 116,000 pounds of honey, 5344 hides and 40,200 gallons of whale oil. Miners had produced $500,000 in gold bullion. The 187 ships which had called at the port had brought 16,025 tons of freight other than lumber; 6,015,185 feet of lumber including the Texas and Pacific stock, 749,000 laths and shakes, 1,403,750 shingles and 1260 split posts.

Gold scales

Horton's bank block at the corner of Third and D Streets was finished in late November, adding another touch of elegance to the downtown area, and the walls of the new Commercial Bank block were going up at the corner of Fifth and G Streets.

Not even the announcement on December 11 that the New York banking house of Jay Cooke & Company, which had been involved in railroad financing, had been forced into bankruptcy, could dampen San Diego's optimism. *The San Diego Union* said that while most people seemed to look upon the progress of the railroad as the basis for the town's prosperity, the Julian mines were free to operate with settlement of the Cuyamaca dispute, the Lower California mines had produced half a million dollars in gold, and a new placer discovery at Japa, below the border, was expected to produce as much. Farmers had had bumper crops, and sheep ranchers were delighted with theirs; blacksmiths and wagon makers in the city were working at full capacity, and at Ballast Point the War Department had fifty men at work erecting earthworks 1100 feet long behind which it planned to install fifteen heavy caliber guns that could sweep the bay from La Playa to the mouth of the harbor. The project was to cost $225,000. The first ten-mile section of the Texas and Pacific roadbed was nearly finished, as Scott had promised.

The second day of the racing season had to be postponed because of rain. The San Diego River went over its banks in one day and several hundred people collected to watch the sight as it washed about Old Town and tore at the new Texas and Pacific roadbed where it crossed the river. In the mountains work at the mines came to a halt as the downpour softened roads and wagons were unable to move ore to the stamp mills. Eight days of rain turned the creek in Banner Canyon into a roaring cataract.

Farmers and ranchers were jubilant at the first heavy rains, for it was their guarantee that they would see no recurrence of the disastrous drought of two years earlier that had forced many to desert their lands and homes. But for them and the rest of San Diego, their troubles were just beginning.

As the calendar turned over into 1874, Alonzo Horton, heavily overcommitted, leased the Horton House to Gilbert Lane for five years for $27,000. A month later Sheriff S. W. Craigue was forced to take over the lease and he made Capt. James S. Gordon, then manager of the San Diego Chamber of Commerce, its new manager.

The frequent heavy rains that had kept the Texas and Pacific grading crews slogging through the mud for more than a month became a steady torrent in mid-January, continuing without pause for six days and nights on land already saturated to its limit. At 2 o'clock on Sunday morning, January 18, a wall of water came down the San Diego River carrying everything in its path. When the first flood crest hit the river mouth, Old Town was flooded, the railroad roadbed was carried away, and only quick work on the part of some volunteers with a boat managed to save a family that lived on a small farm in the flats west of Old Town. Their house, garden, trees and everything they owned were swept away. Again, hundreds of San Diegans gathered on the high ground to watch the river, choked with trees and stumps and drowned livestock, pouring out onto the flats so heavily that no land showed between the river mouth and Point Loma. Several families in Old Town hastily gathered their belongings and moved out of their rain-sodden adobe houses. Among those of the historic adobes that collapsed in the storm was the Lopez House, one of the oldest. It had been built at the foot of Stockton Hill before the American conquest by Bonifacio Lopez, who was known as "The King."

The in-bound Yuma stage was nearly lost at Otay when the driver attempted to drive his team across Otay Creek at flood stage. Virtually every road in Southern California was washed out and the only communication between San Diego and the outside world was by telegraph and the steamers. Rufus K. Porter reported that it took him a full day to get from San Diego to his home in Spring Valley, from where he sent back word that he could hear the roar of the Sweetwater River which was three miles from his house. Residents and squatters in the Tia Juana River Valley hastily moved their stock and belongings to higher ground as the river began to rise and high winds drove the downpour across the land. By January 29 the Tia Juana River was eighteen feet deep in some places. At the ford in the mountains where the road crossed the headwaters of the Tia Juana River, the eastbound Yuma stage lost nearly all of its mail as the driver and team barely made it across the torrent. James Hamilton, an expressman, came into San Diego on February 5 and reported that he and his partner for three weeks had been trying to reach Julian with a freight wagon and had been unable to do so, as roads had gaps up to ten feet deep and seventy-five feet wide. Two weeks later the Tia Juana River was two miles wide on the flood plain, and rising rapidly.

At the height of the flood excitement, on January 28, James A. Evans, chief engineer of the Texas and Pacific Railroad, returned after a six-weeks trip to the East with reassurance for San Diego. Evans said all was well as Scott was sure to get the government subsidy and the 400 miles of Texas and Pacific line in operation in Texas was paying splendidly.

As far east as Phoenix, the land fared no better. Yuma was flooded in three-quarters of the town and many houses were washed away. The Gila River rose twelve feet in one night and the Colorado River was three miles wide at Yuma.

It was during the flood period that the no-fence law was put to one of its violent tests at San Luis Rey. In mid-February, Patrick A. Graham, a rancher, picked up a stray horse from his property and put it in the public corral. When a neighboring rancher, J. Wild, sent his ranch hand, George Blanchard, to go after it, Graham told him he would have to pay the 50-cent feed bill. Blanchard pulled a pistol and shot Graham in the neck, critically wounding him. William Blounts Couts, justice of the peace, arrested Blanchard and set the bail at $5000. Blanchard never had a chance to raise bail. He was found hanged to a tree the next morning on the banks of the San Luis Rey River. A woolen gag had been tied in his mouth and fastened with a rawhide thong behind his head.

Near the end of February word came from the Stonewall Mine that nine days of continuous rainfall followed by a fifteen-inch snowfall had brought everything in the Cuyamaca Mountains to a stop. By mid-March the rivers were still running full. A second ferry had gone into operation at the Old Town crossing of the San Diego River and both were doing a good business. A Los Angeles and San Diego stage coach tried to cross the river near Old Town and was nearly lost when the horses and the coach bogged down in soft sand. The stage was saved by quick use of boats and long ropes.

It was not until the end of March that the first freight wagons were able to haul their loads to the mountain mines. Spring burst

(Next page)
Banner rivaled Julian at the height of the Gold Rush but became San Diego county's largest "ghost town." It sat below the pine hills of Julian, top right, and the Cuyamaca Mountains. Gold-rich Chariot Canyon slices into the mountains, in left center. A hotel, center, and first stamp mill, right, were landmarks. Floods washed the town away. Painting by Marjorie Reed Creese.

115

Ore train

onto the scene and San Diego blossomed into a solid carpet of wildflowers. Campo sent its rainfall figures into town for the five months of November through March. There had been more than thirty inches of rain, including ten inches that had fallen in February.

While the economic scene in San Diego remained rather quiet during the spring, the town of Banner was a scene of furious activity. New construction began almost as soon as the freight wagons could move through the deep mud. By mid-May two stores were under construction, one owned by "The Count," of Julian, and another by A. P. Frary and Solomon Shulz. A Mrs. Koehn was building a two-story hotel; three saloon buildings were under construction and an addition was being put on another building. Two stamp mills were operating full time, the Bailey Mill and the McMechan Mill, and a third mill, the Chariot, was shut down for installation of heavier steam machinery. Within two months the settlement of a few cabins at Banner had grown to a community of forty buildings. Its residents celebrated the Fourth of July with a thirty-eight-gun cannon salute, some thirteen more salutes when the American flag was raised, had a parade and picnic, and finished off with another thirteen-gun salute when the flag was lowered at sunset.

Julian had developed into a settled community. By the summer of 1872 it had about fifty houses, three hotels, four stores, two restaurants, and a schoolhouse, plus saloons. The unpainted hotel and saloon buildings of Julian and Banner were not the large structures common to the raw towns of the Western Plains. Instead of the dust of the windy plains there was the mud of fierce mountain storms. There were no big gambling halls, with their ornate lamps, mirrors, polished bars and elegantly-clothed and painted ladies. Miners and prospectors dealt cards around unfinished tables in front of roughly planked bars. In Chariot Canyon the miners lived in cave-like houses erected with rock slabs and which outlasted most of the mines themselves. There were Indian women of all work and the willing Chinese. As in the North and in other mining towns of the Far West, the Chinese were assigned to the most exposed areas and the meanest of shacks.

Schools, churches and family life appeared much sooner in Julian and Banner than in the mining camps and towns of the Sierra Nevada during the Gold Rush. It was a score of years later and a new generation had come to stay and not just to gamble for sudden riches. A hundred years later unmarked mounds could be traced on a rise of ground across the creek that ran alongside the

Boot Hill, Banner

town of Banner. It was a "boot hill" of forgotten men who cheated history by dying of whiskey instead of bullets.

Horace Fenton Wilcox in his recollections said:

> During the gold rush Julian and Banner was pretty tough places, but I reckon they wasn't any tougher'n most mining camps of that time. Every other place of business was a saloon, a gamblin' joint, or a dance hall. But on the whole things was pretty orderly. We never had much shootin'.

Chuck Wagon

The Wilcox toll road had been carved down Banner Canyon, from Julian to Banner, and the rate was $1 a wagon, and 25 cents for a burro and prospector, if they could catch them. Before its construction heavy equipment had been lowered 1000 feet down the hills in what were called "stone sleds." Joe Swycaffer built a wagon road to the Golden Chariot mine far up Chariot Canyon. The year of 1873 was a good one. The *San Diego Daily World* remarked that the county was developing into a first class mining district even though not a dollar of outside capital had as yet been invested in the mines.

Late in 1873 Don Juan Machado, of the old San Diego family, came in from his ranch in Lower California with a handful of rubies found in the diggings of Japa, 100 miles from San Diego. In February 1874 placer diggings were discovered in San Vicente Creek, forty miles from San Diego, on a headwater of the San Diego River, and the belief that a large vein of gold quartz somewhere in the surrounding hills was the source, drew a great many prospectors to the area.

As a result of the heavy storm damage to the road to the mines, the County Board of Supervisors hired A. P. Frary to build a new road to Julian by way of San Vicente Canyon. On June 11 *The San Diego Union* published a letter from Frary saying that he and his crew of twenty-four men had the road half-finished, but warned that miners had been cutting timber in the Julian area, taking the choice pieces they wanted and leaving the trunks to rot on the ground. If the waste of timber were not stopped, said Frary, "there will not be a stick of wood within five miles of Julian three years from now."

A. P. Frary

The prominent New Town merchant and civic leader, J. T. Nash, announced on May 14 that he had made a huge gold and silver strike near the foot of Smith Mountain, forty-five miles northeast of San Diego, and later known as Palomar Mountain. Nash said he had opened four veins of gold ore and three of silver. He named the gold strikes Shenandoah, Flying Dutchman, Rising Sun and Fleetwing. Two of the silver strikes were the Black Eagle and Silver Rule.

Collis P. Huntington

A few days later the Helvetia Mine Company of Julian announced that it had incorporated for $3,600,000, with its chief stockholders as "Count" Dwarkowski and Solomon Shulz, Julian merchants; Thomas C. Stockton, August Burkhardt and Oliver Sanford, all prominent men in Julian and Banner mining ventures. They said work would begin immediately to install new and more powerful machinery at the mine.

On July 18 the Hamilton Express Company reached Julian with the first wagon load of freight over the new road. The War Department ran short of funds and work halted on the construction of the new fort by Ballast Point. Nothing more was done for twenty-three years. By August work had ceased on the Texas and Pacific roadbed in San Diego. Scott announced that he would make no application for a government subsidy, at least until the next winter. The financial panic and the growing public resentment over the vast land grants for railroad promotions were making the Congress wary of financing Scott's railroad venture, and he faced formidable opposition in Collis P. Huntington, one of the original "Big Four" of California who still intended to dominate the Pacific Coast from the Columbia River to the Gulf of California.

The Chamber of Commerce in 1874 published a pamphlet listing the natural advantages of San Diego, stressing its commercial as well as agricultural possibilities, to counteract what it called false pictures which "are sometimes drawn by jealous and adversely interested parties, many of whom have never seen, and are profoundly ignorant of, the object of their jealousy."

The publication spoke of the Texas and Pacific Railroad, as if nothing had changed, and of the proposed Southern Pacific route to Yuma and the possibilities both held for San Diego as the gateway to the Southwest. But the character of the new arrivals would change. The speculators were leaving and in time they would be replaced by settlers who sought not money but climate. The Chamber of Commerce publication took note of this, and stated:

As a national sanitarium, San Diego is unsurpassed. Hundreds of invalids have been restored to health, or greatly benefited, by our health-giving climate ... the late Prof. Agassiz whose testimony is worthy of the highest consideration, after spending some weeks in San Diego, thus expressed his opinion with regard to the climate, at a public meeting: "There is one advantage that I, as a scientific man, may lay more stress upon than is necessary; but I hardly think it possible. It is the question of latitude. You are here upon the 32nd parallel, beyond the reach of the severe winters of the higher altitudes. This is your capital, and it is worth millions to you."

Prof. Louis Agassiz, an internationally known scientist of Swiss birth, had visited San Diego at the same time as had Scott and the Texas and Pacific officials, as a member of an expedition aboard the United States Coast Survey steamer *Hassler*. He had collected a large number of sea specimens from San Diego's Chinese fishermen.

Not all persons in San Diego believed that its future lay with its climate, or that San Diegans would ever be provident enough to be satisfied with less than the glories which they had glimpsed.

J. A. Shepherd

J. A. Shepherd, Horton's bookkeeper, wrote to his relative in England that "it is a standing joke at our expense, all over California that San Diego has lived on 'harbor' and 'climate' for six years, and at last the people are getting starved out."

The population of San Diego began to decline. Horton no longer seemed to have the enthusiasm of the earlier days. He, more than anyone, probably felt that direct trains from the East would never arrive. It had been a long way from Hortonville in Wisconsin to San Diego in California, and a success beyond his dreams had been within his grasp, but now it was slipping away. He had sold his wharf and had been forced to further mortgage his hotel. Taxes ate away at the unsold lands he had obtained for 27½ cents an acre just seven years before. In a letter, David M. Berry wrote that "San Diego is bankrupt...Horton is busted and property nearly worthless."

The San Diego Union carried long lists of property sold by the County Assessor for failure to pay delinquent taxes. From April 1873 to April 1874 the lists included 468 parcels in sizes ranging from twenty-five-foot lots up to parcels of 400 acres. For the same twelve-month period of 1874 to 1875 the assessor sold 336 more parcels ranging up to 300 acres, a total of 804 parcels in twenty-four months, belonging to more than 450 individuals.

The no-fence law was bringing ruin to many cattlemen, and on June 10, 1874, Cave J. Couts died in the Horton House, shorn at the end of much of the wealth he had acquired over two decades. Once a lieutenant in the United States Dragoons, he resigned to marry a daughter of Don Juan Bandini and built one of Southern California's most famed homes, at Guajome Rancho east of Oceanside. He acquired two more of the original Spanish-Mexican ranchos, Buena Vista and San Marcos, for a total of 20,000 acres, and sent huge herds of cattle to San Francisco during the Gold Rush. But his world, a baronial one typical of the early days of the American period, was vanishing and his burial was reported in only a few inches of newspaper notice.

Despite the new flurry of prospecting, and even though some

outside capital was beginning to appear, the peak of gold production in San Diego County had been reached. Though there were twenty-three mines being worked, eleven of them considered very valuable, and there were mills with a total of seventy-five stamps, production was down sharply in 1874. It was due in some measure to the severe weather. Gold brought out of the Julian and Banner districts in that year was valued at only $193,000, compared to the $500,000 of the previous year. The slump in mining intensified and Rossiter W. Raymond in the United States Mineral Resources Report of 1875 reported that "most of these mills are idle and none of the mining operations have proven permanently profitable."

The depression rolled across the country and slowly settled on California. By the summer of 1875 many banks were in trouble and a run started on the Bank of California, in San Francisco, the most important financial institution in the state. Waves of frenzied people pounded on the closed doors and glass windows demanding their money. William C. Ralston, known as "the man who built San Francisco," and president of the bank, ostensibly went for his usual swim, and waded into the ocean, and died.

The town that had grown from a population of several hundred to 4000 in seven years and had seen the erection of nearly 1000 homes, now slipped back to a population of about 2000. Horton was struggling to save what he could, and his bookkeeper, or business agent, Shepherd, informed him that it was imperative he mortgage his best property to meet pressing debts of more than $17,000, and suggested that he not bring his niece, Mary, out to San Diego until the Spring as it would add at least $35 a month to his expenses. The Kimballs turned to raising sheep on the National Ranch and set out 400 orange trees in the Sweetwater Valley. Fr. Antonio Ubach in 1874 laid out the new Catholic cemetery on the hill above Old Town, where many of the builders of San Diego's first boom would find their final resting places. In the same year, in April, San Diego finally received the patent to its pueblo lands, twenty-eight years after the American conquest when assurances were given that all titles would be quickly and properly recognized.

The idea of a railroad was not entirely dead. The issue in Congress was now whether the Texas and Pacific would be allowed to build to Yuma and through the San Gorgonio Pass, and then to San Diego by way of Temecula Canyon, or whether the Southern Pacific should extend through to Yuma, cross Arizona and meet Scott's line coming west. Huntington, of the original "Big Four" of the Central Pacific, bested Scott at every turn.

A compromise of the railroad battle was in the air, which provided that the Texas and Pacific would build from Fort Worth to El Paso, and thence 100 miles into New Mexico to form a junction with the Southern Pacific, and that the Southern Pacific was to acquire all the rights and lands of the Texas and Pacific in San Diego County and have the right to build from San Diego to San Gorgonio Pass, to connect with its main line to Fort Yuma. As the compromise did not require the Southern Pacific to build the connection, San Diego decided it had been abandoned, or at best, would never be more than a branch-line town. The San Diego Committee of Forty sent Scott the following telegram:

The citizens of San Diego rely implicitly upon your honor and good faith for the consummation of your oft-repeated pledges. You promised that if the route directly east proved feasible it should be constructed. Fulfill your pledge. The direct line is the only route upon which a competing railroad should enter San Diego and they will unanimously oppose any compromise that will not secure that line.

Scott's reply placed the full burden on San Diego:

Have used my utmost efforts to secure San Diego a railroad line on such route as can best effect the object; and if you can effect it in any better shape than I can, I should be very glad to have you take it up and adjust it with any party, or on any terms that you may think best. But in taking these steps, I shall expect you to relieve me of any possible obligation.

San Diego bombarded Congress with appeals to fulfill its promises to the people of San Diego, and sent Horton, David Felsenheld and Col. Thomas S. Sedgwick to assist its congressman, S. O. Houghton, in the wearying and obviously losing struggle. Horton and other citizens induced Huntington and Crocker of the Southern Pacific to visit San Diego, in the hope they could be persuaded to put San Diego on the main line. They asked if San Diego would be willing to donate half as much land as had been given to Scott, and when this proposal was rejected, lost interest.

San Diego's case was summed up in a final and prophetic telegram sent by the Board of Trustees to Col. Sedgwick in Washington. The people saw all too clearly the fate that was rushing upon the town and its port. It read:

It is the deliberate and unchangeable conviction of San Diego, that the proposed connection north of here, in the hands of the Southern Pacific Company, would be an injury instead of a benefit to us, because:

1. It places in control of one corporation for all time every approach to our harbor.

2. Trade and population would be taken away from, instead of brought here, while the road is building. It is now moving from the northern part of the county to Colton.

3. By occupying the only passes it would prevent extension of Utah Southern road and connection with Union Pacific.

4. It would supersede construction of direct line from Anaheim, increasing our distance from San Francisco to 650 miles.

5. It would increase the distance from Yuma by 60 miles.

6. Experience has taught us that the strongest promises in a bill do not protect us against subsequent amendments at the desire of the corporations. Legislation that fails to require immediate beginning at this end, and construction of so much road before next session of Congress as to remove the temptation to amend bill, is worse than worthless.

7. Whatever supposed guarantees may be put in the bill making the road a "highway" it is well known by all engineers that the company building the road holds *in fact* control of it; and no other company can have equal use, or will build parallel road.

8. Southern Pacific Company one year ago agreed to build on direct line, provided San Diego would consent that it should have the western end.

So far from a San Diego standpoint: But we hold no petty local view; we supplicate no favors. The interest of San Diego is here bound up with the national interest. We submit to impartial statesmen the conceded truth that the proposed compromise diverts the Nation's bounty from the original purpose of the Southern transcontinental legislation; deprives all the millions east of San Diego of direct access to their nearest Pacific harbor and destroys competition for all time. San Diego's natural advantages are such, that in asking the Nation's aid for the construction of a railroad to her port, she asks it upon a line, and upon terms that will contribute to the Nation's support and wealth for all time to come; while the compromise plan will be an intolerable and interminable national burden. For these reasons San Diego prefers no bill, rather than the San Gorgonio branch.

Many San Diegans suspected that Huntington had offered a connection with the Southern Pacific only as insurance against the entrance of Scott, and that as the Texas and Pacific was on the verge of defeat, he was under no pressure to please San Diego. Though Huntington was quoted in later years as saying that "grass could grow in the streets" of San Diego for all he cared,

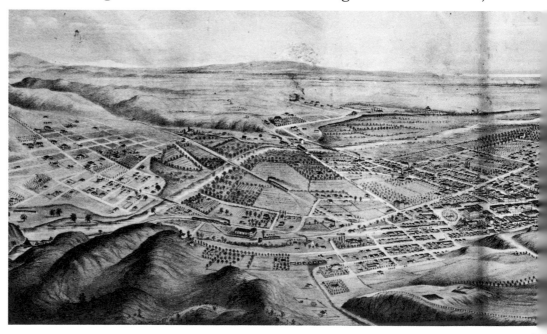

Morse, as chairman of the committee which met with the Southern Pacific people, and Horton recalled that they were courteous and sympathetic but not much interested. They indicated the Southern Pacific was not anxious to compete with water transportation on the coast.

An entirely different account of the attitude of the Southern Pacific was given a decade later in a letter written by Frank Kimball. He stated that Crocker, one of the "Big Four," had told him:

Charles Crocker

> You will never live long enough to see a railroad laid to the Bay of San Diego, nor one laid in the state by a transcontinental railroad which we do not lay... I have my foot on the neck of San Diego and I'm going to keep it there.

Los Angeles sealed the fate of a transcontinental road for San Diego when it and San Pedro gave the Southern Pacific a site for a depot and $600,000 to bring the line directly into Los Angeles through the Tehachapi Pass from the north and through the San Gorgonio Pass from the east. Los Angeles, not San Diego, was left to challenge San Francisco's dominating position in the commerce of California. By May of 1877 the well-financed Southern Pacific, subsidized with 7,500,000 acres of California agricultural land, had reached Yuma and the Colorado River, and before it stretched the land grants originally given to the Texas and Pacific by Arizona and New Mexico. Huntington picked them up.

Once more San Diegans talked of building their own railroad, as they had planned years before, between San Diego and Los Angeles, or San Diego and San Bernardino, and then San Diego and Utah to connect with the Union Pacific, but nothing came of

While San Diego slept, Los Angeles was emerging as a city, as shown by this bird's eye view sketched in 1877. But it had no port.

them. Taxpayer suits were filed against Scott and the Texas and Pacific to recover the more than 8000 acres of lands which had been granted as subsidy. The Southern Pacific was driven across the country to El Paso and eventually to New Orleans.

Though San Diego, in its dream of railroad riches, had not been inclined to pay too much attention to the advice of the late Prof. Agassiz, to build its future on its climate, there soon came an end to the loss of population, and a renewed trickle of settlers were attracted by the warm sun and a mild life. These would be the quiet years, but nevertheless, growing ones.

George W. Marston was beginning his climb to a position of civic leadership. He had left his job in the Horton House to work as a clerk for A. Pauly & Sons and then in the general store of Joseph Nash. There he met Charles S. Hamilton, who also was a clerk, and in the spring of 1873 they had joined forces to buy the store for $10,000. Hamilton gave a promissory note for $5000 at twelve percent interest, and Marston $5000 in cash advanced by his father, also at twelve percent interest. This was just a few months before the railroad bubble burst, but their partnership survived the depression, and in five years they had paid off their debts. In 1878 Marston established his own store in a small wood structure on the northwest corner of what is now Fifth Avenue and Broadway.

The San Diego of that period is best described by Van Dyke:

The real estate offices were deserted; the hotels had more waiters than guests; empty stores and houses became numerous on all sides. Day after day and year after year the bright sun shone upon quiet streets and storekeepers staring out of the door at our almost unbroken vacancy.

There were many like Marston and Hamilton who were to look back on those years not with bitterness, but with some nostalgia. Sixty years later Marston was to write:

The Tom Scott railroad had failed and we were still living mainly on Great Expectations. Steamer and stage lines were in good running order, we had a daily newspaper, water supply was rather scant, streets unpaved, muddy in winter, dusty in summer. It was a frontier town, but not of the western plains type. Rather rough compared to present standards, but having a charm and picturesque quality that is happily remembered by the pioneers. I believe that cultural and moral standards were quite as high as they are today.

Horton had become more petulant with each disappointment, and leadership was slowly slipping from his hands. He had built a town but not a city. The trains would come but in his lifetime they would not bring the goods of America to be traded across the waterfront for the riches of the Orient.

THE BIG GUN FIGHT
AT CAMPO

Border bandits kept the Old West alive.
Armed bands gathered by camp fires
in threat to destroy Campo
following famed gunfight.

CHAPTER IX

One by one, or in small groups, horsemen carrying pistols or carbines filtered into the area of the little Mexican town of Tecate just below the international border, at a point about fifty miles east of San Diego. It is a high country that slides off quickly into the series of low, easy valleys which formed one of the early routes of travel between Yuma and San Diego. This was the railroad route originally favored by Ephraim Morse and Gen. Rosecrans.

Two miles above the border was the settlement of Campo, where the Gaskill brothers had a store, a mill, a small hotel of sorts, a post office, a large residence, a blacksmith shop and a number of houses. It was all theirs. They ran large herds of cattle over a 900-acre ranch, and there were some people who wondered how they accumulated them. They also raised sheep and hogs and had 400 hives of bees, and were the largest shippers of honey in San Diego County and perhaps in the United States.

The Gaskills, Lumen, 32, and Silas, 46, were handy with guns, as men had to be in the remote areas where many staked out their own domains, and before coming to Campo, they had hunted and killed bears for a livelihood in northern California. The reputation of the Gaskills was such that cattle rustlers from Mexico generally gave Campo Valley a wide berth in their sweeps through

San Diego County. They usually crossed the border at Jacumba near Pete Larkin's stage station, and then circled through Buckman Springs, Pine Valley, Descanso, Viejas Valley, Horsethief Canyon, and then turned south through Cottonwood Canyon and crossed the border to Tecate.

While in the mountains, at an elevation of 2500 feet, Campo is east of the higher ridges, and the winter storms usually drop most of their rain and snow before reaching the small valley. In 1875 there were a number of large oak trees scattered across the valley and some sycamores along the creek which ran through the center of the little settlement and passed directly underneath the store. The cold running water was used as an improvised refrigerator.

Campo was an important settlement, as it was there that the stage coaches and the ten-mule freight wagons stopped to rest their animals after the long climb up the mountain slopes from the west and from the east on the new Yuma road by way of Jacumba that ran entirely within the United States. The Army maintained a telegraph office in the rough wooden building which doubled as a store and *cantina*.

Campo Valley was the domain of the Gaskill brothers who beat off a bandit raid. This is how it appeared a few years later.

Tecate, a squatters' settlement and a hideout for cattle rustlers, was on the abandoned Mexican rancho of one of the former grand Dons of San Diego, Juan Bandini. The ranch was raided and plundered many times by Indians during the chaotic period of the

Mexican rule of California.

The armed riders arriving at Tecate included remnants of the outlaw gang of Tiburcio Vasquez who had been captured at Rancho La Brea, near Los Angeles, on May 21, 1874, and tried and hanged. His followers had scattered. One lieutenant, Clodovio Chavez, continued robbing and killing in San Fernando Valley, north of Los Angeles, then drifted into Arizona.

Two other members of the outlaw band, Pancho Lopez and José Alvijo, swung north to the Panamint and Lone Pine areas of east central California, where they murdered a storekeeper and then fled south into Baja California.

While temporarily hiding out and working as a ranch hand on the Barker Ranch at Texas Hills, Arizona, ninety miles north of Yuma on the Gila River, Chavez was recognized and shot to death on November 26 by another rancher, Clark Clotvig, who had tried to take him into custody. Three days later Clotvig's ranch was shot up by six hard-riding Mexican horsemen.

Rumors persisted that the gang was reforming despite the two deaths, under Pancho Lopez, and as they were in need of more guns and ammunition to arm a larger band they were planning to recruit for outlaw operations in Sonora, they intended to conduct a raid somewhere along the border. The apprehensions of the Gaskills at Campo and of other border ranchers were heightened by the appearance of the mounted gunmen at Tecate. They all seemed to have plenty of money. They gathered, camped and waited.

Many years later Silas Gaskill said in an interview:

I was working at the forge when I learned that the robbers were going to raid us. A Mexican was hanging around the shop and he seemed to be pretty nervous. I was busy and paid no attention to him. He waited until he could talk to me alone. Then he slipped up and whispered in my ear. He said Pancho Lopez and his gang were coming to clean us out. I had been on good terms with the informer and fed him occasionally when he was broke. Anyhow, he put me on guard.

The Gaskills weren't easily frightened. They cleaned and loaded six muzzle-loading shotguns and placed one each in the store, the blacksmith shop, the house, the stable, the post office, and one outside near the post office where it could be grabbed by anyone who might want to join the fight.

On November 30, 1875, four days after Chavez had been killed in Arizona, Pancho Lopez was seen in the general store at San Rafael, forty miles below Tecate, and reportedly witnessed Louis Mendleson, the owner, give his clerk, Henry A. Leclaire, $600 in gold to be delivered to Steiner & Klauber in San Diego. Leclaire

131

left San Rafael in a buggy with two horses and a passenger. The passenger was Don Antonio Sosa, former territorial governor of Baja California. That was the last time the two men were seen alive. Sosa himself had been a rough handler of rustlers. Contemporary news reports say that while governor he had pursued five horse thieves into San Diego County and captured and summarily executed them by gunfire.

On the morning of December 4 two farm wagons with their drivers rattled through Campo and down the road toward Tecate. On the way they met six armed horsemen heading in the direction of Campo. They exchanged greetings and went on. The horsemen were to slip inconspicuously as possible into Campo and open the attack, and then the wagons were to return with nine more men who had been hidden in the brush just over the United States side of the border. In mid-morning Pancho Lopez and his band of killers casually rode into Campo and dismounted, attracting little attention as it was a stopping place for many travelers, and sauntered toward the store and *cantina*.

Two of the men, Alonzo Cota and José Alvijo, preceding Pancho Lopez, went into the store. Not much is known about Cota but Alvijo had been with Pancho Lopez in raids at Panamint and Lone Pine. Loafing inside the store was Rafael Martinez, one of the gang who had been sent into Campo several days earlier. He moved outside, where he joined Teodoro Vasquez, a relative of Tiburcio Vasquez, and Pancho Alvitro, a fugitive wanted for murder in Los Angeles. Most reports say six bandits rode into Campo and one was waiting at the scene, making seven in all. Lopez took a position near the store doorway, from where he could be seen by the men both inside and outside.

The Campo Hotel and Store for many years were important stops for both Army wagons and stage coaches on the lonely Yuma route.

At the moment Lopez raised his hand to give the signal for his men to open fire, a Frenchman on a gray horse rode into town to get mail for his employer, a sheep rancher at Las Juntas. He also was armed. As the two men in the store, Cota and Alvijo, reached for their guns, Lumen Gaskill yelled "murder" and dropped behind a counter and scrambled toward his shotgun. Cota and Alvijo dived over the counter. Cota grabbed Lumen by the hair and Alvijo placed the muzzle of a gun against his chest and pulled the trigger. The bullet went through Lumen's chest, puncturing a lung, and he began to bleed from the mouth. The two bandits left him for dead.

Silas Gaskill

Upon hearing Lumen's cry and the shot, Silas Gaskill, who was repairing a wagon in front of the blacksmith shop, leaped after one of his cached shotguns leaning just inside the shop door. He grabbed the gun and whirled just as Vasquez charged into the shop doorway with a six-shooter in hand. The bandit fired first. His shot was followed by the blast of Silas Gaskill's shotgun. The bullet struck Silas in the side and nicked his arm. In return, Vasquez took the charge of buckshot in his chest at close range and was dead before he hit the ground. Alvitro and Martinez scurried behind the blacksmith shop. Silas ran around the other side and met them coming around a corner. He dropped Martinez with a shot from the second barrel. Alvitro then had only one thought in mind, to get away from that shotgun. He raced toward the mill and hid behind a pile of lumber. Silas ran toward the house to get another shotgun.

Meanwhile the Frenchman who had just ridden into town hurriedly dismounted and put the horse between himself and the bandits and began firing at their leader, Pancho Lopez. One of the shots hit Lopez in the neck and knocked him down, though he returned the Frenchman's fire while sprawled on the ground. Cota and Alvijo, coming out of the store after shooting Lumen Gaskill, and seeing the wounded Lopez, opened fire on the Frenchman and wounded him in the arm.

While Silas was shooting it out with the three bandits in the vicinity of the blacksmith shop, and while the Frenchman was shooting it out in the street with the other three, Lumen Gaskill, bleeding profusely but far from dead, dragged himself along the floor of the store and reached his shotgun under the counter. He crawled to the door and from the floor fired at Alvijo who was standing by the Frenchman's horse. The charge smashed Alvijo to the ground.

Running toward the house for another loaded shotgun, Silas

This is the Gaskills' home at Campo. Crack bear hunters from northern California, they were tough customers for cattle rustlers.

passed a stranger named Livingston who had dashed into the settlement to find out what the shooting was all about, and handed him his empty gun. Unable to find another loaded gun, Silas emerged from the house to see Alvitro, who had recovered from his early fright, walking toward Livingston with a pistol pointed at him. Silas grabbed the empty shotgun away from Livingston and aimed at the bandit. Alvitro once again turned and fled behind the blacksmith shop, and as he went around a corner he came into range of the wounded Lumen who was still lying prone in the doorway of the store. Lumen fired the second barrel of his shotgun and wounded Alvitro.

The accounts all differ somewhat, and a correspondent for *The San Diego Union,* the telegraph operator, on the scene at the time, said he also had exchanged fire with one of the bandits and then scurried for safety under the store, where he found Lumen standing in the icy creek. Lumen had emptied his gun and though faint from loss of blood, had slipped down through a trapdoor and into the water.

The fight had lasted but five or six minutes. Lopez and Alvitro, both wounded, and Cota rode out of town. The two wagons which were to have brought nine more gunmen into action never arrived. It is believed the men had heard the furious shooting and decided the battle was not going as had been anticipated and fled across the border. Silas Gaskill's account given forty years later says Alvitro had been wounded so seriously that Lopez helped him off his horse, sat him down in some bushes, and put a bullet through his head.

The telegraph operator who had remained hidden in fear, returned to his key and clattered out the details of the attack to San Diego. Ranchers in the area also began descending upon Campo. The wounded José Alvijo had been left behind and he had crawled away into the brush and rocks where he intended to hide and then make his way back across the border. Rafael Martinez, not wounded seriously, was taken into custody. The body of Vasquez was buried near the blacksmith shop.

Common pistols 1865-90, Colt .44, Remington .44

The same afternoon a hastily-formed posse of ten ranchers went east on the Yuma road in search of the fleeing bandits. Indian tracking parties were sent out to scour the countryside and returned at 3 o'clock with the news they had found one body three miles west of Campo, near the road. It was assumed to be that of Pancho Alvitro. Positive identification was never recorded. Other ranchers brought guns and ammunition, food and supplies for a full-scale defense, as it was anticipated that the bandits would regroup, assemble their companions around Tecate, and return to the fight. Lookouts were placed on the surrounding hilltops.

At 4 o'clock the next morning José Alvijo, cold and riddled with buckshot, staggered up to the Gaskill home and begged for help. Sheriff Hunsaker and three deputies arrived from San Diego and put the two prisoners, Alvijo and Martinez, under guard. That night while the sheriff and two of the guards were away for a few minutes, or so it was reported, a group of ranchers appeared, tied up the remaining guard, and carried off the prisoners. The next morning some Mexicans from Tecate found the two bandits hanging from a tree by a single piece of rope.

The hangings aroused the population of Tecate, many of whom were in sympathy with the bandits and themselves engaged in occasional cattle rustling. Aroused Mexicans for miles around moved toward Tecate, and lookouts on the American side of the border reported as many as eighty camp fires dotting the valley floor around the town.

Winchester 1873, premium model

A short time after the shooting Simon Miller, a rancher on the road from Yuma, arrived at Campo and reported that three Mexicans, two of them bloody and bandaged, had held him up and stolen the two horses he had with him. The body of the clerk of the store at San Rafael, Henry A. Leclaire, who was to deliver $600 in gold to San Diego, was found twenty miles away outside San Rafael. He had been shot through the head. One of the two horses with his buggy also had been shot but the other one was still in the harness almost dead of thirst and hunger. The former governor of Baja California, Antonio Sosa, who had left with Leclaire, was still missing and so was the gold.

Fear was rife in Campo, and Silas Gaskill wrote to Allan Klauber in San Diego on December 14:

We have been told by parties from Ticarte that they intend to try us again; that they are determined to rob us before they give up. They say they will try it next time with a force sufficient to go through us. It seems rather tough that we can't be protected in some way from being robbed and murdered here at home; minding our own business, does it not? I wish you would use what influence you can for us and see if we can't get some protection in some way. The government ought to protect the Postoffice and Military Telegraph Office here. They will have to be discontinued; probably both officers will be killed in the next attack.

Much of Northern Mexico, especially the state of Sonora, was in a state of rebellion and it was not certain whether the armed men gathering at Tecate were to join the revolt or avenge the deaths in the Campo raid, and *The San Diego Union* stated in an editorial:

We cannot afford to have so dangerous a neighbor as Sonora now is. With starvation and anarchy in that state, bands of vagabonds, beggars and bandits will be continually crossing to the American side of the line, as they have been doing for the last two or three months, with such results as we note in the vicinity of Campo and along the whole border east and west of the Colorado.

A committee was formed in San Diego, to augment the guard

Lumen Gaskill, a handy man with a shotgun, survived the gunfight at Campo. The incident brought death to a total of six men.

at Campo, to seek military assistance, and to reach some sort of truce between the American settlement of Campo and the Mexican town of Tecate before a major border clash occurred. On the committee were Ephraim Morse, chairman; W. E. Begole, W. W. Stewart, W. W. Bowers, A. Klauber, H. H. Wildy, Douglas Gunn and Charles A. Wetmore. Wildy, San Diego's district attorney, was placed in charge of the posse and Wetmore was sent to San Francisco to see Gen. John M. Schofield, commander of the Army's Pacific Division.

Wildy found seventy to 100 armed men camped around Tecate, and with food running short, some kind of action could be expected soon. Two of the three bandits who had fled from Campo were reported in the vicinity of San Rafael and the people there were as afraid of the armed bands north of them as were the residents of Campo.

The body of the former governor of Baja California, who had been with the murdered Leclaire, was found on December 16, not far from the scene of the crime. His head had been smashed and his throat cut. Sheriff Will Hunsaker went to San Rafael and learned that at least fifteen men were in the gang that had planned the Campo raid and that Lopez had been responsible for the murder of Leclaire and the former governor.

On January 3, more than a month after the attack, Company G, 1st Cavalry, arrived at San Diego aboard a steamer and moved into the old barracks at New San Diego. They had forty-three men, fifty horses, two wagons and an ambulance. A detachment of ten under a Lieut. Storey reached Campo on January 11, 1876. The situation was quieting down, and Lieut. Storey became the only casualty. He dropped his pistol and shot himself in the hip. He left four men to guard the settlement and returned to San Diego.

The Frenchman who had ridden into the midst of the fight died while enroute to San Francisco, evidently from infection of his wound. As for the bandit leader, Pancho Lopez, Silas Gaskill learned that he had died of a neck wound a year after the fight.

So ended the events that surrounded the famous gunfight at Campo. One man had been killed outright in the gun fight; two had died of their wounds; another had been killed by his companion; two had been lynched, and two others had been wounded. Two other persons had been murdered for gold. Only one identified member of the gang, Alonzo Cota, apparently survived. What happened to the sixth bandit who rode into town, if there was a sixth, was never established. According to the recollections of Silas Gaskill, several years later the sheriff of El Paso notified him that he had Cota in custody and would deliver him for $1000. The Gaskills were not interested. They were busy with the development of the ranch and lived out their normal lives. It was the last raid of organized bandit gangs in Southern California. Cattle rustling, however, persisted on an extensive scale for many years.

In that same year, in midsummer, members of a gang of Sonoran horse thieves were reported operating along the border, and on July 17, a mare belonging to a pupil was stolen from the yard of the little country school in Milquatay Valley north of Campo. Two of the older boys at the school, identified as Andrew and Zachary Elliott, and a youth from Tecate, Manuel Melendrez, started in pursuit and enlisted the aid of local ranchers. Three separate parties were formed to hunt down the thieves, and one of them, led by Deputy Sheriff Charles Hensley, crossed the border and received permission from the *alcalde* of Tecate to pursue, capture and return the thieves.

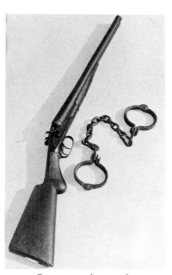

Lawman's equipment, 1870-80

The three boys got to them first. Their story was that the two thieves refused to surrender the horse and opened fire. One of the boys was slightly wounded, but, in returning the fire, they killed both of the Mexicans. In a letter to his brother, Lumen, who was at San Diego, Silas Gaskill wrote:

> The devil is to pay. The Mexicans have arrested the two Elliott boys, and a party went down to see about it and the Mexicans have arrested them—seventeen of our men—the whole neighborhood is up in arms . . . the boys who are at liberty are concentrated on this side of the line.

One of those held was Deputy Sheriff Hensley. Later reports indicated there were only eleven Americans in all in custody, including the Elliott boys. All were taken to San Rafael. San Diego's district attorney, H. H. Wildy, and another deputy, Ned Bushyhead, went to San Rafael in company with Fr. Ubach and finally after many hearings and arguments, all except the Elliott boys were released. Wildy appealed to the United States Department of State and was appointed a special envoy to intervene on their behalf. A trial developed the information that the Mexican youth, Melendrez, also had obtained written permission from the *alcalde* of Tecate directing him to take the thieves into custody, and if fired upon, to shoot back. The Elliott boys were freed and the border once again quieted down. Sometime later according to dispatches in *The San Diego Union,* it was learned that the judge in the case had been arrested and convicted of accepting a bribe of $1000 to release the boys, and had been secured with ball and chain and packed off to seven years of imprisonment at La Paz in southern Baja California.

THE DISCONTENTED
SEVENTIES

CHAPTER X

Across the land the depression that began with the financial panic of 1873 persisted. There was widespread resentment against the railroads. Growers in California in particular felt they were being overcharged on freight rates. State governments were inefficient and usually corrupt. Writers and pamphleteers were condemning big business or espousing socialism. Fledgling labor unions in California harassed the Chinese who had been imported by the thousands, and various regulatory acts were passed which merely added to the confusion and anger.

The discontented Seventies passed slowly for a town that had expected greater things. The population grew, but a decade would pass before it would equal what it was in the time of the last boom. By 1880 the population of the town was only 2637, though the population in the county had doubled, from 4951 to 8618. But its rival coastal city, Los Angeles, was pulling far ahead in the same period. By 1880 it had 11,183, and the county 33,381.

Even so the water supply system in Pound Canyon proved to be inadequate as early as 1875 and the San Diego Water Company began pumping water from the sands of the San Diego River and lifting it several hundred feet to University Heights. This proved to be very costly so a tunnel was driven through the hills from a point in Mission Valley and the water was piped through it to University Avenue, where it was allowed to flow across the empty mesa to a reservoir at what is now Fifth Avenue and Hawthorn Street.

Horton continued in the real estate business, and though he had lost much of his holdings, he struggled to retain the Horton House despite attachments, the efforts of his enemies to take it away from him, and difficulties with lessees. San Diego was a trading and commercial center for 15,000 square miles, and a Chamber of Commerce directory of 1874 listed six churches, three lodges, two newspapers, two banks, five hotels, and one public and three private schools; eleven real estate agents and eleven attorneys; ten general merchants and ten grocery stores; five blacksmiths and wheelwrights, as well as four drug stores and four barber shops, and many specialty shops and supply yards. The town filled with people once again, but Morse wrote:

> The hotels are all full, the town never was more full of strangers than at present but they are all tourists and invalids and no speculators among them.

Many turned to new pursuits and new sources of revenue. Most of the mines and mills in the Julian District were idle and even the Golden Chariot mine in Chariot Canyon had closed down by 1876 and the population of Julian had dropped to less than 100 persons. Frank Kimball received a crate of 1000 oysters from San Francisco and planted them in the bay at the mouth of the Sweetwater River. Life was rather serene, though it was not always easy to live with the thoughts of what might have been, and picnics were the favorite pastime. They were held under the great

Land speculation based on railroad hopes brought about the building of homes such as that of stage operator John G. Capron.

oaks or the pepper trees which were growing everywhere, in town and country, and buckboard buffets dispensed the bounties of good seasons.

The stage to Julian was held up on the Coleman grade and the Wells, Fargo treasure box robbed of $1000. *The San Diego Union* continued publication without interruption, though its rival of the tidelands battle, the *Daily World,* did not last long. Jacob M. Julian and N. H. Conklin, new arrivals from Mississippi, acquired ownership in 1874, and it was soon merged with a new publication, the *San Diego Daily News* started by Julian in 1875.

Ruins, Chariot Mine

The Congress appropriated $80,000 in 1875 to channel the San Diego River to prevent the silting up of the bay. This was the second attempt. In 1853 a timber bulkhead had been constructed across the bed of the channel, where it had swung across the flat land between Old Town and Point Loma and toward the bay; and a former channel, which had twisted toward False or Mission Bay, had been deepened. The work was done under the direction of Lieut. George Derby, of the United States Topographical Engineers and a famed humorist, but, because adequate money had not been provided, the dike gave way within two years.

This time the work was thoroughly planned and executed by the Corps of Engineers. The contract was awarded to Capt. George A. Johnson, owner of Los Peñasquitos Rancho, and Howard Schuyler of San Francisco. They set a charge of gunpowder underneath Presidio Hill on the river side and shook down 4000 to 5000 cubic yards of dirt. The explosion flattened most of the remaining adobe walls of the historic presidio. The contractors employed seventy white men and seventy-five Chinese in scooping out a gently curving channel into Mission Bay and throwing up a levee 7735 feet long, which rested on the east on the base of Presidio Hill and on the west on the base of Point Loma. It was twenty-three feet wide at the top and forty-one feet wide at the base, and rested on a bed of stones three feet deep. It was faced and topped with stones.

San Diegans, knowing the history of the river and its occasional bursts of fury, were skeptical of its ability to hold. Lieut. John Weede, of the Corps of Engineers in charge of the work, refuted the critics in a letter to *The San Diego Union:*

Miner's house ruins, Chariot Canyon

... the plan for the improvement was, after careful study, decided upon by a Board of Engineers who deemed themselves justified in believing that a levee, stronger by far than those which have for years guided the mighty waters of the Mississippi, the Rhine, the Po and the Adige, might possibly control the waters of the San Diego.

The work was completed in 1877. The bay was saved, but each

winter heavy silt from the San Diego mountains oozed down and choked up Mission Bay, a bay that nobody seemed to want. A chronicler from the *Los Angeles Express* described his visit to old San Diego "with its crumbling relics of the past" and told how the levee would confine the "river to the new channel and send it into False Bay, which has no commercial value and can be filled up with impunity."

The Colorado River still held its mighty promise of agricultural wealth. From 1873 to 1875 Commander George Dewey, U.S.N., and later Admiral Dewey, surveyed the Gulf of California on the *U.S.S Narragansett* and visited the mouth of the river. A year later Lieut. Eric Bergland was detailed to determine the feasibil-

ity of diverting the flow of the river onto the Colorado Desert, as Ephraim Morse and others thought could be done, and whether a channel could be built entirely on American soil.

In 1876 the city was reincorporated by the Legislature and its boundaries described as in the Hays survey, except for the waterfront on the bay, "and this shall be the ship's channel of the bay," and the municipal jurisdiction was extended over the waters of the bay and to one mile at sea. Through another oversight, False or Mission Bay was not included within the municipal jurisdiction.

The winter of 1876-77 was a dry one and by May the areas north of San Diego County were feeling the bite of the droughts that had proved so terrifying in the 1860's. Sheep men from northern

In the Discontented Seventies San Diego lost population and waited out depression and drought. This is a bird's eye view in 1876.

145

counties moved their flocks into San Diego County, which still had some grass on the mountains, and the sheep stripped every growing thing before them. In June there was a heat wave and it was 104 in the shade at Poway and 122 in the sun in Spring Valley. Mud springs erupted in the Imperial Valley. As June drew to a close the honey crop was reported as a total loss. The heat wave had killed the blossoms and artificial feeding was begun to keep the bees alive until the Fall. This was a severe blow to the economy of San Diego, as the honey crop in 1876 had been 1,277,155 pounds, and 800,000 pounds had been exported to the East.

As had the Silver Dons and the Spanish and Mexican ranch owners before them, many Americans were losing the ranches they had acquired in previous years of distress. Joseph S. Mannasse and Marcus Schiller saw two of their ranches, San Dieguito and adjoining Las Encinitas, foreclosed for debts. The Fall brought heavy rains and extreme cold and the loss of 300 to 400 sheep a night from exposure. Upon petition of citizens the payment of city taxes was postponed.

The illustrated book, *History of San Diego County,* published in 1883, stated:

The year 1877 will long be remembered as exceptionally rainless and distressing. Scarce a flower bloomed on the dry valleys away from the stream-sides, and not a single grain-field, depending upon rain, was reaped. The seed only sprouted and came up a little way, and withered; and horses, cattle and sheep grew thinner day by day, nibbling at bushes and weeds along the shallowing edges of streams, many of which were dried up altogether for the first time since the settlement of the country.

A letter to *The San Diego Union* from a visitor from Los Angeles in 1877 chided the town for its despondency:

Of what has San Diego really to complain more than other towns? There are none suffering among you—in the East thousands are wanting bread. There are no tramps among you and few are out of employment. Your streets are quiet; they are not filled with idle men asking for work or food. You have hard times, but where can good times be found? The whole country is depressed. A wail of hard times goes up even from this favored locality, and in San Francisco it is much worse. The times are out of joint. The tide is out. We must wait patiently for the flood.

The Chinese held many of the jobs that white men now found more attractive. There was no place for the Indians, who had been replaced as laborers and servants by the Chinese. In 1876 President Grant had set aside nine reservations in San Diego County, and the remnants of the 5000 Indians who once had owned all of the land were being rounded up and driven into the hills and unwanted valleys. The nine Indian reservations embraced ninety-seven and a half square miles of land in fifteen locations in a rough fifty-mile belt from San Diego's present El Capitán Reservoir to the foot of the San Jacinto Mountains in what is now Riverside County. The Cahuilla Reservations included six square miles near El Capitán Reservoir in San Diego County and two areas totaling twenty-four square miles north of Mt. Palomar in Riverside County. The Potrero covered nineteen square miles of Mt. Palomar and the area northeast of it; Santa Ysabel covered twenty-five and a half square miles in two areas near the south end of Lake Henshaw; and Capitán Grande covered two ten-square mile areas on the northwest and southeast sides of El Capitán Reservoir. The Pala Reservation was one square mile, lying east of Oak Grove; Maja and Lycuan Reservations, a quarter section each, were three miles west of Cuyamaca Peak and two miles east of Dehesa; Agua Caliente, one and a half square miles, was five miles east of Lake Henshaw; and Cosmit, the smallest, ninety acres, was two miles northwest of Cuyamaca Peak.

Yellow Sky, Capitán Grande Indian.

The Indians, however, found a defender who stirred the nation's conscience. It was Helen Hunt Jackson, with her book, *A Century of Dishonor,* and her novel, *Ramona.* Though the tragic story of Ramona and Allesandro was laid in the Hemet country of Riverside County, Mrs. Jackson gathered material at Guajome Rancho in San Diego County and the padre of her story was created in the likeness of Fr. Antonio Ubach.

In midsummer of the unhappy year of 1877 a wave of rioting swept the state and many Chinese lost their lives. Chinese fishing villages dotted the coast and their strangely rigged junks were a familiar sight at San Diego. Charles Nordhoff in his book on *Travellers and Settlers in California* had described how the Chinese sailed from San Diego as far south as the Cedros Island, 300 miles down the peninsula of Baja California, in search of abalone. The meat was prized as a delicacy and the shell for ornamentation, and by 1870 the Chinese fishermen in California were exporting $1,000,000 worth of abalone annually to their homeland, as well as dried shrimp valued at $3,000,000. Legislative acts were passed to tax or restrict their fishing. In San Diego, it became evident in 1877 that outbreaks against the Chinese were only a matter of time, and *The San Diego Union* reported:

Cinon Duro, Mesa Grande, last hereditary Too-Ka-Muck chief.

> It was ascertained that an agreement in writing had been in circulation for two days past, pledging the signers to join in ridding the city of Chinese, and persons refusing to sign were threatened . . . in one instance, we are informed, a man who declined to sign was assaulted.

Fleets of Chinese junks, as seen in San Diego Bay, opened fishing areas off Mexico. Abalone was brought up from Cedros Island.

An attempt was made to burn down the Chinese quarter along the waterfront. Several buildings were saturated with gasoline and set afire, but the flames were quickly extinguished by volunteer fire fighters. Sheriff Joseph Coyne appointed a number of special deputies and a meeting of citizens was called to organize a Committee on Public Safety, and D. O. McCarthy, president of the Board of Trustees, telegraphed the commanding general of the Army's Pacific Division requesting that arms at the barracks be issued to the committee's 200 members. A. H. Gilbert was chosen chairman and officers were appointed for each ward. *The San Diego Union* said:

> The Chinese may not be, in any considerable number, a desirable element of the population. But those that are here are under the protection of the laws and must not be molested . . . here in San Diego we do not mean to permit hoodlumism and rioting. . .

The distribution of Army weapons was approved and the full committee marched to the barracks to receive their breech-loading rifles and cavalry revolvers. Its members took up assigned posts and apparently remained on the alert until the threats of rioting had subsided.

In a time of labor unrest the Workingmen's Party brought about rioting in northern cities, and it attempted to dominate the constitutional convention elected to write a new state constitution. One was adopted in 1878, but it met opposition from business and financial interests. When it was placed before the people in 1879, however, the rural vote was enough to assure its ratification. Though a victim of many compromises, it did establish more controls over the Legislature, and provide steps toward equalization of tax burdens and a means of independent assessments of railroad properties.

148

In San Diego, it was a clean sweep for Republican candidates, and the new constitution was approved by a vote of 1004 for it and 159 against it. An expression on the Chinese question resulted in a vote of eleven for further immigration of Chinese and 1325 against it. As the results of the balloting on the constitution became known, *The San Diego Union* reported:

Captain Ferris was on the plaza last night with the "Centennial gun" and fired a salute in honor of the triumph of the new constitution. While the salute was being fired, the bells were rung and cheers given for the people's victory.

Though Horton had worked vigorously to move business uptown to the vicinity of the Horton House, trade tended to concentrate on lower Fifth Street, as it had from the beginning of New San Diego. George W. Marston long since had moved his store from Fifth Street and Broadway and in 1882 was doing business at Fifth and F Streets. In that same year, in June, the San Diego Telephone Company began service with thirteen subscribers.

The growth of population in the county reflected the development of agriculture and the homesteading and settling of the smaller and upland valleys in the manner of the Gaskill brothers at Campo. Cattle, once the prime source of revenue of both the Spanish and Mexican periods, had given way to sheep. In 1882 the county produced 954,354 pounds of wool from 151,000 sheep. Cattle numbered 10,114 and cows, 1459.

By the middle of the seventies the new settlers had found most of the 2,000,000 acres remaining unclaimed in what was called the "agricultural belt" in reality were in scattered valleys or canyons or along rocky mountain masses. Good lands had to be searched out. Even as late as 1880 there wasn't a single irrigation ditch in the entire county despite a meager average rainfall which at that time was estimated at only four inches a year.

By 1882, besides the Spanish and Mexican land grants as yet undivided, there were, according to assessment records, 3052 farms ranging in size from less than ten to more than 600 acres. There were 921,604 acres in all subject to assessment. Of the total, 5162 acres were enclosed, or fenced, and 22,997 acres under cultivation. There were 11,209 acres in wheat, with an annual yield of 142,499 bushels and 3206 acres in barley, with a yield of 58,024 bushels.

The more successful farming was being done in the wet belt which ran through the higher country, from Viejas Valley through Cuyamaca Rancho, the Julian Hills, Warner's, Guejito, Bear Valley, Pauma, and Smith's Mountain, or Palomar. The Bernardo Rancho, northeast of San Diego, and Rincón del Diablo Rancho, the site of Escondido, as well as Santa Maria Valley were on the edge of this belt.

S. G. Blaisdell, a native of Vermont, located in Poway Valley, and though he planted a fine orchard, the roots of his giant grove

"Sunnyside" orchard and farm of J. C. Frisbie in the valley near Sweetwater Dam was to become one of the place names of San Diego County.

San Diego became one of the world's leading producers of honey. These are the bee hives in the Sweetwater apiary of J. S. Harbison.

of eucalyptus trees killed all of his fruit trees. F. R. Sawday produced good crops at Ballena even during the drought of 1877. The inland settlers were from many lands, even as those who had arrived during the mission-hide days and remained to marry the daughters of the Dons.

Bernardo Etcheverry, a native of France, was running 12,000

"Los Peñasquitos," one of the best known of the old Spanish land grants, was the home of cattleman J. S. Taylor who made it a showplace of the West.

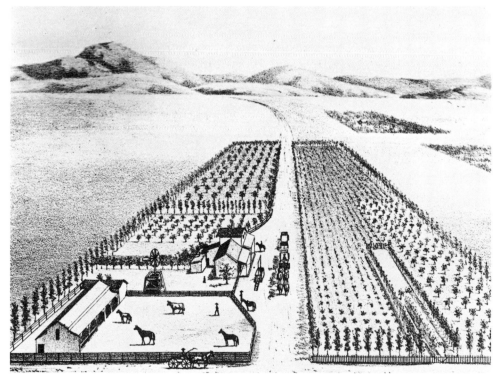

In El Cajon Valley, "Knox's Station" was a stop for overnight travelers and freighters on their way to the Julian mining country. A hotel was built later.

sheep on some of the finest agriculture land, Santa Maria Valley, once the rancho of Edward Stokes, the English sea captain who had married the daughter of José Joaquín Ortega. Herbert Crouch, a native of England, had a ranch in the San Luis Rey Valley where he grazed 4000 sheep. William Thompson, a native of Nova Scotia, settled in San Pasqual Valley.

Juan Forster, the Englishman who had married the sister of Don Pío Pico, the last Mexican governor of California, and acquired the largest rancho in San Diego County, Santa Margarita, fell upon bad days and harassed by debts, litigation and taxes, sold out to Richard O'Neill and James Flood for $250,000 in 1882. He died two years later. Warner's Ranch, the historic stopping place for immigrants who arrived over the Gila Trail, and for the Butterfield stages, passed into possession of a former governor of California, John G. Downey.

The growing of fruit, the enticement of the many advertisements of the wonders and delights of California, was being extensively developed. There were 7359 apple trees and San Diego boasted that the apples grown in the Julian Hills were as fine as any produced in New York State. There were 3309 orange and 1257 lemon trees, but it was generally conceded that their fruit for some reason was not as good as that grown in the Los Angeles area. Olives, a staple of the mission days, continued in production, with 2807 trees. There also were 7833 peach, 2064 apricot, 1820 fig and 648 plum-bearing trees. The National Ranch had strawberries and grapes as well as peach, almond and walnut trees, and 20,000 young orange trees had been set out. El Cajon Valley had 2000 muscat grapevines and 600 orchard and walnut trees. The county in one year shipped eighteen tons of raisins and dried fruits and produced 13,000 gallons of wine. Honey was one of the most valued products and there were at least 20,000 hives in 1880. The shipments in 1878 were 1071 barrels and 15,544 cases, and nearly ninety tons. J. S. Harbison, the pioneer in honey production, had 2000 hives and for himself and others shipped twenty carloads in one season.

Droughts and storms were only occasional hazards in a mild land. The country was young and the settlers ambitious. Wealth was not always measured by the standards of those who so often had seen their investments vanish in the speculation over railroads. Agriculture and climate were the assets on which it seemed the future would have to turn. Success once tasted, however, is not easily laid aside, and for the Morses, the Kimballs and the Hortons, defeat was not acceptable.

J. S. Harbison

THE TRAIN THAT
FINALLY CAME

A train tour through Temecula Canyon —
at long last San Diego had a railroad.
The Santa Fe promised much but
brought disappointment.

CHAPTER XI

The progress of the Atchison, Topeka and Santa Fe Railroad revived in San Diego the hope of becoming a transcontinental terminal. The Santa Fe, with far less subsidies than its rivals, had built slowly across the mid-country and through Kansas, where it fattened on the hauling of cattle. The Santa Fe looked around for an outlet on the Pacific Coast and began building toward El Paso with a view to terminating at Guaymas in the Mexican State of Sonora on the Gulf of California. It also inched a line westward across Arizona toward The Needles on the Colorado River. The powerful Southern Pacific already had thrown out a line into the Mojave Desert to turn back any rival approaching Southern California by way of The Needles.

A few San Diegans, and in particular Frank Kimball, had kept in touch with the various railroad promotion schemes in the East, and had met nothing but discouragement. But now Kimball and a few others met secretly at the home of Ephraim Morse and decided to make a new effort. At the meeting were Kimball and Elizur Steele, representing National City; Morse and J. S. Gordon, representing San Diego; John G. Capron, the stageman, M. A. Luce, an attorney, and several others. Kimball was sent East in June of 1879. At Philadelphia he found there was nothing that

155

could be done about the Texas and Pacific. In New York he learned that the intentions of the Southern Pacific had not changed. The Santa Fe seemed to be San Diego's best hope.

In Boston, Kimball conferred with Thomas Nickerson, president of the Santa Fe, and other officers and directors of the company on the advantage of terminating at San Diego. He spoke convincingly, and after many meetings and periods of waiting, the Santa Fe agreed to build eastward from San Diego to Yuma and then northeasterly to join the Santa Fe at Albuquerque, New Mexico, with the first section of forty miles to be constructed within eight months, and predicated upon San Diego raising $10,000 in cash, to pay for rights of way, and a promise of 10,000 acres of land in National City and any of the railroad lands that could be won back from Scott and the Texas and Pacific. The fact that the terminal was to be at National City was not made public, and San Diegans quickly subscribed the money requested. Horton contributed only $250. Santa Fe engineers arrived and spent three months making their own surveys.

The legal suit over the 8800 acres of land which had been granted to the Texas and Pacific railroad was settled, with Scott and his company retaining half and with the rest put in trust for

Land speculation rose with the excitement over railroads and San Diegans often gathered at the Plaza to hear the latest developments, as shown here in the Eighties.

public use of San Diego, which in this case meant railroad uses. San Diego was ready for final negotiations with the Santa Fe.

The other 4000 acres were deeded by the Texas and Pacific to the Los Angeles & San Diego Railroad Company in 1883, a paper subsidiary of the Southern Pacific and its parent, the Central Pacific, and they were promptly sold off.

Another newspaper, the *San Diego Sun,* which had been started by Mrs. Charles P. Taggart, wife of the city attorney of the tidelands issue, in 1881, commented on the sale of the lands as follows:

> The railroad history of this town is a history of debt, delusion and despair — the Central Pacific, the great highwayman of our coast — has gobbled up 4000 acres of the 8000 acres we so crazily gave Tom Scott without consideration.

But the story had not yet ended. The Santa Fe joined hands with the Pacific and Atlantic Railroad which had been building west along the 35th parallel, from St. Louis into the Oklahoma Territory, and which had gone bankrupt despite a land subsidy of 43,000,000 acres. The Santa Fe abandoned the idea of a southern route and proposed to cross the Mojave Desert and enter Southern California through the Cajon Pass. This, in all likelihood, would mean the terminus would be at Los Angeles or even

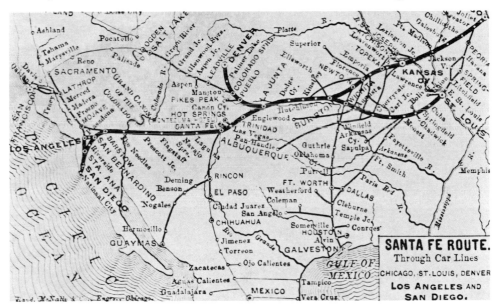

SANTA FE ROUTE.
Through Car Lines
CHICAGO, ST. LOUIS, DENVER
LOS ANGELES AND SAN DIEGO.

The Santa Fe railroad bested its rivals and got a terminus on the Pacific Coast by helping a subsidiary reach San Diego.

San Francisco. The following letter from Nickerson, quoted in part, tells the story:

> Decided to build under the Atlantic & Pacific charter to the Colorado River. When money is raised to cover the construction, then it will be decided whether the next move will be extended to San Diego or some other point or points on the Pacific Coast . . . Whatever you think about that route (Yuma-San Diego), we are satisfied that it is too intensely hot and dusty ever to be a favorite route for passengers.

157

A switch engine puffs along San Diego's waterfront in the 1880's and the commerce of the world was expected to arrive at any time.

Frank Kimball was sent back to Boston and this time he had to argue with officials of the Atlantic and Pacific as well as those of the Santa Fe. In the end, and after many days of seemingly fruitless conferences, the two companies and their banking interests agreed to the organization of a separate railroad line, to run from San Diego by way of Colton, to connect with the Santa Fe. It was promised, however, that the terminus of the entire line would be at National City, on San Diego's Bay.

From Kimball they obtained a pledge that the 10,000 acres he had promised to them would be placed with a syndicate to be controlled by the railroad and its officers and that he would sell to it additional land worth $100,000. Altogether, the Santa Fe obtained from San Diego and National City 17,000 acres of land, including valuable rights of way and waterfront privileges, as well as 485 lots and $25,000 in cash. Kimball returned by steamer in August and was welcomed by a large group of citizens. However, the belated revelation that the terminal would be at National City dampened much of the enthusiasm and there were no fireworks nor firing of cannons in San Diego. The California Southern Railroad was chartered on October 12, 1880, to construct a railroad from National City to San Bernardino, with Benjamin Kimball of Boston as president, M. A. Luce of San Diego as vice president, Thomas Nickerson as treasurer, and Frank Kimball as one of the directors. A large part of the railroad lands returned by the Texas and Pacific was immediately delivered to the new company.

The route selected ran forty-six miles up the coast to the present city of Oceanside, then northeast up the Santa Margarita River Valley through Temecula Canyon and northward across

158

the highlands to Colton, south of San Bernardino. The choice of Temecula Canyon as the gateway through the coastal hills was a surprise. However, it opened up into the Temecula Valley which was on the old immigrant wagon route between Yuma and Los Angeles by way of the San Felipe Pass and Warner's Ranch.

Ground was broken on December 20, 1880. By March of 1881 the roadbed had been graded between National City and San Diego, by following the edge of the bay, crossing creeks and tidelands by low bridges or dirt fills, and the first rail was laid on June 17. Shops, a round house, yard and water tanks were begun in National City. A business center arose just as quickly, with four hotels, the Railroad, the Reed, the Palmer House and the National.

In the next weeks San Diego's waterfront was alive with activity that hadn't been experienced since the Gold Rush. Schooners and brigs arrived with equipment and railroad ties. Large work forces of Chinese were brought down from San Francisco, and while work was proceeding at San Diego, at least a thousand were also put to work carving a roadbed out of the rock walls of Temecula Canyon. Five more ships brought iron rails from Antwerp, Belgium. The bark *James A. Wright* sailed from New York with three locomotives and thirty flat cars. Another locomotive came out overland and at San Francisco it was hoisted onto the brig *Orient* and unloaded at the wharf in National City on July 9.

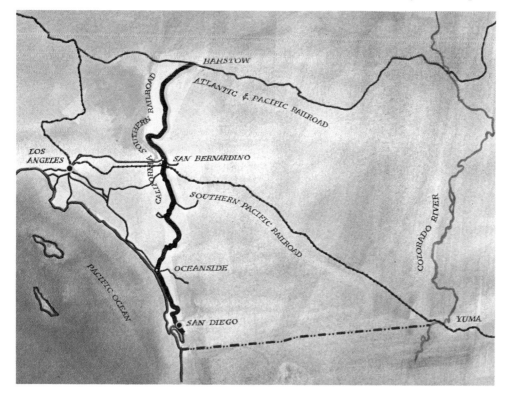

This map shows the route of the California Southern Railroad which linked San Diego with a transcontinental system near Cajon Pass.

It was named the "Urus," the mythical ox, and the engineer, A. D. Xander, described it as a "monster and powerful machine." The honor of giving rein to Urus fell to Frank Kimball and a short ride on the first rails to be laid was a thrill to the San Diegans who had worked and hoped for so many years. By late August the rails had reached the foot of Fifth Street in New San Diego, and this caused *The San Diego Union* to issue a dire warning:

> When the locomotive reaches the wharf, accidents and runaways will occur every day. There is not a horse in the city that ever saw one.

The California Southern inched northward, with hundreds of Chinese toiling with pick and shovel and removing dirt in baskets and carts, crossing the bed of the San Diego River on piling driven into the sands by steam power, passing Mission Bay and going up Rose Canyon, from Elvira to Soledad Hill, then down into Soledad, or Sorrento, Valley, and following up the coast to Oceanside, forty-six miles from San Diego. There were sixty bridges and trestles spanning a river, creeks and tidewater lagoons. By December, the tracks had bridged the San Luis Rey River and engines and loaded flat cars were making two trips a day between National City and the point of progress.

The tracks went inland at the entrance to the Santa Margarita River, north of Oceanside, and followed the river across the Santa Margarita Rancho, which later became the United States Marine Corps' Camp Pendleton. The valley narrowed and grew deeper as the roadbed approached Temecula Canyon. Here the line disappeared from view as it wound and climbed six miles between high and rocky walls. Ignoring the advice of area residents, the engineers built the line as close to the bed of the river as possible, and it crossed and recrossed an innocent-appearing stream of runing water many times before it emerged from the canyon at the southwest point of the Temecula-Elsinore plain. At Temecula the Santa Margarita River becomes the Temecula River, and at the entrance to the canyon it also receives the winter flow of two other streams, the Murrieta and the Pechanga.

The line reached Colton on August 14, 1882, a distance of 127 miles from National City, and service was begun with a fare of $6.00 one way and $9.00 for the round trip, and the *National City Record* commented:

> The person who would begrudge $9.00 for a round trip from National City might be compared with the Southern Pacific Railroad—without a soul. The scenery in Temecula Canyon is well worth the price of the trip.

Station stops were established along the line in San Diego

County. The main passenger and freight depot in San Diego was near the foot of Twenty-second Street, with another passenger depot at the foot of Broadway. Next was the Old Town stop, a block north of the Plaza, near San Diego Avenue and Taylor Street. Selwyn was at the top of Rose Canyon and Cordero in the center of Sorrento Valley. The Del Mar and Encinitas stations were at their present locations. Stewart's was the next stop on the line, and later became known as Farr. Carlsbad and Oceanside stations were near their present locations. Next was Ysidora, four and a half miles north and east of Oceanside on the banks of the Santa Margarita River. De Luz stop, also on the river, was southwest of the present community of Fallbrook. Fallbrook station was near the mouth of Temecula Canyon, about three miles from Fallbrook. Next was Ranchita in Temecula Canyon between the Fallbrook station and Temecula.

San Luis Rey Village, 1883

At Colton, however, the Southern Pacific refused permission to the California Southern to cross its lines and lands in order to reach San Bernardino. A court action followed and the California Southern won. The first train, with the locomotive decorated with flowers, stalks of corn and round squash, pulled into San Bernardino on September 13, 1883. It would be sometime, and after a major disaster, before a connection could be made with the Santa Fe to form a new transcontinental railroad.

All interest was in the railroad. The automobile had not yet appeared on the American scene. San Diegans paid little attention to the unusual son of a local attorney, Zachary Montgomery, who had a large ranch home, "Fruitdale," in Otay Valley. Though John J. Montgomery had a master's degree in science he also served as foreman of his father's ranch. In his spare time he conducted many scientific and engineering experiments, studied the characteristics of seagulls, and began the construction of a glider, or flying machine. One machine with flapping wings failed. The second, with aerodynamically designed fixed wings, was taken out before dawn in August of 1883, placed on a bed of hay in a wagon, and packed up to Otay Mesa. John seated himself in the glider and waited until midmorning for the wind to rise. Then his younger brother, James, took hold of a tow rope and ran down the slope of a hill. The glider, with John controlling its flight by a rudder and shifting the weight of his body, soared 600 feet. This was the first controlled flight in a heavier-than-air machine in the history of man. Though his father was to become an assistant attorney general of the United States, and John was to continue his scientific experiments in flight, more than a half century would pass

John J. Montgomery

*Chamber of Commerce
promotion, 1883*

before this exploit on Otay Mesa would be known and recognized.

In the Christmas period of 1883 stories in the newspapers described the breath-taking beauty of the sunsets with their curious shades of blood-red, orange and yellow, which had begun to appear following the volcanic explosion of the island of Krakatoa in the Strait of Sundra, Indonesia. Most of January was clear and sunny, but on the 24th, it began to rain. By February 4, San Diego had received 4.22 inches. El Cajon measured three inches in one day. Julian was paralyzed by four inches. Corral de la Luz, the railroad station near the Santa Margarita Ranch house, measured thirteen inches in fourteen days. Campo and Laguna had ten inches in five days.

The San Diego Union reported:

> The heavy rain of the past few days has interfered greatly with travel by rail. The train which left here last Saturday night (February 2), returned on Sunday night, not being able to get through Temecula Canyon, and the train coming south, which should have arrived here Saturday night, did not arrive until 2 o'clock this morning. About six miles of track in Temecula Canyon were rendered practically impassable on Saturday by landslides and rocks rolling down on the roadbed.

Construction trains were sent out with repair crews to shore up the weakening roadbed by "cribbing" it with extra ties and timber. At the Cordero station in Soledad Valley two huge landslides covered the tracks and they had to be dug out, but new slides occurred almost as fast as the others were cleared away.

The last train got through on February 14, with the water still rising in Temecula Canyon. Every road in San Diego County had been washed out. On Friday, February 15, the California Southern tried to send through another northbound train. At the Fallbrook station, a washout forced the crew to back the train up to Ysidora, while repairs were made, and finally it started through the canyon once more, only to encounter new washouts, this time behind them as well as ahead of them.

*Building of the
California Southern
Railroad, to connect with
the Santa Fe, required
many bridges. This trestle
was north of Oceanside.*

One of the passengers, Charles A. Wetmore, a San Diego businessman bound for San Francisco, and the engineer, walked to the coast and found most of the underpinning of the San Luis Rey River bridge had been washed out by a raging torrent of water, and in Soledad Valley most of the tracks had disappeared. The hike from the train to San Diego took six days. The fate of the "lost" train had been unknown.

Aboard the stalled train, which was slowly sinking into the river, W. H. Atwater, a Wells, Fargo agent, and the others left behind got up steam in the engine and managed to drive the train a hundred yards ahead to higher ground. There they killed and prepared gophers for food, and finally Atwater built a raft, tied his clothes in a bundle, and floated down the muddy and turbulent river, dropping over two waterfalls, and, after three miles, drifted onto a bank where a sheepherder threw him a rope and pulled him ashore.

The San Diego Union's Temecula correspondent, who signed himself as "C. Senor," reported that every bridge from Temecula to Colton was washed out; timbers, ties and telegraph poles were strewn for miles along the river banks, and several miles of track were completely gone. One entire bridge from forty miles upstream at San Jacinto came riding down the current of the Santa Margarita. Parts of the railroad were reported sighted twenty-five miles at sea. As the flood temporarily subsided, the train was left high and dry in the canyon.

The rains continued intermittently. A cloudburst at Smith Mountain delayed attempts to repair the railroad. At San Diego, Chollas Creek was running 120 feet wide and the flood waters of Switzer Creek through the city park carried away the railroad bed near the waterfront. Early in April the Sweetwater River bridge collapsed when some ranchers tried to drive a herd of cattle over it. And on April 5, the sloop *Brisk* sailed with ten tons of provisions in an attempt to relieve settlers isolated at Oceanside and Encinitas. It was unsuccessful. The sloop spent most of ten days seeking shelter from a gale in the lee of Santa Catalina Island. The railroad began running trains again as far as Oceanside on a "cribbed" track of temporary repairs. Heavy rains continued every day in some part of the county. The heaviest rainfall measured was at Mesa Grande, where on April 17 it was reported that the season total had reached seventy inches. At Ballena, George M. Stone recorded a season total of forty-nine inches.

The slackening downpour of the next three days encouraged

The San Diego Union's
office and press room,
1883

California Southern
Railroad schedule

The San Diego Union to announce that "Spring has come." Nearly every road in the county was washed out; Julian was isolated; telephone lines were down between Julian and Banner; most of the cattle in the county were belly deep in mud; the railroad was barely able to operate as far as Oceanside. But the water in the rivers and creeks was falling and the county chain gang was working daily to repair ruined streets in the town, and the sun began to shine. *The San Diego Union* noted that the town dandies had begun to turn out in the latest fashion of plug hats, tight-legged trousers and "needle-pointed" shoes.

By April 23, melting snow in the mountains sent new freshets down the slopes. Four days later, the rain started all over again. The Casa de Fitch adobe in Old Town collapsed. The California Southern Railroad announced that its damage had reached $250,000, and that it had no money left for repairs. Food became short in the backcountry early in May, and reports from outlying areas noted that the rain had nearly wiped out the gopher and field mouse population, and had brought on a plague of scorpions, rattlesnakes, cutworms and caterpillars, and later an army of grasshoppers appeared.

The same storm wrecked a Southern Pacific train at Seven Palms in the desert, and the railroad bridge over the Colorado River was carried away at The Needles. By the second week in June the rains began to die away, and by July 1, the rainy season was over. The city's official recorded rainfall for the 1883-1884 season was 25.97 inches, the heaviest on record. More than inconvenience and monetary loss was involved as it was now obvious that the Temecula route could never become a major railroad artery, though the Santa Fe agreed to further financing for the California Southern. The Temecula portion was rebuilt with Chinese labor and service was resumed on January 6, 1885.

The Southern Pacific now was facing determined opposition at The Needles gateway to California and the threat of competition by sea with a Santa Fe terminus at Guaymas on the Gulf of California. The Southern Pacific sold its 242-mile line between The Needles and Mojave to the Santa Fe and received in exchange rights to Santa Fe's line from Benson, Arizona, to Guaymas. The Santa Fe conquered Cajon Pass, and by way of another subsidiary, reached San Bernardino.

In New York the *Daily Graphic* proclaimed a future in which San Diegans themselves had begun to doubt:

The last spike on the extension was driven on Monday, November 9, 1885, which completed the link connecting San Diego with the entire East via the

The age of comfort in transcontinental travel arrived, and luxury Pullman cars heralded a new and richer development of the Far West.

Atlantic & Pacific and Atchison, Topeka & Santa Fe.

Today the people of San Diego are celebrating the event in a manner that proclaims the awakening of the city to new life, from which, as long as the sun shines, under no matter what rulers she will never again slumber until ages have filled her lap with the wealth of nations.

The first through train left San Diego on November 15, 1885, from a small frame depot costing $300 at the foot of D Street, or Broadway. The National City terminal was a two-story building. San Diego set Wednesday, November 18, as a day of celebration.

The aging Alonzo Horton was named chairman out of respect for his founding of New San Diego. But the end for him, as a man of power and influence, had come four years before, when the mortgage on the Horton House had been foreclosed by a San Francisco investment firm. An invitation to attend the observance was sent to all leading citizens, and read:

You are respectfully invited to be present at the Celebration of the Opening of the Through Railway Line of the Atchison, Topeka & Santa Fe System to the Pacific Ocean, at the Port of San Diego, to be held in this City on Wednesday, November 18th, 1885.

The completion of this line, establishing a Fourth Great Highway between

Oceans in the United States, is an event whose importance, not alone to this City, but to the State and Coast, cannot be over-estimated. The people of San Diego, with persistent energy and steadfast faith, have for a long period of years, looked forward to the day that is now so close at hand. They will cordially greet you at their jubilee.

The town was gaily decorated and there was a parade with brass bands and marching units of the Grand Army of the Republic and the Knights of Pythias. There were many speeches and expressions of welcome to visiting railroad officers at a public gathering in a gymnasium which had been converted into Leach's Opera House. It was on D Street, between First and Second Streets.

The first transcontinental train to arrive reached San Diego on November 21, in a driving rain. About a hundred persons were on hand to greet the sixty passengers. Somehow, for all the bands and speeches, the great hour when San Diego at long last was connected by rail with the East seemed to be an anticlimax to the thirty years of struggle running back to 1852, before many of those who were present at the train's arrival had ever heard of the town. The day of the stagecoach and the mule freight trains was vanishing. Business in San Diego increased, with the greater possibilities for trade between towns and regions, and the quiet years were over. But the wharfs and warehouses did not fill with the goods of the world. The big cargo ships never came, and the Santa Fe was determined to push on from San Bernardino directly into Los Angeles and leased the tracks of the Southern Pacific. But a boom such as San Diego could not anticipate lay just ahead. It would not be the result of a flow of commerce but of a passenger rate war between rival railroads.

The railroad building era threw together many diverse peoples. Here Mexican ranch hands, Americans and Chinese workmen mingle at bar.

A BOOM NOBODY
WOULD BELIEVE

CALIFORNIA

The CORNUCOPIA OF THE WORLD

ROOM FOR MILLIONS OF IMMIGRANTS

43.795.000. ACRES OF GOVERNMENT LANDS UNTAKEN

Railroad & Private Land for a Million Farmers

A CLIMATE FOR HEALTH & WEALTH WITHOUT CYCLONES OR BLIZZARDS.

CHAPTER XII

"I wouldn't have missed it for all I have lost. It was worth living a lifetime to see." These words were attributed by Theodore S. Van Dyke to a Californian he described as an ex-millionaire of the Boom of the Eighties. Van Dyke was an unusual person in his own right—engineer, farmer, writer, lawyer—and in later years, in his book about the Boom of the Eighties, *Millionaires of a Day,* Van Dyke wrote:

> The Californians have been accused of shearing a drove of innocent lambs from the East. If true, this would have been one of the most interesting features of the times; for, as we shall see, the lambs afterward sheared the shearers in charming style.

Prosperity was returning to the United States, and with the availability of capital and the development of power-driven machinery, the second phase of the Industrial Revolution was getting into full swing and industry was advancing faster than agriculture. The railroad companies, with their millions of acres of land to sell or lease, began advertising heavily and describing the wonders of the West.

The boom was touched off when the Santa Fe Railroad withdrew from the Transcontinental Traffic Association and the Southern Pacific accepted this action as a declaration of war. The $125 passenger rate from the Missouri Valley to Southern California dropped to $100 and it continued to drop as the railroads sought to undercut each other.

San Diego, feeling the first touches of a new wave of immigrants who already had been coming into Los Angeles in considerable numbers, and perhaps a little jealous of its northern neighbor, organized the San Diego County Immigration Association, for the purpose of supplying reliable information and describing opportunities available. It stated:

> San Diego County ... has been the last to improve, and as time passes onward ere long will furnish additional evidence of the truth of the saying that "the last shall be the first."

The town had grown to 5000 population and land was being taken up in the backcountry. The entries made for government land in 1884 embraced 24,960 acres. In the town, the health seekers were supplemented by those who came because they could afford to live in a climate of their choice. Van Dyke wrote in 1890:

> It was plain that they were in fact buying comfort, immunity from snow and slush, from piercing winds and sleet-clad streets, from sultry days and sleepless nights, from thunderstorms, cyclones, malaria, mosquitos and bedbugs. All of which, in plain language, means that they were buying climate, a business that has been going on now for fifteen years and reached a stage of progress the world has never seen before and of which no wisdom can foresee the end.

H. L. Story

Not all persons, of course, reacted with enthusiasm at their first glimpse of a country that had become known in the East as a "regular little paradise." Van Dyke, in another book, *Southern California,* wrote:

> People have actually entered San Diego Bay in the morning, intending to spend the winter, and left for home the same evening without getting off the steamer, simply because it was raining.

These persons were in the minority, however, and for a short time the health seekers in numbers would give way to a stampede for the land of Southern California that rivaled that to the gold fields of northern California more than three decades before.

One of those who came for the climate was Elisha S. Babcock, a railroad financier from Evansville, Indiana, who arrived with H. L. Story, of Chicago, a piano manufacturer. Both men were not in the best of health and spent a good deal of their time in the open air, and one of their pastimes was to row across the bay to Coronado and hunt jack rabbits. A San Diego group headed by Milton Santee had platted Coronado as a site for a resort community, and though the project had failed, Babcock was quick to realize its possibilities. In 1885 he and Story organized a syndicate of outside capital, and after settling the question of title, bought the

E. S. Babcock

4185 acres known as the Peninsula of San Diego, which included both Coronado and North Island, from Archibald C. Peachey of San Francisco and William Aspinwall of New York, for $110,000, and began clearing off the brush.

The coastal railroad was opening new territory to settlement. A. Jackson Meyers, who had been granted 160 acres on the dry coastal mesa on the south edge of Rancho Santa Margarita, built a house and laid out a townsite to become known as Oceanside. It was from here that the California Southern proposed to extend a branch line directly east to open up the lands between the coast and Rancho Rincón del Diablo, or Escondido. A colony of Germans settled on an inland portion of Las Encinitas Rancho and founded Olivenhain, or Olive Grove. John A. Frazier had a grant of land on the coast at the north edge of Rancho Agua Hedionda, where upon drinking the water from a natural spring he found relief from his rheumatism. In El Cajon Valley, which had been opened to settlers, Amaziah L. Knox had built a hotel and livery stable, and Knox's Corners was a stopping place for stages enroute to Julian and the gold country. Milton Santee, the civil engineer who had hoped to develop Coronado, purchased 6000 acres of Rancho Santa María, halfway between the coast and the gold country, and surveyed it for sale into small farms and ranches.

After nearly four decades of hearings, the 58,000 acres of the lands of the San Diego Mission which adjoined the pueblo of San Diego were confirmed to the descendants and assignees of the family of Santiago Arguello, and under the pressure of speculative anticipation, they were opened to settlement. As most of it was on the higher tableland that stretches along the coast and extends perhaps ten miles inland, drilling for water was not always practical and real development had to wait for another day. In time, however, here was to grow the heart of a metropolitan area.

For a time, San Diegans went about their business as usual.

Knox's Hotel, El Cajon

This was "downtown" Oceanside in 1885, destined to become within two years one of the state's best known recreational areas.

171

*Railroads brought
tourists, speculators,
immigrants*

The City Trustees instructed a committee to prepare a contract with an Indianapolis firm to provide for street lights to be installed atop high masts, or towers. Jacob Julian, who had sold his newspaper, the *Daily News,* to the *Sun,* started another one, the *San Diegan,* Democratic in policy, in 1885, in association with several partners. Van Dyke and W. E. Robinson sought to organize an irrigation company, but had difficulty in arousing any interest. Alonzo Horton was selling real estate in a town he had once virtually owned. No one could foresee what was going to happen.

Babcock retained the architects James W. Reid and his brother Merritt to design Hotel del Coronado. To raise the money to build it, he marked out the island in lots, began laying a water line under the bay from San Diego, built railroad tracks down his principal street, Orange Avenue, organized the San Diego and Coronado Ferry Company, placed an order for a ferry boat, and meanwhile pressed Story's steam yacht into service. His nationwide advertising campaign, in newspapers, magazines and railroad publications, spurred a migration that was being experienced with a rising intensity in all of Southern California.

All of a sudden the incoming boats and trains were crowded with passengers. Land in San Diego began to sell as it had before the panic of 1873. The ring of the hammer was heard on every corner. By the summer of 1886 Horton's Addition had acquired 306 new homes and 200 more were under construction. To Van Dyke, there were several aspects to this migration:

. . . the majority cared nothing about the solid resources of the land, and were looking only for amusement or a chance to make some money without work. For the news was already widely spread in the East that the land was "booming," and it was more widely spread by the papers in all directions. There were still many who felt nothing but contempt for a country they did not understand and that they did not try to understand; but the majority were on the other extreme and finding the land rapidly growing, with crops all good and money plenty, fell at once into blind, unreasoning love with it. Hence a rapid increase in the letters, already too abundant and silly, sent to Eastern papers.

The growth of San Diego now began in earnest, and Van Dyke wrote:

. . . by the end of 1885 its future was believed to be plainly assured. A very few who predicted a population of 50,000 in five years were looked upon as wild, even by those who believed most firmly in its future. Even those who knew best the amount of land behind it and the great water resources of its high mountains in the interior believed that 25,000 in five years would be doing well.

Not so optimistic was Harrison Gray Otis, who visited San Diego to describe its boom for the *Los Angeles Times.*

She has got it and is holding on to it with the tenacity of death and the tax collector. I hear of a score of men who have made their "pile" within a twelve-

Theodore S. Van Dyke

172

month, and I know that a score more are pursuing the eagle on Uncle Sam's twenties with a fierceness of energy that caused that bird o' freedom to scream a wild and despairing scream . . . this is peculiarly a San Diego pursuit; you never see anything of the sort in Los Angeles, where the populace take care of the noble bird and encourage him to increase and multiply . . .

While not as successful as had been anticipated, the lighting of the town with electric carbon arc lamps on a half dozen 110-foot high masts cast a glow that matched the optimism of the day. Life grew gayer, if less sedate. Sunday buggy riding through the town became the fashion. The City Guard Band gave a concert each Saturday night in Horton's Plaza. The Birch and Cotton Minstrels came to town, paraded through the streets, and performed in the Leach Opera House before the largest audience ever assembled in it. Enthusiasm recognized no geographical limitations. The area of the Florence Hotel, on Fir Street between Third and Fourth Streets, was being described as San Diego's "Nob Hill." On July 4, the California Southern Railroad's Cannonball arrived two hours late with 400 passengers and the drum corps of the Los Angeles Turnverein Society which marched in uniform to Mayrhofer's Beer Garden where they joined the City Guard Band in celebrating Independence Day. They all sang to the music of the San Diego Coach Whip Waltz-Quadrille String Band.

Hotels and rooming houses rapidly filled and *The San Diego Union* warned:

The transient population of our city is so large that notwithstanding our many good hotels, an unwary stranger who neglects to engage a room immediately on his arrival here is often compelled to sit in a chair through the night for want of a bed.

Rowdyism became more prevalent and the enforcement of the laws more difficult as well as neglected. There were at least sixty

Arc lamps on 110-foot tower at Fifth and F Streets, 1887

The boom also brought an era of lawlessness and saloons were scenes of nightly brawling. This typical painting is by N. C. Wyeth.

saloons, ten opening within eight days, and as many of them were the scenes of nightly brawling, the City Trustees raised the license fee from $200 to $600 a year and required them to close at 11 o'clock at night. Thievery and burglaries increased. "Missiles" were thrown at performers in the Leach Opera House.

The gamblers and the boomers followed the speculators who had followed the settlers. Van Dyke wrote of the boomers:

> The business of this class is to follow up all lines of rapid settlement, chop up good farming land into townlets 25 or 30 years ahead of the time they are needed, and sell off in the excitement enough to pay for the land and have a handsome profit left over. The boomer came from Kansas City, Wichita, Chicago, Milwaukee, Minnesota, New York, Seattle and everywhere, and with the aid of a brass band and free lunch (which had a marvelous influence on the human pocket) he began his work. Most of them were in Los Angeles but a few found their way to San Diego, to leaven up the whole lump.

Hotel Corona del Cajon, El Cajon

By mid-1886 several thousand persons were arriving in San Diego monthly by train and ship. Seeking speculative markets, outside capital reached into the county. Land speculators boarded incoming trains at Oceanside, offering land in that area at "bargain prices," or at any place else. The Escondido Land and Town Company subdivided Rancho Rincón del Diablo into small farms and laid out another townsite. A syndicate organized the Santa Maria Land & Water Company and acquired 3200 acres for a townsite in the Santa Maria Valley and named it Ramona, after the novel of Helen Hunt Jackson. A townsite was laid out in El Cajon Valley by the El Cajon Valley Company, of which Ephraim Morse was a principal figure. A second hotel, the Corona, had an observation tower from which prospective buyers could select their lands. The Pacific Coast Land Bureau loaded fifteen carriages and coaches with prospective buyers and took them to see the beauties of the valley. Lots were sold in a spirited auction. The El Cajon Valley Company also laid out the inland town of Lakeside and construction of a hotel there was begun. A few houses and stores appeared at the site of the present town of Encinitas. The lands of nearby Los Vallecitos de San Marcos were opened and another town, San Marcos, got its start. Lots were offered on the installment plan near the railroad depot at the foot of Twenty-second Street. Jacob S. Taylor, a Texas cattle man, was erecting a hotel at Del Mar which, it was noted, was becoming a popular health resort.

By November Babcock in Coronado was ready to cash in on the incoming tide of buyers and speculators. On November 13, 1886, in response to his advertising and offers of free rides across the bay on his new ferry boat and various yachts and boats, 6000 persons arrived to attend a public auction of land on Coronado. The first purchase reputedly was made by Levi Chase, the lawyer who

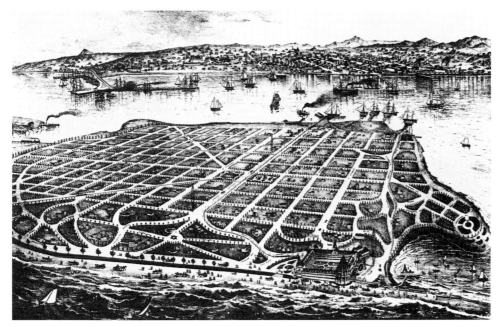

*The most spectacular
promotion of the Boom of
the Eighties was
Coronado. This sketch
shows what it
was expected to become.*

was one of the original subdividers of the El Cajon Rancho, and by
nightfall he had resold it at twice the price. In this and subsequent
auctions land sales totaled $100,000 to $400,000 a month, and the
construction of the hotel had not been started. At the end of the
year realty sales in San Diego had reached a total of $7,000,000,
new construction was valued at $2,000,000, and 26,281 persons
had arrived and 13,938 had departed. San Diego had gained 12,343
residents in a single year.

Water, not land speculation, was the key to a permanent prosperity, and Van Dyke and Robinson were at last able to convince
a large group of investors of the feasibility of reaching into the
mountains to bring irrigating water to the arid coastal mesa and
for domestic use in the town of San Diego. They organized the San
Diego Flume Company in May of 1886, with a capital stock of
$1,000,000, and construction was begun on Cuyamaca Dam at the
headwaters of Boulder Creek, a tributary of the San Diego River,
and on a lower divisionary structure and a wooden flume, or aqueduct, thirty miles in length.

In the same year, in order to promote the sale of lands in National City and a proposed subdivision at Chula Vista, south of it,
the San Diego Land and Town Company, the syndicate controlled
by the Santa Fe Railroad, began the construction of a dam on the
Sweetwater River in a narrow gorge eight miles upstream at a
point previously selected by Frank Kimball. By June of 1887 the
dam had reached a height of sixty feet when it was realized that
the capacity could be more than tripled by raising it to ninety feet.

On the morning of March 6, 1887, the Southern Pacific followed
the Santa Fe in dropping the passenger rate from Missouri to
Southern California to $12. In a few hours it went down to $8,

*Lakeside was the
"garden of San Diego
County" in this
advertising folder on
the advantages
of El Cajon Valley.*

Magazine advertisement, 1888

then to $6, then to $4. By noon of the same day the rate was $1. A rush to California beyond any possible anticipation was under way. Land advanced in price with each passing day. Business lots rose from $500 to $1000 and then to $2500 a front foot. Corner commercial lots were listed at $40,000. Rents became almost prohibitive. Ships arriving with lumber were besieged by builders. Shaves went up in price to 25 cents and baths to 40 cents.

The firm of Howard & Lyons advertised that the lots they were offering for sale in Middletown on India Avenue overlooking the bay, could be purchased that week for only $125 and "they will be worth $1000 each within a year." After an ode to rain and its beneficial effects the advertisement proclaimed:

> When you behold the earth covered with fragrant children, born of her marriage to the clouds, and when you know that this charming effect of a few showers can be increased and perpetuated the year round with a little water from the mains and a little labor with hoe and rake, you will be thankful to us for having called your attention in time to the Middletown Heights lots.

Frank Terrill Botsford and George W. Heald bought a large part of the La Jolla area, subdivided it, and scheduled a public auction under the auspices of the Pacific Coast Land Bureau. It was to have its own hotel. The auctioneer, Wendell Eaton, told the eager customers about the future of "La Jolla Park:"

> This is the natural watering place of this whole Southern country, and nothing can turn the tide from it. It is simply nature working... today the property is as free as air, and you can buy it at your own price.

Frank T. Botsford looks out from his real estate "office" and over the land which he developed as the famed La Jolla Park.

Rancho Peñasquitos, the first of the Spanish grants, was offered in tracts of ten acres for $250 each, with the added attraction of a lottery. Purchasers were to select their lots and put their names in a hat for a drawing. Winners were to be awarded some specific improvement on their property or a choice of another lot or house on the ranch or one in Del Mar. One prize was listed as the $25,000 Peñasquitos ranch house being used as a hotel.

Van Dyke, the most descriptive of the writers of the period, recorded how the boom became a fever and all reason cast aside:

Barbecues, dazzled buyers, the auctioneer's chant and the clink of dollars were daily events in 1887, such as this land sale at Morena.

> Speculation in city lots, which soon went beyond the scope of moderate resources in money and skill, found avenues to the country; and for twenty miles about the town the mesas and valleys were checkered with this or that man's "Addition to San Diego." Numberless new townsites were nearly inaccessible; one was at the bottom of a river; two extended into the bay. Some of the best had graded streets and young trees. All were sustained in the market by the promise of future hotels, sanitariums, opera houses, soldiers' homes, or motor lines to be built at specified dates. Few people visited these additions to see what they were asked to invest in, but under the stimulus of band music and a free lunch, they bought from the auctioneer's map and made large payments down. In this way at least a quarter of a million dollars were thrown away upon alkali wastes, cobble-stone tracts, sand-overflowed lands and cactus, the poorest land being usually put down on the townsite market.

San Diego now had eight hotels with accommodations for 1110 persons, Dr. P. C. Remondino's St. James, formerly the Santa Rosa, being the largest with 160 rooms. There were ten rooming houses and each could accommodate from thirty to 125 persons. Hotel rates were $1 to $4 a day and meals cost from 25 cents to $1. By midsummer of 1887 the Chamber of Commerce reported that 41,356 persons had arrived and 18,155 had departed in the fiscal year from June 30, 1886, to July 1, 1887. Passenger arrivals by train alone had risen from 2313 in July, 1886, to 4755 in June, 1887.

Hotel St. James

One day in July the pleasure schooner *Lurline* slipped into the harbor and aboard her was the master and owner, John D. Spreckels, who was a son of Claus Spreckels, the "Sugar King" of San Francisco. Claus Spreckels had fled a revolutionary Germany, landed in New York with no knowledge of the language and no money, and had gone on to make a fortune. John D. was one of three sons and already he had established himself in his father's company and in related businesses. San Diego meant little to him at the time, but on this casual visit he walked the streets, talked with the town's leaders, and felt the exhilarating surge of the incoming tide of people. He agreed to a suggestion that he accept a franchise to build a wharf which was needed to handle coal for the California Southern trains. His promise went no further than that. But the name of "Spreckels" already was on many lips on both coasts and speculators were alert to its possibilities.

A headline in *The San Diego Union* of September 2, 1887, reported a "Great Panic" in New York, and that depots, ticket offices and steamships had been "seized" by immigrants:

> The greatest excitement ever known in this city has been prevailing for the last twenty-four hours. Men gathered in crowds upon the streets talking in frantic manner, in front of a broker's office in Wall Street. Six mounted policemen were sent for, and with great difficulty made room for carriages to pass. Crowds gathered around all the principal hotels. Express wagons, loaded with trunks, rushed through the streets to the Union Depot. All available vehicles have been pressed into service to convey the fleeing populace.

The cause of all this "terrible panic" was credited to a letter received by a Wall Street broker from a source in San Diego. The letter stated that J. D. Spreckels, the great "Sugar King" of the Sandwich Islands, had recently made arrangements to have a steamship line connect at San Diego with the railroad, for mail, freight and passenger transportation to New York, that a large wharf franchise had been secured, and "in a very short time it was expected that his ships, laden with the products of foreign countries, would cast anchor in San Diego Bay."

According to *The San Diego Union's* report, the letter also disclosed that the Southern Pacific Railroad was making efforts to extend its line to San Diego and that the San Diego and Lower California Railroad had sold its bonds in the East and the road soon would be running trains through Tia Juana City, "the only mountain pass into Lower California." Tia Juana City was the subdivision laid out in the Tia Juana Valley and which drew its name from the old settlement known as Tijuan which straddled both sides of the international border. The original name is believed to have been of Indian origin, meaning, "By the Sea." The

*John D. Spreckels
as a young man*

THE SUCCESS OF SUCCESSES

TIA : JUANA : CITY !

Messrs. Hart & Stern the enterprising real estate firm, are building a city (not on the plan of Romulus and Remus, the founders of Rome), but by selling lots in San Diego's greatest suburb at moderate prices, and encouraging the construction of hotels, stores, sanitariums, railroads, and all the essentials that go to make up a prosperous place.

OVER $70 000 WORTH OF LOTS

were sold on the day of the auction, and the record of sales shows astonishing progress, the demands for lots being rapidly on the increase. Prices range from $100 upwards. There are a number of acre tracts also desirable for villa homes.

COMMERCIAL ADVANTAGES

Tia Juana is fourteen miles south of San Diego. The situation is unequaled in Southern California for a suburb city. It is abundantly supplied with wood and water. It is situated in the most fertile valley in San Diego county. It has a perfect climate. Tia Juana is on the highway between two counties, and the San Diego and Coronado Railroad will undoubtedly pass directly through the town. It commands the only natural pass to Lower California. In speaking of Tia Juana, one writer has graphically described it as follows:

Tia Juana will become a second El Paso. As a health resort it has no equal in San Diego county.

This valley is five miles from the sea, sheltered from the rigors of fog and spray, secure from excessive humidity at night, and open to the ocean's gentlest breeze, being neither damp nor warm, but uncommonly serene and mild in atmosphere. In fact, no better climate, no superior spot can be found on earth for invalids or persons with delicate physique. It contains 40,000 acres, is sixteen miles in length, and averages some five miles in width. It is among valleys what a diamond diadem is in jewelry, it is a partition of Paradise. No purchaser of such property can ever wax indignant and loudly affirm it a sub-division of sheol. It is not, and cannot be made, the matter of a speculative sin or dangerous feline game. Tia Juana has oranges of finer flavor than those of Cypress, rustling corn equal to that of Illinois, lemons superior to those of Italy, figs more delicious than those of Smyrna, grapes more lucious than those of Portugal, olives equal to those of Italy, vines like those that creep and trail along the castled Rhine, peaches like those of Delaware, finer pears than can be found in Maryland, apples not inferior to those of New England, prunes unequaled in any land, vegetables to which for size and quality, Southern California only can lay claim. Soft and pure mountain water is within a few feet of the surface of the soil, hence there can be no necessity for irrigation nor lawsuits over riparian rights. The land of peace and plenty. Tia Juana—the best and richest soil in San Diego county Tia Juana—the purest, most convenient and natural water supply. Tia Juana—one of the most accessible localities outside of the city. Tia Juana—the valley where magnolias, oleanders, crysanthemums, tube-roses, calla-lilies, pinks, pansies, gladiolias and all the most exquisite and tropical flowers are blooming in the open air in utter wantonness—Tia Juana.

Messrs. HART & STERN, Real Estate Brokers and Auctioneers, of 827 and 829 Fifth Street, San Diego, Cal., will give full particulars. Call or write.

The "Tijuana City" or "Tia Juana" of the boom days was on the American side of the border, and lots were sold across country.

report continued:

Most of the farsighted and shrewdest speculators have concluded that better opportunities are offered in the growing city of San Diego than there are in New York, and consequently, . . . they are leaving this city on every train for the metropolis of the Southwest.

A few days later the trap was sprung. A bulletin reported that a committee of the New York Stock Exchange had asked that all lots for sale in Tia Juana City be taken off the market "and we will take them all at the price offered." However, *The San Diego Union* reassured its readers that a reporter had called on the agents for the land, Hart & Stern, and they stated that before complying with the request they intended to give all of their friends in San Diego a chance to buy. Lots worth $70,000 were sold in a few days to "friends."

Their money evidently purchased lots in a land of plenty, as specified in the advertisements:

Tia Juana has oranges of finer flavor than those of Cyprus, rustling corn equal to that of Illinois, lemons superior to those of Italy, figs more delicious than those of Smyrna, grapes more luscious than those of Portugal, olives equal to those of Italy, vines like those that creep and trail along the castled Rhine, peaches like those of Delaware, finer pears than can be found in Maryland, apples not inferior to those of New England, prunes unequaled in any land, vegetables to which for size and quality, Southern California only can lay claim.

The town soon acquired a drug store, boot shop, several grocery stores, a land office, a hotel and saloon, and a federal customs house.

John D. Spreckels also purchased the interest of W. W. Story in the Coronado Beach Company and thus, perhaps more than he had ever intended, found himself drawn into a situation where, as Alonzo Horton before him, he soon would be instrumental in shaping a community. Horton built a town and Spreckels would make it a city.

The lower bay area had a strong attraction for speculators, as the lands had been subjected to general "jumping" as the result of the rejection by the United States government of the claim of the family of Don Santiago Arguello to all the territory between the tip of the bay and the Mexican border. One of the principal promotions was a town named Oneonta, which was to remain a name on the map, lying just south of the present Imperial Beach and north of the Tia Juana River. "Oneonta" is a Mohawk Indian name of a town in New York State and was imported from there by settlers. Oneonta, it seems, had everything. Promotion material stated that it was the Pasadena of San Diego County and that

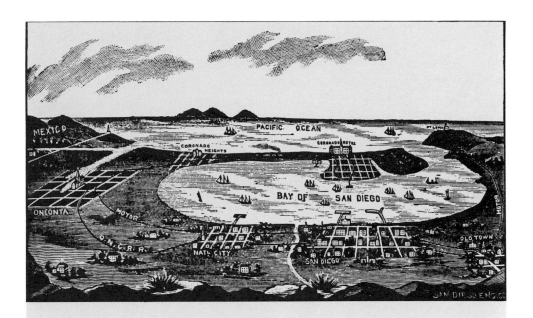

ONEONTA!

BY THE SEA!

(Incorporated Dec. 17, 1887.   Capital Stock, $300,000.   A. E. Young, Prest., A. C. Mouser, Sec'y.)

The Pasadena of San Diego County, the Terminus of the National City & Otay Railway, and for Healthfulness and Beauty of Location without a Rival.

It now has: Six round trip passenger trains daily to San Diego ; good water ; a $20,000 hotel ; a telephone line ; a lovely bay ; the best fishing and hunting on this coast ; a rich soil ; a climate unsurpassed ; a combination of ocean, mountain and valley scenery unequaled ; a beautiful park site almost surrounded by water ; a combination of beauties and advantages that must be seen to be believed ; and it is conceded by all to be the loveliest place for a home, and the most desirable as an investment in this county.

HEALTHFULNESS OF CLIMATE.

Dr. C. M. Fenn, of San Diego, in speaking of the mesa land in and adjoining Oneonta, in an article published in the May number, 1887, of the "Southern California Practitioner," a medical work, published at Los Angeles, California, says: "The air of this entire belt, partly because of the ocean breezes which constantly fan the heated soil, is wonderfully soothing to lesions of the lungs and mucous membranes generally. Fogs are seldom known here. During seven months' sojourn here the writer completely overcame rheumatic proclivities, which had driven him away from San Francisco, and parted company with a catarrhal trouble which had annoyed him for years. Another medical gentleman, a victim to one of the severest forms of ozœna, was measurably relieved during a short stay. Besides these cases, an aphonic consumptive entirely recovered her voice and a fair degree of health in less than four months after arrival. Within my observation, also, were several phthisical incurables, whose lives were unquestionably prolonged by residence here. In addition to its hygienic advantages, this locality furnishes a rare opportunity for all kinds of sea-bathing, fishing, pleasant walks and drives, on land and beach, and a varied landscape of plain and ocean, mountain and valley, upon which the eye cannot dwell without increasing interest. As an adjunct to pneumatic differentiation, inhalation or medication of the lungs, by any method whatever, I can cordially recommend the Tia Juana (referring to this mesa), for suburban residences also—it can have no formidable rival in this vicinity."

Dr. T. B. Taylor, of Philadelphia, for years in charge of a sanitarium, says Oneonta is by far the most desirable place for a sanitarium he ever saw.

Its wonderful healthfulness is conclusively proved by the fact that Dr. P. A. Wood, Leon Young, G. E. Hargis, Charles E. Smith, J. H. Folk, W. D. Foot and others living in and adjoining Oneonta have been cured of catarrh, rheumatism, lung, throat and other diseases, and unitedly testify that every one, without a single exception, living there for any considerable time has been restored to perfect health.

For Sale by ARNOLD, JEFFREY & MOUSER, 862 Sixth St. and by THOMAS & HINKLE, 1429 E St.

A hotel, a New York Indian name on the Mexican border and sure cures for anything from headache to flat feet sold lots at Oneonta by the Sea.

181

those "living in and adjoining Oneonta have been cured of catarrh, rheumatism, lung, throat, and other diseases, and unitedly testify that every one, without a single exception, living there for any considerable time, has been restored to perfect health." The honor of having the "Pasadena of San Diego County" also was claimed by the San Diego Development Company for its subdivision, La Mesa, lying east of San Diego.

The new community of Otay, south of Chula Vista, was one of the largest of the boom promotions and acquired a factory, the Otay Watch Works, around which future development was to take place. Largely financed by Frank Kimball, it even manufactured some watches. The Babcock organization also promoted South Coronado and Coronado Heights.

Otay Watch

Otay was to become the great city of the South Bay, and a watch factory was to be the core of a new Western industrial empire.

OTAY !

"THE MAGIC CITY,"

So the National City *Record* calls it, and so it is. Lying ten miles southeast of San Diego, in one of the finest fruit-growing regions in in the county, in a beautiful valley, long having stood in need of a town. Just the right distance from the city for suburban homes. Far enough inland, so that the ocean's raw winds are melted into delightful zephyrs. Being the terminus of the steam motor line—is it strange that it is the coming suburb of San Diego? Lots in this splendid property are for sale by

Guion, Hamilton & Hartley,

S. W. Cor. Sixth and E Sts., SAN DIEGO, CAL.

They also have constantly on their books some special bargains in the city, in fruit and grain farms and stock ranches. They invest for non-residents when desired, and invite the readers of THE GOLLEN ERA to write them for any information regarding the country or city. M. D. Hamilton, of their firm, being President of the Board of City Trustees, can give any information regarding city matters.

Don Antonio Arguello, son of Santiago Arguello, also subdivided 26,000 acres of the huge Mexican ranch the family had retained, just below the international border, into town lots and five-acre tracts and laid out another town. The speculation in land in Mexico was not confined to that near the border. In 1883 the

182

Mexican Congress passed the Law of Colonization, which provided that colonization companies surveying land in Lower California should have one-third of all they surveyed and the right to purchase the other two-thirds at 10 cents per hectare (one hectare equals 2.471 acres), and before 1888 some thirty concessions were granted. Four companies, however, managed to gain control of 7,642,543 hectares of land, or approximately four-fifths of the entire peninsula. A firm named Hansbury and Garvey, the San Diego agent for the International Company of Mexico, was advertising that it had 18,000,000 acres for sale in Lower California. Steamers and overland stages were leaving San Diego loaded daily for Ensenada and returning empty. The International Company was building a hotel at Ensenada and purchased horses, buggies, carriages and wagons in San Diego to be sent there to haul purchasers out to the tracts. Tents and bedding were sent down to provide for them until the hotel could be completed.

The Chamber of Commerce Report of 1887 recorded glowing civic progress and the rapid development of local transportation:

Two years ago the present city of San Diego was a quiet, inactive village. The one short local line of railway had been almost destroyed and inoperative by reason of floods for a year past. Communication with the outside world was to be obtained only by steamship and a miserable stage service. The local road was not only rebuilt, but San Diego was made the Pacific coast terminus of the great Santa Fe transcontinental line of railway. Now began an era of progress and development unprecedented in the history of California.

The ungraded streets were leveled to beautiful driveways; electric lights provided for the city and private consumers; street railways started; new lines of steam ships put on to accommodate the increasing commerce; new manufactories, while the capacities of the old ones were more than doubled; motor and electric railroads, communicating with the progressive suburbs fast springing into existence; magnificent business blocks, costing from $20,000 to $75,000; Coronado Beach, with its $2,000,000 worth of improvements, sprang up like an Aladdin lamp scene in less than a year; new water and gas pipes laid down and extended; a city increased from a population of 4000 to that of 20,000, and brimming over with business enterprise and liberality.

Such is the history of the city within the past two years. Its unquestioned excellence of climate and its peculiar commercial advantages has drawn the attention of business from all parts of the union to it. The settling and development of the interior part of the county is also going ahead rapidly. It is now traversed by two steam broad-gauge railroads, with two now building, another one to be commenced shortly by the Southern Pacific, and all to terminate upon the Bay of San Diego.

The National City and Otay Railway Company, owned by the Land & Town Company, built twenty-nine miles of road, including the main line from Fifth and L Streets in San Diego to National City, Chula Vista and Oneonta, with branch lines to La Presa, Sweetwater Dam and Tia Juana. It used steam "dummies," little boxlike steam engines, to pull passenger cars. The Coronado

Railroad Company used steam dummies and one full-sized steam engine on the Coronado Belt Line that ran from Fifth and L Streets in San Diego, around the bay shore through National City, and up the Silver Strand and along the east side of Coronado Island to the ferry terminal. At the height of the boom the Coronado Belt Line and the National City and Otay Railroad ran a total of 104 trains a day.

The Ocean Beach Motor Railway began running steam cars from Roseville to Ocean Beach through the cleft on Point Loma that some day would become a freeway. The San Diego, Old Town and Pacific Beach Railroad, a subsidiary of the Electric Rapid Transit Company, began existence as an electric streetcar line, using an overhead power line, one of the first in the United States. It ran down Kettner to Old Town where it cut diagonally across

San Diego & Pacific Beach Motor train, a "steam dummy" line eventually extended to La Jolla, furnished passenger service for many years.

the historic Plaza. The electrical equipment was soon removed and it operated as a steam power line and the tracks were extended to Grand Avenue and then westward to Pacific Beach and eventually to La Jolla. A horse track was built where the line turned from its northerly course onto Grand Avenue.

On April 15, 1886, a group led by Babcock and Story had organized the city's first transit system, the San Diego Street Car Company and the first mule-drawn cars began running on July 3, from the ferry landing to D Street and up D to Fifth. Construction continued until eight and a half miles of tracks had been laid and cars were serving most of the business and residential area, from the bay east as far as Thirty-first Street on National Avenue. The Coronado Beach Railway soon extended its horse-car line from the hotel to a racetrack at the Spanish Bight, the inlet between Coronado and North Island, and later to the extreme tip of North

By 1888 transit systems
served most of the
city, predominantly
horse cars such as this
one seen at
Fifth and E Streets.

Island to haul rock for the construction of Zuniga Shoal Jetty. It
soon switched to the little steam "dummies." Another line organized by Babcock and Story and using steam power was the
University Heights Motor Road, called the Park Belt Line, which
ran from Eighteenth and A Streets up Switzer Canyon across the
southeast section of Balboa Park land and came up onto the mesa,
or University Heights, at Marlborough Street and University
Avenue, and then turned west to Fifth and down Fifth to Fir, to
connect with the San Diego Street Car Company's system.

San Diego's Electric
Rapid Transit in 1887
was truly electric and
rapid, though somewhat
uncertain due to the
primitive power
system used.

185

Bands, balloons and free lunches were employed to attract eager settlers to land auctions, as shown in this photo of Ocean Beach.

186

The electrical equipment was shifted from the Old Town line and used on a route that ran north from the foot of Fourth Street to University Avenue and then east to Normal Street, ending at the present El Cajon Boulevard. The electric cars were two-unit trains using power to pull a passenger car, though there was space for some passengers in the power unit. Service frequently was interrupted by power failures.

The Cliffs Hotel, Ocean Beach, later the Beacon Hotel

The line between Roseville and Ocean Beach was built by William H. Carlson, an enterprising young politician who had got his start as a page boy in the State Legislature. He joined Albert E. Higgins of San Diego in laying out a new town at Ocean Beach, which was then known as "The Mussel Beds." Prospective customers, after being ferried by steam launch across the bay, were taken in style to the Cliff House erected in Ocean Beach. A flood tide of cash set in and on the first of each month the happy promoters raised the prices of the lots ten percent, and perhaps several hundred were sold for as much as $300 each. A single auction in another new beach community, Pacific Beach, on the north side of Mission, or False Bay, resulted in sales amounting to $200,000.

Carlson had borrowed a steam engine from the Pacific Coast Steamship Company, which operated a line for its wharf, to haul passengers over his line, but when he neglected to pay for its rental the company sent a crew out to rip up and store his tracks for security. A feeder railroad line for the California Southern, known as the San Diego Central Railroad Company, was building a line through the backcountry, where so much land speculating was going on, from Oceanside by way of Escondido, Bernardo, Poway and El Cajon to San Diego. Service on the twenty-one mile section between Oceanside Junction and Escondido was started on December 31, 1887.

Old Town Plaza slept through boom

The California Central was building a branch line down the coast from Los Angeles by way of Santa Ana as part of the Santa Fe system to connect with the California Southern near Oceanside, "which will bring Los Angeles within four hours of San Diego Harbor." This was a fateful move in the destiny of San Diego in view of the serious difficulties still being encountered in trying to keep the railroad line open through Temecula Canyon. There was no one to reflect on its implications amid the cries of the auctioneer and the din of the builders' hammers.

The San Diego, Elsinore and Pomona Valley Railway also was under construction from its northern point, crossing an inland empire and pointing hopefully toward the harbor of San Diego. The San Diego, Cuyamaca and Eastern Railroad was organized

Gov. Robert W. Waterman

and was surveying the backcountry for a proposed line through El Cajon Valley, thence by way of Santa Maria Valley to Warner's Ranch, a route rejected many years before by United States Army engineers. At Warner's it was to proceed down San Felipe Pass and cross the desert to intersect the Southern Pacific. Then it was to turn northeast to also meet the tracks of the Santa Fe, or the Atlantic and Pacific as it was known along its western section. Mexican interests were planning a line down the peninsula from San Diego to San Quintin Bay, with a branch to Yuma, thus giving San Diego another outlet to the East.

The principal organizer of the Cuyamaca Railroad was Robert W. Waterman, the governor of California from 1887 to 1891, and he also purchased the Cuyamaca Rancho and reopened the Stonewall mine. In 1888 two new and apparently rich mines were opened, the Gold Queen and the Gold King, about four miles southeast of Julian, and this promptly resulted in the reopening of mines at both Julian and Banner, in particular the Owens and the Helvetia. Gold deposits also were worked near Mesa Grande, east of Santa Ysabel, and at Escondido. The Dulzura District in the Otay Mountains, not far from the Mexican border, also yielded small amounts of gold.

Even the desert was not spared. The Hon. William Williams of

Indiana made a speech in the Plaza and called for the irrigation of the desert to make it "blossom as the rose" and provide "prosperous and happy homes to thousands of homeless Americans." The San Felipe and Desert Land & Water Company was organized and proposed to build a reservoir in Banner Canyon, drill a 3000-foot tunnel up into the snow country of the Cuyamacas, and bring life to the "rich empire plains known as the Colorado Desert," which it said contained 5,000,000 acres and almost all of it arable. Incidentally, the dizzying prospect that the tunnel might pierce many new rich gold veins was an added inducement to invest.

Perhaps in some ways these promoters, and many others in Southern California, were merely a century ahead of their times, for in describing the desert's Borrego Valley, the company's brochure stated:

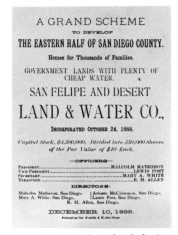

A little north of the dam, lies Borrego Bay, an arm of the Desert, embracing in its mountain-girted area, 100,000 acres of rich, clayey soil, under a tropical sun. Completely sheltered by high mountains, excepting in the gap, through which it looks out into the Desert, it can, with a wind-break of ever-green trees in the gap, be made comfortably cool in the warmest weather. Beyond this gap, is an empire of rich, clayey soil, almost perfectly level.

To those who might shun the desert and yet still have money in their pockets, the brochure pointed to the dry eastern slopes of the

Promoters ahead of their time saw a future for the desert

A contemporary pictorial folder contained this fine etching of the San Diego that had reached some level of sophistication in 1887.

great mountains:

> To him who, notwithstanding . . . successful experiments of the French colonies in the heart of the burning plains of the Great Sahara of Africa . . . to him who still dreads the Colorado Desert, we offer a home on Government land in the beautiful valleys of the eastern slope of the Cuyamaca range, completely sheltered from the warm Desert winds and the fogs of the Pacific Ocean . . . These gentle mountain slopes, naturally charming to the eye, when covered with vineyards and orchards, will excell the far-famed vine-clad hills of France and Italy.

The general impression, according to Van Dyke, was that the Californians had worked up the boom, but "the sad and homely truth is that nearly all the innocents were wise and successful men, who insisted on being shorn."

As had happened in the founding days of New Town, when they had happily sold to the "crazy" Alonzo Horton a large share of the pueblo for 27½ cents an acre, the San Diegans had been only too eager to again dispose of their idle lands to the supposedly unwary newcomers. But, as they watched the rising boom, they began to have second thoughts, as related by Van Dyke:

> Shall I, who have lived on beans and peppers and rustled clams these many years on the salt-sea shore so as to hold my lots, now see some rich old duffer from the East get still richer at my expense?
> Not much! I haven't skinned dead cattle to save their hides in dry years, and drunk mescal instead of good whiskey, for nothing. We never knew what the cussed country was worth until outsiders found it out, and now we are green enough to let them make all the money out of it.

As the banks were full of the money deposited by the strangers, which they were willing to loan "the solid old citizens" at fifteen percent, the natives had little difficulty, as Van Dyke expressed it, "in rescuing enough of the precious soil from the hands of the unworthy stranger." They bought on contract, a third or a fourth down, as had become the custom, at prices five to fifteen times the original prices "and they went around the corner and smiled in their sleeves at the way in which they had again taken in the 'tenderfoot.' "

WHEN THE GAMES
RAN ALL NIGHT

Lures such as this drew thousands
to Southern California in the Great Booms.
Health and wealth were
sure to be every man's lot.

CHAPTER XIII

The two years that began in 1886 and ended in 1888 were the
most gaudy, wicked and exciting in San Diego's history. The
boomers and gamblers had followed the speculators to San Diego
and now came the entertainers and the criminals. It was San
Francisco of the Gold Rush all over again. The town even acquired
its writers, poets and musicians, who gathered around the magazine *The Golden Era* which James Harrison Wagner brought to
San Diego in 1887 from the Mother Lode Country where it had
once flourished with such grand contributors as Mark Twain and
Bret Harte.

The extravagances of the Victorian age flowed with the language by which a golden land was sold and resold, from one person
to another, and back again. The most eloquent of these super-
salesmen of yesteryear was Thomas L. Fitch, known as Col. Tom
Fitch, a former New York lawyer who played various roles in the
West, as an editor, orator, and promoter, and earned a dubious
distinction of being portrayed as one of the characters in Mark
Twain's *Roughing It*. He wrote most if not all of the promotion
literature for the real estate firm of Howard & Lyons which was
republished in a souvenir booklet.

As far as the advertising writers were concerned, in two or three

*Fifth Street, south
from Broadway, 1888*

years there would be no more prosperous city in America than San Diego, with five trunk railroad lines centering on the shores of the bay; with four lines of ocean steamships coming and going from her wharves; and with 50,000 persons dwelling within its confines.

Words were sharpened into spears as San Diego and Los Angeles vied in the rate of growth and fought each other for the privilege of trimming the newcomers, and Col. Fitch joined in this struggle with ability and relish. In one of the advertisements in the souvenir booklet, Fitch challenged the contention of Los Angeles — and even San Francisco — that San Diego had no backcountry worthy of mentioning. It read:

"No backcountry at San Diego," — sneers Los Angeles squatting among her sloughs and fearful that the scepter of empire may be speedily snatched from her fever-flushed hands.

"No backcountry at San Diego," — sneers San Francisco gathering tolls upon highways she never built, watching with anxious eyes her dwindling commerce.

"No backcountry at San Diego," — squeek the little towns that fancy there will be no feast for them except in the crumbs that fall from Los Angeles' table cloth . . ."

Fitch proclaimed that the resources of San Diego County, let alone the advantages of climate, were sufficient to attract a population of 1,000,000 persons, but this was considered an obvious literary license. In contrast, he wrote:

Los Angeles is part of our backcountry. Flea-infested in summer, mired in winter, roasted at noon day, chilled at night, unsewered, typhoid-afflicted, pneumoniated Los Angeles.

As for backcountry, he insisted that San Diego's also included Ventura and San Bernardino Counties as well as Tia Juana; and in addition, it had a "front country," which took in Japan, China, Australia and the west coast of Mexico and Central America, though perhaps they weren't exactly contiguous.

Los Angeles was a subject of which San Diego never tired, and the citizenry became thoroughly aroused over the attempts of northern real estate promoters to "steal" the name of "Ramona" for their own subdivisions. "Ramona" had become a byword in the East. In another promotional article in the souvenir booklet, Fitch wrote of *Ramona*, though perhaps somewhat irreverently:

Only a few years ago that interesting squaw was wandering up and down San Diego County with never a corner lot she could call her own, and only the sheep-shearing, horse-nipping, sad-eyed son of the soil, to wit: "Allesandro," for company. Now under the inspiration of Helen Hunt Jackson's genius, every enterprising land speculator who is lying in wait for the soft and sentimental side of a Boston tenderfoot rushes to name a creek or a town, or a street "Ramona." We do not complain of this, but we think that Los Angeles real

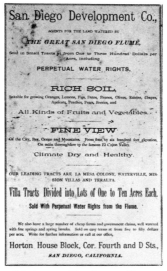

*Water, soil, view, climate,
easy terms
were magic words*

194

estate sharps who are trying to carve sanitariums out of fog banks ought to keep their predatory hands at home.

With Los Angeles properly rebuked and put in its place, the promotional writers turned their attention back to their own wares, the beauties of San Diego, and their efforts achieved a flowering unequaled in Southern California before or since. Of Oceanside, the Howard & Lyons' "Special No. 1" began with a flourish of rhyme that read, "This is the place I long have sought, and mourning because I found it not." Oceanside, it was said, had plenty of room for 10,000 to 15,000 persons:

Go to Oceanside next Saturday week and take with you all the cash you can raise and buy at auction, and keep buying until your money and credit are both exhausted. It will not be possible for you to make a mistake . . .

If you buy to hold you will be able to put up a cottage from the front windows of which you can behold a panorama of sea and shore, of cloud palaces and white-winged ships such as can be seen nowhere else in this land.

There was but one other place as salubrious as Oceanside in the world, it was stated, and that was the little city on the Mediterranean at the foot of the Alps, called Mentone, which Sam Cox had immortalized in his *Search for Winter Sunbeams*. While lots in Mentone cost 50,000 francs, lots in Oceanside could be purchased for only $5000!

The memories of Spain, which had influenced events and formed traditions in California for three centuries, had long been forgotten. Italy was the magic country, in popular imagination. Roseville, the town along the base of Point Loma, which Louis Rose had struggled to develop for so many years, now was considered certain to be the terminus of the Southern Pacific Railroad—if it ever built into San Diego. In an article in *The Golden Era* magazine, on the joys of buying and residing in Roseville, the author was carried away by scenes of bay and city:

From the townsite of Roseville the gaze goes beyond the three inlets or reaches from the bay, and we rest our eyes on the city that already hugs the hill in so compact a way, with a certain newness about it, to be sure, and a deal of character of its own, and yet betraying a form and a suggestion of the Bay and City of Naples, with Table Mountain, far away in Mexico, and San Miguel a little to the left, the two standing instead of Vesuvius, the dust in lieu of the smoke from the crater, and the adjacent mountains lying back in sullen grandeur like those frowning over Naples . . . "Is this the busy nineteenth century in America, or the seventeenth in Italy? Is the reality a dream, or the dream a reality?"

The promoters of Pacific Beach had one thing their rivals lacked, a real poet. He was Joaquin Miller, the "Poet of the Sierras." Miller came to San Diego at the behest of the publisher of *The Golden Era*. For a time he was enthused about San Diego and

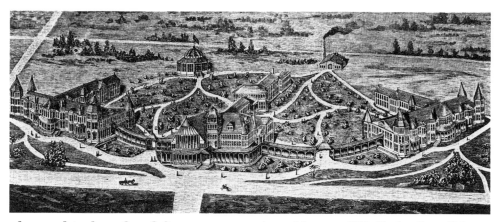

Daniel Choate

planned to buy land for permanent residence. While in San Diego he wrote *Perfumed Nights* and *San Diego,* and for the dedication of the area's first institution of higher learning, the San Diego College of Letters at Pacific Beach, which had been started by Wagner and other friends, he composed *The Larger College* to express the higher cultural sentiments which all believed surely must lie somewhere within the eager immigrants and land buyers. A second institution of higher learning, the College of Fine Arts of the University of Southern California, was projected for University Heights, the subdivision above the northern boundary of Balboa Park. If all the schemes had materialized, San Diego most certainly would have been the educational center of the Southwest. Daniel Choate, a native of Maine who came to California during the Gold Rush, was the principal promoter behind the College Hill Loan Association which laid out the subdivision of 1600 acres north of the city park. Every other block was donated to the Methodist Episcopal Church and the first $200,000 realized

A College of Fine Arts was proposed for University Heights as shown in etching from the town's literary magazine, The Golden Era.

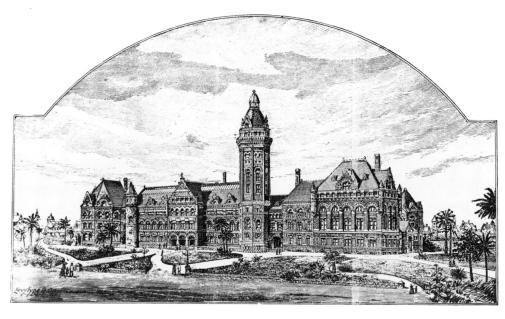

Culture came to a border town with The Golden Era magazine, which had writers like Mark Twain when it was published in the north.

Rose Hartwick Thorpe

from the sale of these blocks was to be used for building the college. It was to be a branch of the University of Southern California which at that time was supported by the Methodist Episcopal Church.

San Diego also acquired Rose Hartwick Thorpe, who at the age of sixteen had written the poem *Curfew Shall Not Ring Tonight*. By the time she arrived in San Diego from Litchfield, Michigan, with her ailing husband, Edmund Carson Thorpe, its fame had preceded her. Poetry about San Diego sprouted with editions of *The Golden Era*. Rose Hartwick Thorpe composed *The Little White Lady of La Jolla* and Madge Morris, wife of Harr Wagner, the pub-

Dr. P. C. Remondino

Jesse Francis Shepard

lisher, wrote *At San Diego Bay.* Helen Hunt Jackson died before the boom got under way, though she had written about San Diego for several magazines. In *The Youths Companion* she expressed enchantment with San Diego where "one views scenes of beauty and promise rarely equaled in the world."

Benjamin C. Truman, who had assisted in the establishment of the Butterfield Stage route in 1858, and had been a newspaper correspondent during the Civil War, came to San Diego to serve as editor of the *Bulletin* in the civic fight over the city's tidelands, and later became chief publicist for the Southern Pacific Railway Company and the author of a number of books, including *Homes and Happiness in the Golden State of California* and *Semi-Tropical California.* One of the most unusual persons was a physician, Dr. Peter C. Remondino, who was intensely interested in the climate and its effect on health. He wrote extensively on various subjects and engaged in many business enterprises. A native of Torino, Italy, he came to the United States with his father on the ship that brought the Italian marble for the Capitol in Washington. They settled in Minnesota, where he learned to speak Sioux and French, and after serving in the Civil War as a physician and surgeon, he was commissioned in the French Army in 1870 and 1871. Upon returning to Minnesota he found the climate incompatible with the malarial fever he had contracted, and after studying the science of climate, selected San Diego as his home. He was fond of comparing Southern California with the shores of the Mediterranean Sea, and wrote that "to the north of Oceanside on the Temecula Canyon route in the Santa Rosa Mountains the scenery reminds one of the upper valley of the Po in Northern Italy, in its valleys, and of the Tyrolese Alps, in its mountains." He assured one and all that in Southern California it was "never necessary to close the houses, either to exclude the heat of summer or the cold of winter." While Dr. Remondino favored the higher inland country lying between Alpine, at 1800 feet elevation, and the Cuyamaca Valley, at 4500 feet, the promoters of a subdivision in the coastal belt which they named Glen-Barnham, seven miles east of Encinitas, asked, "What is the matter with Glen-Barnham? Nothing. This is God's own arrangement for the consumptive, the dyspeptic and the broken-down."

The most celebrated person, at least locally, of the cultural infiltration was Benjamin Henry Jesse Francis Shepard, who was known as Jesse Shepard, a tall, ascetic-appearing musician with a handle-bar moustache and long, tapering fingers who, before he was induced to come to San Diego at the age of thirty-eight, had played the piano before the crowned heads of Europe and the Czar of Russia. He was a native of England and though he studied literature under Alexandre Dumas, he became a concert pianist without having taken a lesson in music.

In San Diego he built a home with stained-glass windows, known as the "Villa Montezuma," at 1925 K Street, which was financed by his admirers and in which he gave intimate private concerts for the town's leading citizens. As he was interested in spiritualism and mysticism, his concerts were presented in an atmosphere of dramatic lighting, in which he would appear out of the dark, play in the light of a single lamp, and then, as the music ended, the light would go out. When it came on again, he would be standing by the piano to make his bows. San Diego loved it.

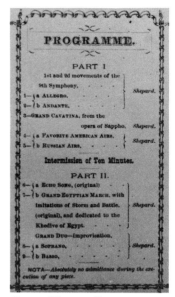

Jesse Shepard's
Concert Program

*Villa Montezuma
was the home of musician
Jesse Shepard. It was
a showplace of
stained glass windows,
rich woods
and much "culture."*

Newspapers and periodicals sprang up as if by magic. San Diego had three daily newspapers; the monthly magazine, *The Golden Era*; a scientific monthly magazine, *West American Scientist*; and a general monthly magazine, *San Diego Magazine*. Outside the city, in the area now embracing San Diego, Imperial and Riverside Counties, soon appeared sixteen newspapers including ones at Coronado, Pacific Beach, National City, Oceanside, Escondido, Carlsbad, Fallbrook, Encinitas, Otay, San Marcos and Julian. It was an articulate as well as a flowery age.

Reports of persons being cured of many illnesses by drinking natural spring waters gained wide circulation. The "Fountain of

199

Youth" that had eluded Ponce de León in Florida perhaps was in Southern California all the time! The noted writer Charles Dudley Warner, who had christened Southern California as "Our Italy," in his articles in *Harper's Magazine* described the long life of the Indians of San Diego County. He reported that Fr. Ubach knew a number of Indians who had been employed in the building of the San Diego Mission in 1769-71, and that there were Indians living at the village of Capitan Grande whose age he estimated at more than 135 years. A Dr. Edward Palmer, once associated with the Agricultural Department of the Smithsonian Institute, was quoted as saying he knew a squaw estimated to be 126 years of age whom he once saw put six watermelons in a basket and carry them for two miles. Dr. Remondino told Warner that Philip Crosthwaite, who had lived in San Diego since 1843, knew an old man who had been breaking horses when Don Antonio Serrano was an infant. Don Antonio himself was now ninety-three years of age, and riding his horse with grace and vigor, and yet the man who held him on a knee as a child was still alive and active enough to also mount and canter a horse. W. A. Winder, of San Diego, reported that thirty-five years before he had visited a house in which aged Indians were cared for:

There were half a dozen who had reached an extreme age. Some were unable to move, their bony frame being seemingly anchylosed. They were old, wrinkled, and blear-eyed; their skin was hanging in leathery folds about their withered limbs; some had hair as white as snow, and had seen some seven score of years; others, still able to crawl, but so aged as to be unable to stand, went slowly about on their hands and knees, their limbs being attenuated and withered. The organs of special sense had in many nearly lost all activity some generations back. Some had lost the use of their limbs for more than a decade or generation . . .

The elixir of life was thought to be in the climate or the water, or both, and Warner was certain that many white people in the United States could prolong life by moving to Southern California. In 1887 Capt. Charles Fitzallen had brought his steamship *Challenger,* out of Cardiff, Wales, into port with the crew suffering severely from scurvy, the ailment of the sea. Upon the advice of Dr. Remondino, Capt. Fitzallen turned his ship over to another officer and became a sheep herder on the Jamacha Rancho lying along the south side of Sweetwater River in southern San Diego County. His recovery was swift, and attributing it to the water from mineral springs in the area which had been recommended by Dr. Remondino, he and a traveling salesman, Alfred Huntington Isham, began bottling the water and selling it internationally as "Isham's California Waters of Life" or as the "Original California Waters."

The character of the town was changing under the impact of its

Therapeutic claims brought visitors

invasion, and a young newspaperman, Walter Gifford Smith, the city editor of the *San Diego Sun*, in his little book on the *History of San Diego*, published in 1892, wrote:

Naturally, a population drawn together from the adventurous classes of the world, imbued as it was with excitement and far from conventional trammels, contained and developed a store of profligacy and vice, much of which found its way into official, business, and social life. Gambling was open and flagrant; games of chance were carried on at the curbstones; painted women paraded the town in carriages and sent out engraved cards summoning men to their receptions and "high teas." The desecration of Sunday was complete, with all drinking and gambling houses open, and with picnics, excursions, fiestas and bullfights...Theft, murder, incendiarism, carousals, fights, highway robbery and licentiousness gave to the passing show in boomtide San Diego many of the characteristics of the frontier camp. Society retired to cover before the invasion of questionable people, and what came to be known as "society" in the newspapers, was, with honorable exceptions here and there, a spectacle of vulgar display and the arrogant parade of reputations which, in Eastern states, had secured for their owners the opportunity and the need of "going West."

One of the enterprising operators of gambling places was Wyatt Earp, the famed marshall of the Western plains. He was undergoing some legal embarrassment at the time, having been indicted for murder in Arizona in the shooting of the men who had slain his brother. He had fled to El Paso, Texas, and attracted by the reports of the boom sweeping Southern California, had come to San Diego, where with his wife he invested in business and speculative property and opened three gambling halls. One was on Fourth Street between Broadway and E Street and fronting on Horton's Plaza; another in the 800 block on Sixth Street, next to the Hotel St. James; and the third on the north side of E Street, near Sixth. He conducted twenty-one different games of faro, blackjack, poker, keno, and other lesser known games of chance.

Little mention of him is to be found in contemporary newspaper files, perhaps out of respect to his difficulties with the law. The San Diego city directory of 1888-89 lists him as "capitalist." He refereed a prize fight which was the feature of a day-long Sunday fiesta, with cockfights, bullfights and a lassoing contest across the border below the town of Tia Juana.

Civic corruption kept pace with the boom. In January of 1888 Police Chief Joseph Coyne was indicted by the Grand Jury for violating the election laws. *The San Diego Union* accused the president of the Board of Trustees, W. J. Hunsaker, who generally was referred to as "mayor," of failing to supervise the police department and that as a lawyer he was representing criminals and gamblers; and Judge C. F. Monroe of using the police court for private business and collecting fees in justice cases. Ephraim W. Morse and George W. Marston, the merchant and a new member

Wyatt Earp

*Chief of Police
Joseph Coyne*

*(Next page)
The famed marshall
Wyatt Earp deals cards
in one of the
gambling houses he
operated in San Diego in
the wild days
of boom and bust.*

201

of the Board of Trustees elected on a reorganization ticket in 1887 when San Diego became a city of the fourth class, led a fight to increase the license fees of saloons, which numbered at least 100, from $600 to $1800, in the hopes of forcing many of them out of business. Mayor Hunsaker vetoed the move.

In an editorial which resulted in a boycott of the newspaper by many elements in the town, *The San Diego Union* stated:

> The professional criminals from all along the coast are flocking to San Diego attracted to this paradise of such characters . . . and the novel experience of being enabled to carry on their usually dangerous avocation without perilous interruption . . . Houses in the most crowded part of the city are broken into and burglarized; men are pounded into insensibility and their pockets rifled on the most public streets; life and property become every day more insecure . . .

Old castle overlooks Moosa Canyon

The police arrested a Los Angeles man as he was setting up a San Diego headquarters for a ring of child pickpockets under the direction of a female "Fagin" known as "Mother Nelson." When the Santa Fe passenger train was halted at Oceanside because of the wreck of a freight train, thugs went through the cars and ransacked all of the passengers' baggage. Armed robbers herded eighteen sailors behind boxcars and took their money.

Guns were again carried openly on the streets and were still a necessity in the lonelier areas of the backcountry. Three persons died in one fight in a little, high-walled, well-watered valley isolated from the main courses of travel. It was the eastern area of what is known as Moosa Canyon, eighteen miles inland from Oceanside. Levi P. Stone, a bee rancher who had claimed 180 acres in the canyon, went East on a visit and when he returned he found his ranch had been "jumped" by squatters, Mrs. Elizabeth Going, her son, Percy, four in-laws and two small children. Stone obtained an eviction notice and with a posse of five men that included a constable, a deputy constable, a special deputy, Stone's brother and a rancher, headed for Moosa Canyon.

The date was January 18, 1888. A row ensued and Mrs. Going appeared in the doorway of the shack with an old musket. The accounts differ on how the shooting began, but those killed were Percy Going, John McConahay, a son of Mrs. Going by a previous marriage, and Mrs. Jennie Burnham, a married step-daughter. Constable A. H. Breedlove, leader of the posse, was wounded in the face and hand, and Stockton Reed, the rancher with the posse, was wounded so seriously he died a day later.

Testimony at the coroner's inquest into what happened at the lonely ranch was conflicting. Constable Breedlove ordered Reed and George L. Morris, the special deputy, to restrain Mrs. Going's son, Percy, while he attempted to disarm her and take "Peg-leg

Johnny" McConahay into custody. A general scuffle ensued and McConahay snatched a pistol from Breedlove's pocket and shot Reed. Morris and the Stone brothers, who were unarmed, fled from the scene. Perhaps a dozen shots were subsequently fired. Mrs. Burnham was found to have been shot three times; Percy, who was only sixteen years of age, twice; and McConahay, three times. At the inquest Mrs. Going and Annie McConahay swore that Deputy Constable Arch Freeman had shot all three from behind a tree trunk.

After some deliberation, it was decided that although the Goings were bad citizens, Levi Stone in the first place had had no title to the land on which the gun fight took place, and the Goings had as much right to it as he did; the writ of ejection had been issued without legal authority, and the Goings had a right to resist its enforcement. The posse was adjudged the "first aggressor." Nothing more came of the case, however.

...a rowdy gambling town

While Fifth Street was the center of gambling and dance halls, Third Street, at about I Street, was the heart of the "Stingaree" district and its more than 100 houses employed an estimated 350 women. The similarity of gambling houses and dance halls in this section of San Diego's downtown area with those of the Wild West was very marked. A graphic description of one dance hall in the "Stingaree" district was provided by a sleuth hired by *The San Diego Union*. This particular hall, when he visited it, was crowded with at least 400 persons, many of them "callow youth and balding rakes," who sat around drinking beer and listening "to the alleged music of an alleged orchestra and feasting their eyes on the alleged charms of stage 'daisies.' " There was a stage at one end of the long hall and on the other side there was a long row of "private boxes" in the shape of a balcony from which "the gaudy women, scantily dressed, display themselves on the railings . . . and wave their handkerchiefs at the crowd below."

Strolling the town among the gamblers and the sporting women, and yet retaining a dignity they did not seem to have, was Pablo, an Indian chief. Pablo wore a plug hat several sizes too small perched atop his head and around which was a bright red band with the letters "Big Chief." His coat had gaudy epaulets, a row of homemade tin medals and a wide sash of many colors. Very popular with all the Indians of the county, he was much respected by San Diego authorities.

There was a steady procession of road shows, touring actor troupes, circuses and minstrel shows through San Diego. Most of them played from three days to a week at either Leach's Opera

"Big Chief" Pablo

One-armed bandit of Old West

House or the Louis Opera House. Nearly all of them drew full audiences. Minstrel shows were most popular with the citizenry while Indians flocked in from miles around to ensure good audiences for the circuses. But the thespian event that crowned the boom-days' theater in San Diego was on May 4 and 5 of 1888. Jersey Lily Langtry came to town.

As the California Southern's Cannonball rolled into the city, a huge crowd turned out at the depot at the foot of D Street hoping to catch a glimpse of the famed beauty, but they were disappointed. The train stopped and Miss Langtry's repertoire company climbed down with the other passengers, but "The Lily" remained hidden in her own private car with the curtains drawn. *The San Diego Union's* reporter fared no better when he followed her car to the Twenty-second Street railroad yards in quest of an interview. She first appeared that night on the Louis Opera House stage, playing the lead in a drama called *A Wife's Peril*. It was a smash hit. San Diego's social register turned out in full plumage and such was the demand for seating that the management moved the orchestra to one side and sold the space to seat the elite. *The San Diego Union's* critique on the drama held that "The Lily's" dramatic talents and beautiful costumes were comparable to her legendary beauty.

In time the rowdy element broke out of the confines of lower downtown, and *The San Diego Union,* continuing its campaign for reform, stated:

> The bawdy houses have begun to infiltrate every part of town, in residential . . . areas and in business districts. The evil does not hide itself nor shun publicity. It obtrudes its hateful presence in the public thoroughfares and walks abroad in the open light of day. The police need no guide to enable them to arrest the inmates of the vilest dens of "Stingaree." No officer can walk his beat in that quarter without seeing enough to warrant him making arrests. The growth of the evil has gone on through the sufferance of the authorities and it is high time the law was enforced . . .

Under the pressure of an aroused citizenship and the reorganization ticket, and after being threatened with prosecution, the mayor and police chief finally got into action and began closing down some of the more obnoxious of the hundred or so gambling rooms and dance halls. One of the last of the gambling rooms shut down was in the Horton House.

Though the peak of the boom had been reached, no one was aware of it. Coronado land sales paced all the others. In midsummer of 1887, 2834 lots had been sold for $1,787,303 and a large newspaper advertisement warned that there were only 700 lots left. A special train left Chicago on December 7 with an oper-

South San Diego and Imperial Beach

YOUR ITINERARY
IS NOT COMPLETE UNTIL YOU
VISIT THE HEAD OF THE BAY

ROUND TRIP 25 CENTS

Take the boat at McKinley wharf, foot of H Street, at 9:20 a. m. or 1:00 p. m., landing an hour later at South San Diego, nine miles distant, every minute of which has been enjoyed. You will find the motor car waiting to take you to beautiful Imperial Beach, where you can enjoy yourself surf fishing, bathing, or taking in the sights until 4:00 p. m., when the car will carry you to the landing and the boat returns you safely to San Diego, making a trip of nearly twenty-five miles by boat and car, besides a day of unexcelled pleasure.

Take Coronado Ferry car to foot of H Street.

CAPT. L. B. RHODIMER, Manager

Phone Sunset 2117   McKINLEY WHARF

Boat rides and excursions enticed real estate prospects

ating staff of 324 for Hotel del Coronado. Without doubt the high point of the boom was the partial opening of the still uncompleted hotel on January 29, 1888. Prominent figures from the Pacific Coast and Eastern business and financial centers registered for the occasion. Though it had been built largely with unskilled Chinese labor, and additional rooms had been added as the work progressed, it was to become known around the world for its architecture and spaciousness. It was sometime, however, before the main dining room, or Crown Room, was opened. *The San Diego Union* described it as follows:

This vast and elegant room, with its wealth of appointments is a rare sight, especially under the brilliant incandescent lights that illuminate it. The polished floors, over which an army of trained servants noiselessly glide, the high inlaid ceilings, the snowy linen and the glitter of the silverware and glass, combine to make a most charming picture. The room may have its equal, but it certainly is not surpassed anywhere.

Towns were still springing up everywhere as the year of 1888 approached. The statistics of 1887 recorded an increase in property values in one year from $4,582,213 to $13,182,171, and the number of business firms and professional men from 340 to 975. Hundreds of new arrivals had been sleeping in tents rented for $1 a night and in sheds and barns, but now 2000 lodging rooms had been completed and 2500 more were under construction. Fifteen lodging houses alone would contain 1100 rooms. A realty firm proclaimed that "in fact we may say that San Diego has a population of 150,000 people, only they are not all here yet." The *National City Record* reported somewhat sarcastically:

At the present date there are only nine cities laid out about the south end of the bay. They are as follows, in their order: Otay, Tia Juana, South San Diego, South Coronado, Coronado Heights, Pacific Park, International City, and "Head of the Bay" . . . and this has not been a good season for towns, either.

One of the last to be subdivided in this period was Chula Vista, south of National City, where W. G. Dickinson, a professional planner and business manager for the San Diego Land and Town Company, planned a "suburbia" not unlike those of ninety years later, with fruit farms of from two to ten acres each with individual homes costing not less than $2000.

As the Christmas and New Year holidays came and went, and civic conditions began to improve, real estate sales began to decline. *The San Diego Union* dismissed this as unimportant and said that it had:

. . . caused needless uneasiness among weak-kneed people . . . and that . . . no man with common sense—blessed with judgment superior to that of an idiot—can traverse this city and witness the astonishing extent of permanent

(Next page)
For a time it appeared that the Kimball Brothers' National City would become the metropolitan center. This is how it looked in 1888.

207

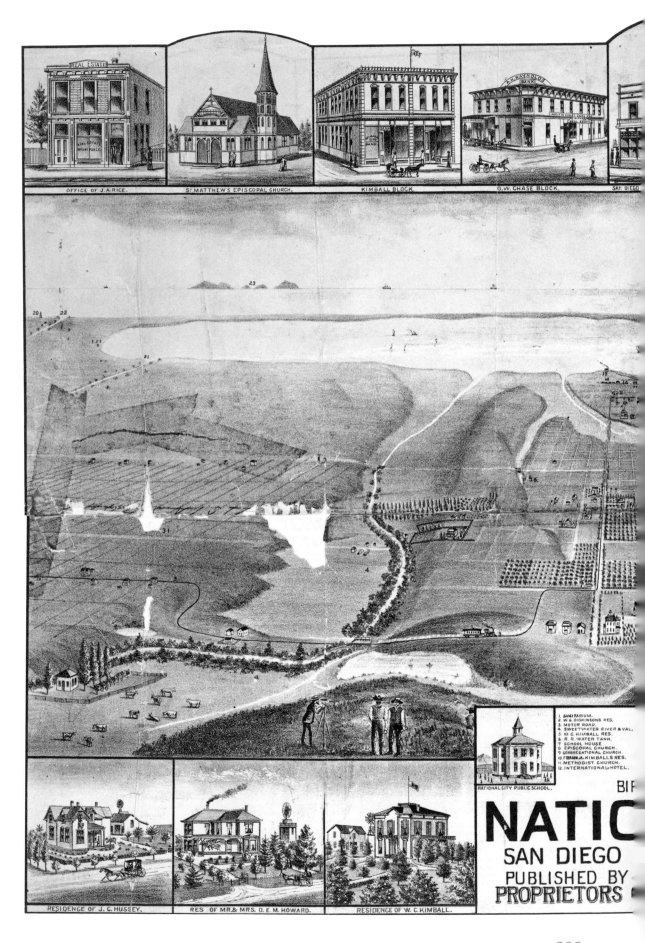

OFFICE OF J.A.RICE.

St. MATTHEW'S EPISCOPAL CHURCH.

KIMBALL BLOCK.

G.W. CHASE BLOCK.

SAN DIEGO

NATIONAL CITY PUBLIC SCHOOL.

1. SANITARIUM.
2. W.G. DICKINSONS RES.
3. MOTOR ROAD.
4. SWEETWATER RIVER & VAL.
5. W.C. KIMBALL RES.
6. R.R. WATER TANK.
7. SCHOOL HOUSE
8. EPISCOPAL CHURCH.
9. CONGREGATIONAL CHURCH.
10. FRANK A. KIMBALL'S RES.
11. METHODIST CHURCH.
12. INTERNATIONAL HOTEL.

BI F

NATIO

SAN DIEGO

PUBLISHED BY

PROPRIETORS

RESIDENCE OF J.C. HUSSEY.

RES. OF MR. & MRS. O.E.M. HOWARD.

RESIDENCE OF W.C. KIMBALL.

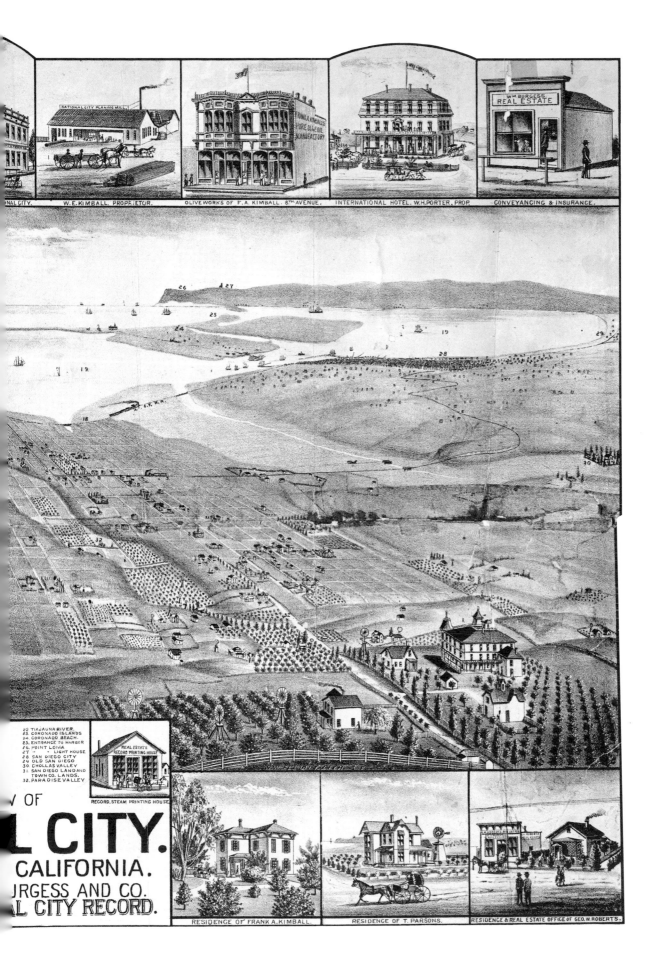

NATIONAL CITY PLANING MILL

W.E.KIMBALL, PROPRIETOR.

FRANK A. KIMBALL'S PURE OLIVE OIL MANUFACTORY

OLIVE WORKS OF F.A. KIMBALL. 8TH AVENUE.

INTERNATIONAL HOTEL, W.H.PORTER, PROP.

WM. BURGESS REAL ESTATE

CONVEYANCING & INSURANCE.

22 TIAJAUNA RIVER.
23 CORONADO ISLANDS
24 CORONADO BEACH.
25 ENTRANCE TO HARBOR
26 POINT LOMA
27 "   " LIGHT HOUSE
28 SAN DIEGO CITY
29 OLD SAN DIEGO
30 CHOLLAS VALLEY
31 SAN DIEGO LAND AND
   TOWN CO. LANDS.
32 PARADISE VALLEY

REAL ESTATE RECORD PRINTING HOUSE

RECORD, STEAM PRINTING HOUSE.

V OF

L CITY.

CALIFORNIA.

URGESS AND CO.

L CITY RECORD.

RESIDENCE OF FRANK A. KIMBALL.

RESIDENCE OF T. PARSONS.

RESIDENCE & REAL ESTATE OFFICE OF GEO. W. ROBERTS.

improvement . . . and conclude that San Diego's prosperity is not anchored to a firm and lasting foundation . . . The boom has settled among us to stay.

How could anything go wrong? San Diego City now had a population of at least 35,000, and at times it seemed that more than 50,000 persons roamed its streets and crowded into its hotels, rooming houses and places of entertainment. Lack of a certain water supply was the only thing that could hold back the development of San Diego and the fulfillment of all the hopes of the faithful. For more than half a century the waters of the winter runoffs had wasted into the sea, and no attempts had been made to conserve them for the long and harrowing dry periods. In 1816 the

On to La Presa! It was another "town" rising in the minds of land speculators who sold and resold lots at ever-increasing prices.

Franciscan padres had completed a small dam across the San Diego River in narrow Mission Gorge, to store water and regulate its flow to the fields of the San Diego Mission in Mission Valley. The works had long since been abandoned, and the tiles of the marvelous aqueduct system stolen for other construction purposes.

In March of 1888 the San Diego Land and Town Company, the subsidiary of the Santa Fe Railroad, completed the building of Sweetwater Dam, eight miles upstream on the Sweetwater River, to supply water for National City and the new subdivision of Chula Vista. The site was at a point where the river valley suddenly is tightly pinched together by rock walls before widening again into a natural basin. At ninety feet, the dam was said to be the highest in the United States and held back waters which Rufus Porter, the newspaper correspondent, reported had run so strong in 1874 that he could hear the roar three miles away. It was constructed of stone heavily impregnated with iron and which weighed 200 pounds per cubic foot. The stone was quarried a mile downstream and imbedded in cement shipped from Belgium.

The completion of the dam in March was followed by a celebration on April 19, when the first water in the reservoir was turned into the mains. More than 3000 persons took part in a Water Festival at National City and most of them arrived by train, either over the National City and Otay Railroad or on the initial trips

over the Coronado Belt Line. The City Guard Band played, and there were many speeches expressing confidence and allaying doubts. For Frank Kimball it was the high moment of the long struggle which had taken so many years out of his life and had sapped his strength and absorbed much of his land and wealth.

In the Cuyamaca Mountains the San Diego Flume Company had completed the building of its earth-fill dam about thirty-five feet high on Boulder Creek, a tributary of the San Diego River, where it emerged from the wooded valley which contained the *Laguna que se Seca,* known to the Indians as the lake that dries up. Below, another small reservoir was constructed to divert the released waters of Cuyamaca into the wooden flume being laid on

Not all was speculation. Sweetwater Dam was the first reservoir built to assure water supply for development of the South Bay area.

The little National City & Otay train hauled land buyers back and forth from promotional ventures that even included Tijuana.

spindly trestles down the mountain sides to assure the future of San Diego. Babcock and his Coronado company had begun the building of another dam on the Otay River, to serve Coronado and other regions south and east of the bay, but the work had been quietly brought to a halt.

The Santa Fe completed its "Surf Line" between Santa Ana and Oceanside on August 12, 1888, reducing the railroad distance from San Diego to Los Angeles to 127 miles. The implication of this move, however, was beginning to be realized. Trains were being dispatched from San Bernardino instead of National City and large shops and buildings were being erected in San Bernardino. On May 3 a fire started in San Diego and in two days it burned over the entire business block bounded by F and G Streets and Fifth and Sixth Streets, with losses estimated at between $150,000 and $200,000. It was more exciting than foreboding. But the country was running out of land speculators and the winter tourists were going elsewhere. Investors became wary and banks more cautious. By the late Spring of 1888 it all suddenly ended. Thomas J. Hayes, who had been selling real estate, he recalled later, until he got tired of taking in the money, told the story as follows:

I remember one day we had a big rain, and after it was over I went downtown. The streets that had been jammed with people as is the case in the streets of Chicago or some other big city, seemed to lack something. The bottom had dropped out of the big boom. From whence the boom came I do not know, and I have never been able to learn to my complete satisfaction. It stopped more suddenly by far than it came. It reversed motion and went down like a chunk of sawed-off wood.

212

OUR 'INNOCENT' LAMBS
ARE SHEARED

One morning, it was all over.
The boom had ended. The Lakeside Hotel
stands in the emptiness
of a town that was never even born.

CHAPTER XIV

One of the characters in *Millionaires of a Day* complained that "I had a million dollars wiped out in the crash, and what's worse, $500 of it was in cash."

Within six months the population of San Diego dropped from 35,000 to about 16,000. Even at that it was three times as large as it was before the boom. Many did find themselves holding inflated property which the speculators had unloaded when the first signs of trouble appeared on the horizon and while San Diegans were still blinded by the blaze of golden expectations. Being sheared twice in the selling and buying of their own land was an experience most of them would never forget. But the real assets were in resources and climate, and remaining, after the boomers and speculators had departed, were those who had come, as they always had, to build homes, to plant trees and to bask in the sun. As Van Dyke wrote:

A grand and everlasting crash had been generally predicted for San Diego. That it did not happen, its people may thank, not themselves, but that kind of providence that watches over children and fools, and that, with not one in a hundred either caring or knowing anything about it, put a prosperous population in the country larger than that of the city itself . . . It is a hard thing to say . . . but if ever a people deserved utter ruin for ignoring and despising great and valuable resources, it is those people who have made San Diego what it is today.

"California, here we go!" Settlers flee San Diego by horse and wagon after the collapse of the boom. Some day, many would return.

There was distress, of course. Public and private improvement work was delayed or halted. More than $2,000,000 in cash was withdrawn from the eight banks and they struggled to remain solvent. San Diegans consoled themselves that much had been accomplished as the result of the boom. Hotels had been built, fifteen business blocks added, a $400,000 sewer system laid, and public transportation begun. The city now had nine miles of gas mains, 230 miles of streets, of which forty miles were graded; an electric light circuit of twenty-five miles; forty-six miles of water mains; twenty-four churches, eight piers and wharves, plus two at Coronado and two at Roseville. The courthouse had been improved and twenty-seven new schools had been opened in the county and eighteen more were to be finished in another year. Fifth Street, the principal avenue, had been paved from the bay north to B Street.

In the county as a whole, the population after the boom was about 35,000, four times what it was in 1880, and more than a million fruit trees had been set out and there were 12,000 acres devoted to raisins and grapes. There was little decrease in population in the county areas, where newcomers had arrived to reside and not to gamble. The passage of the Wright Act in 1887 by the State Legislature, providing for the organization of irrigation districts, brought about rapid agricultural development and within a few years San Diego County had a dozen districts and 10,000 acres under irrigation.

City and county assessments, which had risen to $40,000,000 in 1888, dropped to about $25,000,000 by 1890. At that, they were far above the $2,382,795 of a decade before.

Twenty towns had been started, though some of them quickly

disappeared, among them Englewood, in the Sweetwater Valley; Hyde Park, on Point Loma; Glen-Barnham, east of Encinitas; Richland, east of National City; Morena, near Mission Bay; International City, Monument City and Pacific Park, all in the area south of the bay; and Helix, Waterville and Teralta, east of San Diego. La Playa, another subdivision on Point Loma, died, but was revived in later years. The names of other towns or subdivisions survived, but became attached to other places or settlements, as was the case with Helix. Some of the areas settled during the boom acquired other names as the years passed.

Within the boundaries of the city, subdivisions, or additions, as they were called, had reached a total of 103, ranging in size from a few blocks to tracts as large as the original Horton grant.

The San Diego College of Letters at Pacific Beach soon faded and its one building was converted into the Balboa Hotel. In Escondido, where the Land & Town Company had donated 1000 lots for a seminary as a branch of the University of Southern California, one structure had been erected at a cost of $40,000, and it soon was converted into a combined elementary and high school. The first of the major fires that were to take out the boom-time hotels occurred in 1890. The Del Mar resort hotel, which stood alone in a sparsely settled area, was destroyed by fire

Del Mar Hotel, 1886

217

National City &
Otay Railroad

on January 17.

All of the local steam motor railroads went out of business except the National City & Otay, the Coronado, and the San Diego, Old Town and Pacific Beach Railway. The San Diego, Cuyamaca and Eastern Railway was built as far as El Cajon and its promoters still clung to the dream that it could be extended to provide a direct line to the East. The tracks of the San Diego Central feeder line, from Oceanside to San Diego by way of Escondido and El Cajon, never got beyond Escondido. The Spreckels brothers, John and Adolph, continued to put money into San Diego, in particular into the Babcock enterprises, and Hotel del Coronado weathered the storm.

The depression was well under way when in 1889 a cable car system went into operation. The San Diego Cable Railway Company ran its cars from a turntable at L Street, up Sixth to C and west on C to Fourth, and then up Fourth to University Avenue.

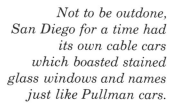

Not to be outdone, San Diego for a time had its own cable cars which boasted stained glass windows and names just like Pullman cars.

From there they were pulled to Normal Street and out what is now Park Boulevard to Adams Street, where a five-acre recreation park was being developed. The power house was situated at Fourth and Spruce Streets. The little cars were painted maroon and white, had names just as did the Pullman cars of the transcontinental trains, and narrow stained glass windows along the upper sides.

The ascendancy of Los Angeles over its more southerly rival was complete. The federal census of 1890 gave San Diego a population of 16,159 and the county, 34,987. Los Angeles came out of the boom with a population of about 50,000 and the county, more than 100,000. In 1889 Los Angeles moved to acquire a harbor, the one factor it lacked for the growth of commerce, and members of the United States Senate Committee on Commerce were invited

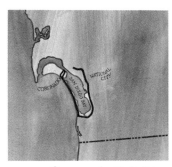

Coronado Belt Line
Railroad

to inspect a number of projects. San Pedro Bay seemed the most logical site, but Sen. William B. Frye, of Maine, after looking it over and concluding that it would cost more to develop than the value of Los Angeles, suggested that if Los Angeles wanted a harbor the city be moved to San Diego. Los Angeles was properly outraged and a fight over whether a harbor should be constructed at San Pedro Bay or Santa Monica Bay, and to obtain federal participation, was to continue for a decade. A few years later, in 1892, Edward L. Doheny, a prospector who had failed in his quest for gold and silver, sank a crude drill into the ground in a residential area of Los Angeles and struck a heavy upswell of oil. Though oil had been taken from the ground in other sections of Southern California for some time, the oil boom that was to transform Los Angeles and all of Southern California was at last under way.

At the lowest point in the fortunes of those who had banked so much on the future of San Diego, the flume to bring mountain water to the semi-arid coastal lands was completed in 1889. The wooden flume, six feet wide, sixteen inches deep and lined with redwood, was laid in a bench cut into the mountains or on 315 trestles carrying it across canyons and depressions. The longest trestle was 1800 feet and at its highest point it was eighty feet

Water, not speculation, was the key to the future. Here a wagon train hauls lumber to build a system to bring mountain water to a dry town.

219

above Los Coches Creek. There were five tunnels, the longest 1850 feet.

The building of the flume was a stupendous task. More than 100 wagons and 800 horses and mules were employed to transport nearly 9,000,000 feet of lumber. In many instances roads had to be constructed up almost impassable mountain slopes. The flume company experienced its own financial difficulties, and at a crucial period Ephraim Morse stepped in to temporarily accept the presidency and to arrange more money and credit for its completion.

During dry seasons the water was to be released from the Cuyamaca Reservoir and let flow twelve and a half miles down Boulder Creek to another dam on the San Diego River, at which point it would be diverted into the flume and carried down the south side of the San Diego River to El Monte Tunnel, about two miles east of Lakeside. From there the water was to be turned south to follow around El Cajon Valley to a terminus at a small reservoir. Here it was to be fed into a steel pipeline laid on the mesa for about ten miles and then into the city mains.

The San Diego flume was thirty miles long and had 315 trestles and five tunnels. This is the highest trestle, Los Coches.

The terminal storage, Eucalyptus Reservoir, on a small branch of Alvarado Canyon, was not completed until the following year. A second, known as Grossmont Reservoir, was built soon afterward. San Diegans, eager for prospects, hailed the flume as the most important enterprise in the history of the county and said it assured the irrigation of from 40,000 to 80,000 acres of land.

Bryant Howard, president of the Consolidated National Bank who had taken over the direction of the flume company from Morse, was named president of a celebration scheduled for February 22, 1889. The event was considered so important that it rated nineteen vice presidents and ten scheduled speakers. A parade started from Sixth and H Streets with A. G. Gassen, the grand marshal, wearing a scarf of red and a big red plume in his hat. His adjutants wore blue scarves and white plumes in their hats, and their aides wore yellow scarves. It being Saturday afternoon and Washington's Birthday as well, most of the downtown area was draped with red, white and blue bunting and flags were displayed in front of houses and stores.

Every organization that could muster a unit was represented, including the City Guard Band, the City Guard, the Grand Army of the Republic, the Knights of Pythias, the Pacific Beach Cadets, the Ancient Order of United Workingmen, the International Order of Odd Fellows, the Turnverein, Atherton's Commercial College, S. White's and Schiller & Murtha's baseball clubs, the Excelsior Rowing club, the Golden Eagle Society, the League of Freedom, and the Red Men. The most popular of the commercial floats was a brewery wagon dispensing free beer to parade viewers along the way.

In the principal address, Howard caused San Diegans to re-experience the hopes of the past. He said the arrival of the water and construction of a railroad to Yuma would make San Diego the hub of territory from South America to Australia, from China to the Sandwich Islands, and from California to Sonora, Mexico:

San Diego is more fertile than Palestine when Solomon reigned . . . more than Greece where Pericles reared the Parthenon . . . one of the most favored regions on earth . . . with a climate that gives life to the blood, elasticity to the step and bloom of health to the cheek.

A visiting member of the United States House of Representatives from Sioux City, Iowa, John Brennan, concurred in the long-range prospects and said that when the Panama Canal became a reality San Diego would realize a fulfillment beyond its wildest expectations, and he cautioned against dividing real estate into small pieces in order to sell it more easily. A subsequent speaker, M. A. Luce, however, held out the tempting prospect that with an assured supply of water, land which had been selling at $10 an acre was now worth from $100 to $500 an acre.

The celebration served as a "wake" for the boom. *The San Diego Union* said editorially:

Judge Moses A. Luce

The sleepy San Diego of the past, the struggling ambitious town of years ago, the "boom land" of a less remote period, are all things of yesterday, and with today's sun dawns a new era in our growth. Some decry the boom, but San Diego's flume is one of its bequests to the present. While we welcome the water

Douglas Gunn

*George W. Marston
about 1890*

*Ephraim W. Morse
in late years*

from Cuyamaca, can we not at the same time use it to brighten a few flowers to strew on the bier of the boom? With present increased prosperity we shall find that the boom was but a greedy worm that, after a natural period of dormancy, has hatched out into the bright-hued butterfly that will be coveted and pursued by many eager followers of the attractive things on earth.

The climax of the celebration came when two streams of water from fire hose nozzles were shot into the air, one at the corner of Fifth and Beech Streets and another at the corner of Fifth and Ivy Streets. There were many compliments on the quality of the new water. However, as valves had not been installed, the water was air-locked, and other water had to be substituted. It was three weeks before the mountain water reached the city's mains.

Before the year of 1888 had come to its sad close, the city's voters had chosen a commission to frame a new charter which was adopted on March 2, 1889, and approved by the State Legislature on March 16. The first election followed on April 2, and at long last San Diego acquired its first formal mayor in thirty-seven years. He was Douglas Gunn, the former editor of *The San Diego Union*. The charter provided for a cumbersome, two-house legislative system based somewhat on the form of state and national governments. It provided for a Common Council consisting of a Board of Aldermen, with nine members elected at large, and a Board of Delegates of eighteen, two to be elected from each of nine wards. Both bodies had to approve measures, the mayor had a veto power but no vote, and many administrative duties were assigned to councilmen.

The campaign for mayor was a bitter one, and Gunn led a Non-Partisan Citizens ticket against a Republican organization that was still dominated by remnants of the San Francisco carpetbaggers known as "Gallaghers," who had arrived as Democrats and changed affiliations in order to gain control of vice and gambling in San Diego's boom days. Gunn and most of his ticket won in an election where a Republican majority of between 500 and 800 normally could be expected. Democrats failed to enter a ticket of their own. The new form of city government went into effect on May 6.

The same charter extended the city's boundaries beyond the pueblo limitations as defined in the Hays survey, to once again include Coronado and North Island and all of the bay, to the strenuous complaints of Coronadoans who objected to paying taxes to San Diego. A campaign to "secede" from San Diego was successfully executed at an election in Coronado in 1891.

The years of careless handing out of community lands also were over. An amendment to the charter prohibited the further sale of pueblo lands, until the year 1930, though 43,000 acres of the almost 49,000 acres originally within the city limits already had passed into private hands.

Elegance in railway stations was a matter of civic pride. This was the San Diego station built for the California Southern Railroad.

For more than a year machinery and equipment of the California Southern Railroad had been quietly moved to San Bernardino, and the Santa Fe now was dispatching all its trains from there instead of from National City. The Santa Fe officials appeared before a meeting of the Chamber of Commerce and acknowledged the impending removal of its shops and its general freight offices to the inland point. The Santa Fe technically had met its commitments to San Diego and National City, in the bringing of a line into the county and in the location of its shops and offices. But there was nothing in the agreement that stipulated how San Diego was to be served and that the terminal was to be permanently located in National City. The decision was a staggering blow to the Kimball brothers, who had given up most of their land and fortune to acquire a transcontinental railroad terminal, but the Santa Fe was entering serious financial troubles.

Frank Kimball wrote:

. . . on looking back over the occurrence it has every appearance of an ingeniously planned scheme, which only experts could plan, to secure a vast waterfront adapted to railroad purposes, with no intention of using it, but rather prevent anyone else from using it . . .

223

Most of the traffic now was routed through Los Angeles and down the coast over the "Surf Line" instead of directly from San Bernardino and through Temecula Canyon. Another season of heavy rain came in 1891 and a roaring flood again tore out the railroad tracks in Temecula Canyon, and the section of the line from Fallbrook station to Temecula station was abandoned. San Diego was left at the end of a branch line. It meant that the town was to experience very little growth in the next decade.

For its brief duration, scarcely more than a week, the storm that struck Southern California and Arizona in February of 1891 was probably the worst on record.

On February 19 heavy rain was welcomed as a guaranty of good crops. Four days later the city was isolated from the world. The San Diego River quickly rose to flood level and hundreds of residents flocked to ride the cable cars to the pavilion park overlooking Mission Valley. A solid sheet of water spread across the valley floor and over the tide flats to False Bay. Every telephone and telegraph line was out, railroad connections were severed and a heavy storm at sea with gale winds interrupted shipping. Virtually everything that had been built in the riverbeds or on the alluvial plains between the great watersheds and the sea was gone or reduced to wreckage.

Droughts and floods were occasional but devastating hazards. In 1889 the San Diego River once again flowed from bank to bank.

Bear Valley reported thirty inches of rain in thirty-seven hours; Cuyamaca, eighteen inches in forty-eight hours. The city, however, recorded only 2.56 inches for the storm and 4.77 inches for the month.

In that day the town of Tia Juana straddled the border and consisted of thirty or forty residences and business houses. The storm washed away perhaps twenty-five of them, as well as the trees which shaded the town. Those who rebuilt moved to higher ground, and laid the foundations for the present cities of Tijuana and San Ysidro. Elsewhere in the county, Campo suffered heavy damage and the little settlement of Foster, three miles north of Lakeside at the end of the San Diego & Cuyamaca Railroad track, disappeared. The Lakeside Hotel was nearly wrecked. Seven months later, the tiny settlement of Campo was deluged by another cloudburst which in 1964 still stood as a world record measured by an accredited weather station, 11.5 inches in eighty minutes, on August 12, 1891.

The San Diego River had dropped almost to normal by February 25 and San Diego discovered that it had been the most fortunate of all the Southern California towns. Mojave, Calico, Barstow, San Bernardino, Pasadena, Los Angeles, and San Juan Capistrano all were far worse off than San Diego. Yuma reported that the Colorado River was twenty miles wide at the former crossing. The local militia had evacuated the town.

Two days later a wall of water from the western slopes of the Rocky Mountains passed through Yuma, raising the river thirty-three feet above low water mark. The next day nothing remained but a railroad bridge, the Southern Pacific Hotel and the Yuma prison. The town was gone and twenty miles of railroad were gone with it. Fourteen hundred people had been made homeless. Lakes formed in the Salton Sink, in the deepest depressions of the Imperial Valley.

Late in the year the California National Bank, which had been opened a year after the boom had burst, failed. A federal investigation indicated that the bank's two organizers, J. W. Collins, president, and D. D. Dare, vice president, had systematically looted the bank; that Collins had been associated with a similar bank failure in Cheyenne, Wyoming, before coming to San Diego, and that Dare was an ex-painter and photographer who bought in with Collins for $7000. When the crash came, Dare was in Europe and apparently never returned. Collins, with his arrest impending, shot himself to death.

Less than two years later in June of 1893, during the "Tidal Wave of Distrust" which swept over banking in the United States during another financial crash and depression, the Consolidated National Bank and the California Savings Bank failed. The president of the Consolidated National Bank was Bryant Howard, who had headed the flume company and had proclaimed San Diego one of the most favored places on earth. The crash also wiped out

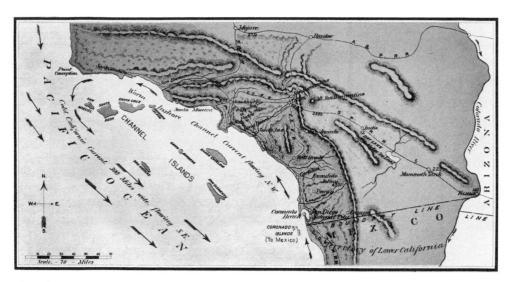

the fortune of Oliver S. Witherby, one of San Diego's early pioneers who had owned Rancho Rincón del Diablo, the site of Escondido, and he died a short time later. The Santa Fe railroad was thrown into receivership for two years, from 1893 to 1895.

Wyatt Earp, the frontier marshal, sold out the investments he had made in San Diego with the aid of boom-time gambling, and departed. The magazine *The Golden Era,* which had exemplified the robust years of California's literary youth, withered away. It lived only eight years in San Diego, from 1887 to 1895.

Horton had come out of the real estate boom with enough money to erect a new home, his fifth and last in San Diego. Three stories in height, it was at State and Olive Streets and commanded a sweeping view of the bay. Not long afterward his wife, while on a visit to one of her sisters in Washington, was thrown from a carriage when a horse bolted, and fatally injured. In 1890 he married Mrs. Lydia M. Knapp, the widow of a retired Navy officer.

Horton remained a staunch Republican to the end. President Benjamin Harrison visited San Diego for one day on April 23, 1891, and he and Mrs. Harrison were taken on a parade through festooned streets. They passed the new home of Horton which he had blanketed with calla lillies, marigolds and geraniums. The Stars and Stripes flew from the roof and all garden statuary was draped with patriotic bunting.

Bad times came upon him again, and in 1894 he decided to sell the Plaza across the street from the hotel he had once owned. The city agreed to buy it for $10,000 by paying him $100 a month, "during the lifetime of said A. E. Horton." The payments in time actually amounted to $16,000, and it was this $100 a month on which he lived out his days. His associate in the founding of San

Horton's fourth home, on First Street, overlooked his lost empire

Alonzo Horton's fifth and last home was completed in 1889

Diego, Ephraim Morse, also experienced severe financial losses from which he never fully recovered.

In January of 1892 the Spreckels interests through the San Diego Electric Railroad Company began buying the local steam horse and power streetcar lines and by the end of the year owned all of them except the cable car system. They were converted to electric power by the simple expediency of installing electric motors in old horse cars. The cable car system had gone bankrupt following the failure of the California National Bank.

Those who stayed and those who came were of many types and many classes. In the waning months of the boom a youth named Ed Fletcher in Ayer, Massachusetts, which is about twenty-five miles from Boston, read with excitement letters from his married sister in San Diego describing the wonderful possibilities for the future. The Fletcher family was one of many by that name in that area of Massachusetts. Ed Fletcher was born in Littleton, not far from Ayer, which in 1964 was still a typical New England town of large and old two-story houses, with a little triangular park and surrounding fields neatly squared off with low stone fences. He was one of six children whose mother died when he was four years old. They tried to keep the family together, but after one sister had married and another had gone to Boston to work, the father placed the other four children with relatives or neighboring families and left for Florida in the hope of making a new start in life. At the age of fifteen, and after having saved $126.50 by working at odd jobs, Ed Fletcher purchased a scalper's train ticket to San Diego for $20 and arrived on September 3, 1888.

Ed Fletcher
as a young man

The future, however, was not waiting; it would have to be earned in a town that was feeling the first effects of the collapse of the boom. But he stayed, as did many others, and after a few odd jobs, one of them selling boxes of apples from a wagon, became a regular employee of the produce firm of Nason and Smith. While riding a bicycle many miles across the mesas and up into the hills, he became impressed with the struggle for water, and he learned, as he expressed it years later, that "water is king; and the basis of all value in this county is water."

One of the banks to survive the crash was established by a native of Mechanics Town, Maryland, who had made a fortune in manufacturing by the time he was thirty-four years of age. He was Joseph Weller Sefton. Sefton, his family and a group of friends from Dayton, Ohio, wintered for several seasons at the Florence Hotel, until in 1888, at the height of the boom, he succumbed to the climate and decided to remain. He founded the bank in

May of the next year, even when signs indicated that the tide had turned against San Diego. One of his early depositors was young Fletcher, who entrusted the bank with $5. But to a man who loved to drive fast horses and race buggies, adversities were challenges.

The son of a President of the United States, U. S. Grant, Jr., who had served as secretary to his illustrious father, drifted from law to finance and real estate and arrived in San Diego in 1893. He and a brother, Jesse Grant, of Arizona, were drawn into a scheme promoted by George Puterbaugh to bring water from Warner's Ranch, with a dam and reservoir on the San Luis Rey River, all the way to San Diego, to irrigate 40,000 acres on the Linda Vista Mesa, where land was being offered for sale at speculative prices on the gamble of attaining water.

Joseph Jessop

At the time of Southern California's boom, in far distant England in the town of Lytham, between Liverpool and Blackpool, during a period of high incidence of tuberculosis, a jeweler named Joseph Jessop worried about the health of his wife and seven children. He subscribed to twenty-one newspapers for a year and studied them to find a new place in which to reside. One of the newspapers was *The San Diego Union.* He finally settled on two choices: South Africa and Southern California. The latter won out, and the family arrived in New York by steamer and went to California by train, arriving at San Diego in 1890. Jessop left his family in San Diego while he looked over Oakland and the San Francisco Bay region, but returned and decided to buy a farm on Linda Vista. Though the whole family improved in health, there was little money to be made in farming dry land while waiting for water, and in three years, as business began to recover, he reentered the jewelry business in San Diego.

John F. Forward

John F. Forward was a grandson of a secretary of the treasury under President Tyler. But there was no money in the family when young Forward's father died and he went to work at the age of fifteen to help support the family. He became a locomotive engineer for the Pennsylvania Railroad, lost an arm in a railroad accident, and faced with a life of service as a railroad clerk, decided to go West, to the San Diego of opportunity. He arrived in 1887 and obtained a job as a clerk in a cigar store. The mayor's chair was twenty years away.

A search for health, not for himself but for an ailing brother, also had brought a utility company owner from Aurora, Illinois, to San Diego. He was Ira C. Copley and the year was 1881. Nine years later his parents, Ira Birdsall and Ellen Copley, arrived to take up residence. On one of his visits, in 1891, the son read an edition of *The San Diego Union* and remarked that he would like to own it. That ambition was years from realization, and the newspapers of San Diego were still going through troubles of ownership and finance that had characterized their existence. The majority of the newspapers that started with the boom had faded away. *The San Diego Union,* which had been acquired by a group of investors from Douglas Gunn in 1886, purchased a rival, the *Daily Bee,* also backed by local residents, in 1890, and the new publication became *The San Diego Union and Daily Bee.* Though both were residing in San Francisco, the Spreckels brothers were still investing money in a town which 15,000 persons had deserted, and they acquired the combined newspaper in 1890. The *San Diego Sun,* that had been founded by Mrs. Charles Taggart, passed through several ownerships and apparently was headed for bankruptcy.

Artist's version of enlarged County Courthouse, 1889

In the winter of 1890 while on the West Coast to visit an ailing sister in Alameda, E. W. Scripps, the successful Eastern newspaper publisher, made a side trip to San Diego, and he later described it as a busted, broken-down boom town. Though he was only thirty-six years of age, he was ready to retire from business and San Diego appealed to him because "it was 3000 miles from the people who bothered me about my newspapers and about their own political or business ambitions."

The region proved to be more attractive than at first glance and after riding around the countryside for a few days, he became aware of its similarity to the Mediterranean area:

> The climate seemed identical with that of North Africa, especially Algeria. Trees and plants growing about the houses of San Diegans were the same I had seen in Algeria. As I had always suffered from colds in the East, and had been free from them in Algeria, Mexico, Egypt and Syria, it occurred to me that I should have a winter home near San Diego.

He promptly purchased 400 acres about sixteen miles outside San Diego, which became the Miramar Ranch. A few years later Scripps advanced money to Paul H. Blades and E. C. Hickman to acquire the *San Diego Sun,* which soon absorbed the *San Diegan.* And thus he, too, would be drawn into events shaping a new course for the "broken-down" town that had been all but abandoned by the railroad barons.

E. W. Scripps

Agriculture developed and the fishing industry expanded. Immigrants of Italian descent were building their own fleet of ships, though there were complaints that the sixteen Chinese junks in the harbor were fishing out the bay with the use of fine nets. Use of nets in the bay was illegal so the Chinese operated largely at

night and with little interference. Large fish were sold on the local market and the small fish were dried and exported to San Francisco. The Chinese fishing camps were south of Roseville, along the base of Point Loma, where they had huge drying racks. Most of the homes of the Chinese fishermen, however, adjoined the old "Stingaree" district and were little shanties standing out over the water on stilts, and, as has been described, backed by irregular streets of the Chinese quarter "where John chatters with his neighbor or gravely smokes his pipe while watching the group of children, with almond eyes and dangling queues of silk, playing in the doorway." The Chinese also began moving into the crumbling adobes of Old Town, a community by-passed by time and events. They covered the open windows with red posters and converted one large adobe into a joss house, or temple.

In the winter of 1889 the United States steamer *Albatross* investigated the offshore fishing grounds south of San Francisco and explored the possibilities of Cortez Bank, lying 100 miles nearly due west of San Diego. *The Golden Era*, in its report on "Prospective Fisheries of San Diego," stated:

It is very probable, judging from the rapid progress made in nearly all the industries of San Diego, that the time is not far distant when the primitive and Oriental type of fishing boats which are now engaged in fisheries of Southern California will be supplanted by a type of vessel similar in construction to those engaged in prosecuting the fisheries of New England. It is not to be supposed that vessels over fifty tons will be used, for the present demand . . . is not sufficiently large to warrant safe investment in vessels of larger tonnage. A small fleet ranging from twenty to fifty tons could find profitable employment off the coast of Lower California and on Cortez Bank.

The difficulty of keeping fish in a fresh state limited the range of fishing fleets but there was considerable discussion of solving this problem, perhaps by keeping the fish alive in tanks of water,

Hotel Brewster

and that long voyages down the west coast of Mexico might be a possibility. By 1897 fresh fish and lobsters packed in ice were being shipped from San Diego by Wells, Fargo to all major cities in the north and as far east as Denver and Kansas City.

The extension of the San Diego, Cuyamaca and Eastern Railroad as far as Foster, about twenty-three miles from the city, brought about another resumption of gold mining activity. Using rolling equipment borrowed from the National City & Otay, the Coronado, and Southern Pacific railroads, it ran trains over a line from Ninth and Commercial Streets in San Diego, through Lemon Grove, La Mesa, Lakeside and to Foster, at the foot of the swiftly-rising hills. That's as far east as it ever got.

San Diego, Cuyamaca & Eastern Railroad

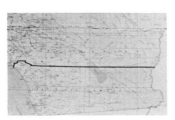

The railroads failed to breach the mountains and stages met the trains and hauled passengers to the gold country and high ranches.

The two daily trains were met by Frary and Foster's four-horse stages which provided a direct service to Julian and Banner. The two mining districts had been combined into one and by 1894 twenty mines were in operation, mostly under new and stronger companies. Two new ones were opened, the Ranchita and the Elevada. The richest producer of them all, however, the Stonewall mine, of which Gov. Waterman had been the principal owner, closed down in 1893 after having given up about $2,000,000 in gold. Total production from the Julian-Banner mines probably reached between $4,000,000 and $5,000,000.

On the high hills above Pala, the site of the little *asistencia* of the San Luis Rey Mission and twenty-eight miles inland from Oceanside, rich tourmaline gem stones were being taken from the earth. That gem stones existed in San Diego and Riverside Counties had been known for many years, as they had been found in ancient Indian burials, and Henry Hamilton in 1872 made the first important recorded discovery, on the slopes of Thomas Mountain in Riverside County. Some years would pass before extensive

San Diego County, 1893-1907

231

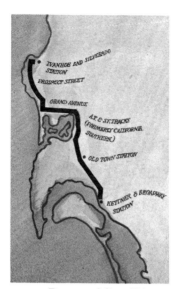

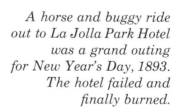

Route of San Diego, Pacific Beach and La Jolla Railroad

mining would begin and many more rich deposits be uncovered. Red tourmaline was to be particularly sought after by Chinese merchants for shipment to distant China.

San Diego County was reduced in size by 6000 square miles when Riverside County was formed in 1893, and $4,000,000 worth of taxable property and many settlements were lost. The county, however, still contained more than 8551 square miles and extended in width all the way to the Colorado River.

In the mid-1890's San Diego recovered some of its confidence and developers were offering land and lots and once again comparing San Diego with Italy. A report issued by the Chamber of Commerce in 1895, entitled *Our Italy*, commented that while San Diego might not be the "Promised Land" of the Children of Israel, it still flowed with milk and honey and how foolish it was for American tourists to spend forty million dollars annually in Italy.

Land developers began to recover some of their courage. The San Diego, Old Town and Pacific Beach Railway was reorganized to permit an extension of the line to La Jolla, which had languished without transportation facilities. The La Jolla Park Hotel, though completed in 1888, did not open its doors until 1893. The last railroad spike connecting San Diego with La Jolla was driven on May 15, 1894, but the line soon was extended 1500 feet to the area of the hotel.

A horse and buggy ride out to La Jolla Park Hotel was a grand outing for New Year's Day, 1893. The hotel failed and finally burned.

Time had removed the Horton House from its place of eminence, and the Chamber of Commerce report stated:

On Florence Heights, overlooking the city, bay and islands, is another big hotel, the Florence. The first families fill its spacious rooms. The Brewster, corner Fourth and C, has most comfortable quarters and accommodates large crowds. It is the home of the traveling man. Opposite the Plaza on D Street is the Horton House—the old reliable, everyday businessman's hotel.

It was estimated that there were now more than 3,000,000 fruit trees in the county, 2,000,000 more than at the end of the boom, of which about 300,000 were orange and 400,000 were lemon trees. The report continued:

Our mountain districts are devoted largely to apple culture, but nearly all deciduous fruits thrive and produce the highest grades of fruit, while some of the valley districts, such as Cajon and Escondido, give preference to deciduous fruits with good citrus orchards in lands a little elevated above the level of the valleys. On the mesa land about Fallbrook citrus fruits and the olive take the preference over all else, the olive being more extensively planted there, probably, than in any other district of similar area in the state, there being over 800 acres now growing within a few miles of the town of Fallbrook. Next in order comes the lemon, then the orange; yet this country with the mesas and small valleys near Escondido, and in Bear Valley, produces apples only second to those of the mountain regions. In the district about San Diego bay the lemon appears to find nearly or quite everything necessary for the production of perfect fruit, and hence it is being extensively planted, but not to the exclusion of the orange and deciduous fruits.

A new subdivision, with the improbable name of Minneapolis Beach, was platted thirty-five miles north of San Diego and just south of the present Carlsbad. Former residents of Minneapolis had purchased 1500 acres, but were offering lots to other settlers from Eastern and Middle states, and special attention was being given to the development of a silk industry. A Japanese expert was imported to superintend the cocooneries and the care of mulberry trees. Women were assured that within eight weeks, by working in their own homes, they could be ready to sell commercial silk for which there were immediate markets.

Kate Sessions

The 1400 acres laid aside for a public park, as yet unnamed, were barren and there were few to envision what might be done. In 1892 a former school teacher from San Francisco, who operated a nursery in Coronado, asked for a lease of thirty acres of park land to start another nursery. She was Kate Sessions. The lease was granted on condition that she plant 100 trees in the park each year and donate 300 more for setting out in the town. For years she planted trees, mostly from seed, in the park and directed the planting of others along the sun-drenched streets. She imported seeds from far away places, Australia, Asia, South America, Spain, Lower California and New England.

The Santa Fe railroad which had so easily abandoned its promises to San Diego joined with the Southern Pacific to form a citrus pool to control freight rates and they threatened to break the citrus growers in San Diego and other counties of California. It became cheaper to ship citrus from the Mediterranean to New

York than from California. Trains were wrecked in the north and San Diego ranchers resorted to shipping by wagon trains. The Santa Fe retaliated by raising passenger rates to San Diego.

Los Angeles became the hub of commerce that San Diego had so yearned to be. The larger growth of Los Angeles, and the prospering of such surrounding communities as Riverside, San Bernardino and Redlands, diverted much of the trade with the interior that San Diego originally enjoyed. As early as 1890 the Southern Pacific was running thirty freight trains a day in and out of Los Angeles. The Santa Fe had never envisioned San Diego County as originating much freight, and despite the belief of Frank Kimball and others, had expected to use the waterfront for transshipment of goods to and from the many ports of the Pacific. For a time some commerce was routed between Los Angeles and San Diego, over the "Surf Line," in preparation for an Oriental steamship line proposed by the Santa Fe. But this dwindled and then disappeared with the development of San Pedro Harbor.

The day of power had arrived but the sailing ship lingered on the ocean. Here, sailing ships are shown unloading at Santa Fe Wharf.

THE TOWN THAT
WOULDN'T GIVE UP

Climate and leisure combined to give the
Victorian Age an unusual flavor
in Southern California. Life was serene
at Hotel del Coronado.

CHAPTER XV

The past had not been forgotten and anyone who could revive hopes for a direct railroad connection to the East was certain of success in politics. William Carlson, the former legislative page boy who helped develop Ocean Beach, was a successful candidate for mayor in 1893 and William E. Smythe wrote in his history of San Diego published in 1908:

As soon as Billy got into the mayor's chair there were to be new electric car lines on every street equipped in an impossible manner, hotels fitted up *a la* Edward Bellamy, lines of steamships to every port on earth, transcontinental railroads galore, the park was to be improved at once, everybody was to have plenty of work at the highest wages, and, in short, the millennium was to come then and there.

In the election which he won handily, Carlson defeated two opponents, one of whom was a Capt. James E. Friend whose nominating petition was signed by 1100 well-wishers. He received only 98 votes, and in his chagrin, he sat down and wrote a book about the town which he entitled *1000 Liars*.

Once in the mayor's seat Carlson was instrumental in the organization of a company to build a railroad from San Diego to Phoenix, Arizona, in coordination with the Coronado Belt Line of the Babcock and Spreckels interests, and the *National City Record* sniffed that "this looks like warmed-over porridge." Franchise difficulties and law suits over rights of ways plagued the line's advance, and when more money was necessary, Mayor Carlson held a mass meeting in the Fisher Opera House at which $5000 in small contributions was raised. The mayor told his listeners:

> San Diego needs salvation as much as a sinner's soul needs it. It is a groundhog case. If you don't help yourself the Lord won't help you.

He disappeared with the money and turned up in Mexico City, where he announced he had obtained a franchise from the Mexican government to build a line across the Lower California peninsula, on the old wagon route from San Diego to Yuma, with a branch line to Ensenada.

There were excursions over the tracks already laid as far as a place called Phoenix Park in Otay Valley, and more fund raising events and much excitement, but no more rails were laid and the San Diego and Arizona Railroad disappeared from public attention. There were other schemes, almost too many to mention, including one inspired by working railroad men themselves, with shares in the project selling for as low as 50 cents, though nothing ever came of any of them.

No civic miracles had come to pass under Mayor Carlson, though he did succeed in getting reelected in 1895, whereupon he quickly found himself in political trouble. The flume and its inadequate storage reservoir had never delivered the volume anticipated and over the years the water had become somewhat slimy and odorous. As the champion of the people, Mayor Carlson led a campaign to purchase the flume system. The company refused to sell.

For the townspeople there were circuses and Wild West shows. This shows an old-time circus parade proceeding up Fifth Street.

U.S. Grant, Jr., the son of the former President, and his partners in the projected San Luis Rey-Linda Vista development, offered to sell 1000 miners' inches of water to the city for $1,000,000. Babcock promptly offered to sell the city the Otay system which he was developing. In his political innocence, Grant heeded the suggestions of Babcock that in the interest of the good of the city the Common Council should be allowed to decide between the two offers. Babcock, through his henchman, Charles Hardy, controlled the Council majority. Grant's project never got off the ground because of the loss of its principal prospective customer, even though E. W. Scripps, the publisher, urged him to repudiate his agreement with Babcock and fight on. But it was a point of honor with Grant.

Meanwhile, Babcock, now further reinforced by Spreckels' investments, began the building of another dam, Morena, on Cottonwood Creek, at a site fifty miles east of San Diego, with the intention of becoming the principal supplier of water for the city. The Southern California Mountain Water Company also had resumed work on Lower Otay Dam; planned another, Upper Otay, at the lower end of Proctor Valley on the west branch of Otay Creek; and a third, Barrett, ten miles below Morena, all to be part of one system.

The people of San Diego in 1896 voted to issue $1,500,000 worth of water bonds, part of the money to be used in helping to develop the Morena system and the rest for distribution facilities. The drought of 1897-98 emptied the Cuyamaca Reservoir and wells had to be sunk in the gravel beds of the San Diego River above El Cajon, to supply water for the flume system.

A few days before a city election in 1897, in which the operators of the flume property and the Babcock and Spreckels interests supported rival candidates for mayor and the City Council over the issue of which company should be allowed to serve the city's water users, Babcock accused the mayor of running out on his promise to support the Southern California water company. *The San Diego Union* could not restrain itself in its contempt for Mayor Carlson, and labeled him "a relic of the boom," a charlatan, faker, traitor to the people, a cigar-and-smile trickster, political quack, pretender, clown, cheap gambler, bamboozler and a liar. Carlson was defeated and Republican D. C. Reed was elected mayor, but the civic fight over the water issue ran into the next century.

Though not all things had come to pass as so many had wished, the decade from 1890 to 1900 always was recalled with nostalgia.

William H. "Billy" Carlson

First National Bank Block

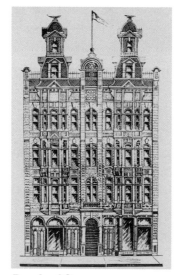

Bank of Commerce Building

There were experiments with raising tobacco and pineapples, and a farm for ostriches, valued for their feathers, was a tourist attraction near Hotel del Coronado. Cuba was engaged in a revolution against Spanish rule and the supply of tobacco to the United States had been curtailed. Tobacco was grown at Nestor, Otay, Campo, El Cajon Valley, Poway, Escondido and Pacific Beach, and a factory began producing cigars under the label of "Hotel Brewsters." The San Diego County Tobacco Growers Association proposed that the city park be diverted to raising tobacco.

With local financing Louis Fisher had built the new opera house on Fourth between B and C Streets, and it was the pride of San Diego. Fisher later went to New York, and with the help of six girls from San Diego, he put the famous Floradora extravaganzas on the road. There were leisurely sight-seeing rides on new double-deck streetcars. There were carnivals and the appearances of Buffalo Bill Cody, the actress Anna Held and John Philip Sousa's Band. Gentleman Jim Corbett, the one-time boxer, performed at the Fisher Opera House and shared the social light at Hotel del Coronado with Prince Albert of Belgium. As for the society of Coronado, it enjoyed a form of "fox hunting" by riding to the hounds after rabbits over the flat lands of North Island. Two more newspapers made their appearance. The *Evening Tribune* was founded on December 2, 1895, by T. D. Beasley and F. E. A. Kimball. The *San Diego Vidette* was established on August 6, 1892, by D. O. McCarthy, though it was leased in 1894, for a time, to Harr Wagner who published *The Golden Era*. Babcock opened a new spa, Los Baños Bathhouse, at the foot of D Street, with 2000 guests. Women's suffrage was the burning issue of the day, but

Harr Wagner

The quiet years brought the double-deck street cars on which sight-seeing rides were highlights for local residents and visitors.

240

*In Coronado they rode,
not to the hounds,
but to the rabbits which
ran by the thousands
over the flat lands
of Coronado
and North Island.*

ladies' large "picture" hats were prohibited in theaters by city ordinance. The Klondike gold fever swept San Diego and there was a rush to secure passage to Alaska. One company tried to buy the Coronado ferry, the *Silvergate*, to use in the Yukon. The last of the chiefs of the marauding border bandit and cattle rustling gangs, "Borada," was killed near Tecate.

Though the "Stingaree" district was not what it once was, as in days of the boom, the stagnation along the waterfront resulted in a "squatter town" that contrasted sharply with the stately Victorian residences of uptown areas. Squatter-town included some

*Characters from around
the world gathered at
waterfront squatter-towns.
San Diego's stretched
from the foot of
Market Street
to Gumbo Slough.*

The Richelieu Block

Pierce-Morse Block

fifteen blocks around the foot of Market Street, and the area from there to Gumbo Slough at the mouth of Switzer Creek, near the foot of Eleventh Street, was always referred to as Pirate's Cove. According to reports in *The San Diego Union*, Pirate's Cove was a strip of crowded, rickety shacks. Those on the bayshore line stood on rotting stilts over the tideflats, "their backyards fenced by the horizon," and the others stared from the landward side from a sea of hundreds of thousands of rusting tin cans under a latticework of crisscrossed clotheslines. Here, "dwarfed geraniums gasped for breath in the dust" and the people lived on "bread and barracuda." Its inhabitants were largely *guano* pirates who pursued a popular trade of the day, of poaching small boatloads of valuable fertilizer from Mexican-owned islands without the benefit of a costly government license. Poachers could make $65 to $100 for a two to four weeks' trip in a small schooner, most of which they drank up in Monongahela whiskey in the "Tub O' Blood Saloon" in Stingaree town, two blocks northward across "Wildcat Alley," the Cove's dusty thoroughfare.

Citizenry of the Cove included "Portuguese Itata Bill;" "Scowegian;" "Chou," the Chinese skipper of the junk *Hong Kong*; "Fan" and "Con" Murphy; "Mizzentop, the Dane;" "Tildy MacCready of Gumbo Slough;" "Sam Mallory of Needles;" and "Lola Osuna, the Tamale Man's Woman," who, when on speaking terms with her husband, could be seen boiling a tubful of tamales every day amid the tin cans and goats.

The financial distress in the country had not run its course, however, and another bank, the Savings Bank of San Diego County, failed in the middle 1890's. In the thirty years between 1870 and 1900 there were fifteen banks established in the city of San Diego, but with the four failures and numerous mergers and closings, only five survived into the Twentieth Century. Within two days, two of the most prominent structures of the old boom days, the Oceanside Hotel and La Jolla Park Hotel, both of which had fallen on bad times, caught fire in June of 1896. The La Jolla Hotel had been closed for some time but the Oceanside Hotel still had guests who threw furniture out of the windows until they were forced to flee. Both hotels were burned to the ground but were reported to have been heavily insured.

Adversity had turned the Kimball brothers against each other. Warren Kimball lost a law suit and his own empire began to collapse. A court decision in 1896 ordered foreclosure on his interests in Rancho de la Nación, part of Chula Vista, and all of Encinitas, except for Olivenhain, which he had acquired. The bank which he controlled in National City was pronounced "insolvent." Within a year his brother Frank Kimball was almost destitute. He wrote in his diaries that from "absolute owner of $1,384,000" he had been reduced to poverty and that he was living in an empty restaurant building without home, money or friends. He said he had been robbed by companies in which he had invested "as well as by some persons nearer home."

*Frank Kimball
in late years*

In the East, Katherine Tingley, the "Purple Mother," emerged as the undisputed leader of the Theosophical Society of America and she proposed the establishment of a School for the Revival of the Lost Mysteries of Antiquity, which also would serve as a "White City," or ideal community, and as a center for a new worldwide crusade for theosophy. A number of religious sects already had found a haven in Southern California, as would many others in the next half century. The theosophy movement as practiced in the United States had its origin with Helena Petrovna Blavatsky, a Russian seeress who died in 1891, and for a time attracted many persons prominent in national life.

Miss Tingley was searching for the "Golden Land" for her "White City" when she encountered Gen. Frémont, who had figured so prominently but indirectly in the fortunes of San Diego for decades. In her own words, as published in *Theosophical Path* in 1914, she wrote:

I told him this story, this fairy story; that in the golden land, far away, by the blue Pacific, I thought as a child that I could fashion a city and bring the people of all countries together and have the youth taught how to live, and how to become true and strong and noble, and forceful royal warriors for humanity. "But," I said "all that has passed; it is a closed book, and I question if it will ever be realized."

He said, "There are some parts of your story that attract me very much. It is your description of this place where you are going to build your city. Have you ever been in California?"

"No," I answered.

"Well," he said, "the city you have described is a place that I know exists." And he then told of Point Loma. He was the first to name the place to me.

While Madame Tingley and her "crusaders" were on a world tour, a site committee purchased 130 acres on Point Loma and obtained an option on forty additional acres. The crusaders reached San Diego in February of 1897, and an elaborate ceremony was arranged to lay the cornerstone of the School for the Revival of the Lost Mysteries of Antiquity. Hundreds of San Diegans in buggies and on bicycles rode to Point Loma. While in Ireland, Madame Tingley had located a greenish stone in Killarney which was to be the cornerstone for the new school, but as it had not arrived, a local stone was substituted and Madame Tingley, using a silver

Katherine Tingley

243

trowel, sealed up a metal box containing a history of the movement and unidentified parchments, and remarked, according to *The San Diego Union*:

> I dedicate this stone; a perfect square, a fitting emblem of the perfect work that will be done in the temple for the benefit of humanity and glory of the ancient sages.

Some of her supporters, however, in walking along the ridge of Point Loma, treeless and windswept and far from the centers of learning and influence, referred to it as a Godforsaken spot. But she persisted and within two years structures that were to become known around the world began to rise on a point of land projecting seaward from the most southwesterly corner of the United States.

Early in 1896 the Cuban revolution for independence from Spain had already become front page news in San Diego newspapers, with the Spanish Monarchy shown as the oppressor. Congress nodded approval to War Department thoughts on strengthening United States coastal defenses and the die was finally cast for San Diego's future as a major military base.

The Spanish-American War saw Southern California spring to the alert. The monitor Monadnock guarded the harbors of San Diego and San Pedro.

By mid-year the Army had dusted off its long-forgotten plans to fortify the entrance to San Diego Harbor, where partially finished revetments lay eroded and weed-grown after years of neglect. By fall, Maj. Charles E. G. B. Davis, U.S. Army, was directing active work on the expanded new plans. They called for six ten-inch Buffington-Crozier disappearing rifles in concrete emplacements at Ballast Point, covering the main channel entrance. Atop Point Loma, 2000 feet north of the Old Lighthouse, were to be sixteen twelve-inch mortars, and on the beach at the extreme tip, two swivel station rifles. Sixteen more twelve-inch mortars were to be installed on a fifty-acre site the Army purchased 6000 feet south of Hotel del Coronado. In addition, there was to be a torpedo casemate on the seaward side of Ballast Point for firing wire-controlled torpedoes, and a remote-controlled system of electrically-detonated mines.

The entire system was to cost $1,500,000. The work went on for two years under continually increasing pressure from the War Department for more haste. Secrecy measures increased and only Army officers were allowed to see the blueprints. San Diego's civic pride swelled with the knowledge that it was important enough to need such elaborate defenses. On the road to Roseville heavy freight wagons hauling steel and cement to the armaments at the foot of the hill ran nose-to-tailgate with equally heavy wagons hauling lumber and materials.

The United States Navy's first real interest in San Diego as a potential base resulted from a celebration of Washington's Birthday on February 22, 1897. A mid-winter carnival had been planned with the usual fancy dress ball, parades, horse races, a water parade on the bay and band concerts, and Rear Admiral Charles Beardsley, U.S. Navy, retiring commander of a Pacific

Long-planned forts were thrown up at Ballast Point to protect the town from the Spanish Navy. But they never fired a shot in anger.

squadron, was invited to be guest of honor. The admiral accepted, and so did a large portion of the Pacific Fleet. When he arrived in his flagship, the heavy cruiser *Philadelphia,* he was greeted by the coast defense monitors *Monterey* and *Monadnock;* the gunboats *Marion, Adams* and *Corwin;* the steamer *Albatross;* and a British heavy cruiser, H.M.S. *Camus.*

Carlson was still in office as mayor and he wired Washington for permission for British marines and sailors to march under arms in the parade in celebration of George Washington's Birthday. The United States and British ministries were nonplussed but permission finally was granted. Two hours before the parade, the British Admiralty signaled that it would not be in "keeping

Heavy cruiser U.S.S. Philadelphia

New San Diego Barracks

First San Diego-based warship, U.S.S. Pinta

with tradition." But the *Camus* did join in firing a full salute with all the other vessels at high noon. Admiral Beardsley reviewed a military parade in front of the Horton House and a sham battle was fought from Mission Hills down to Old Town. An estimated 10,000 tourists, 190 of whom had come from Boston, were in the audience, along with John Philip Sousa's Band, which played two concerts.

At 7:30 o'clock that night there was not a light to be seen on the water or along the shore. Then at a signal from the U.S.S. *Philadelphia's* salute gun, every electric light in the fleet was turned on and hundreds of colored torches were lighted. Aboard the H.M.S. *Camus* lighted Japanese lanterns were passed from hand to hand to the top of her rigging. As they reached the mast-heads a bugle sounded and the *Camus* fired a barrage of colored rockets. Other men-of-war followed suit. The crowds on the beach gasped in wonder as the thousands of electric lights against a black velvet sky revealed the fleet anchored close in, bow on stern. More than fifty small boats rowed by Navy seamen led a procession of yachts and civilian craft lighted by electric lights and 6000 colored torches. Then with fireworks rocketing overhead and star shells bursting, a band and a hundred-voice chorus on barges rendered *The Star Spangled Banner*.

A year later as crews were preparing to install the third of the big disappearing guns at Point Loma, word was flashed on February 16, 1898, that the U.S. battleship *Maine* had been blown up and sunk in Havana Harbor. A national military buildup began at once. The Navy assigned San Diego its own warship for use in training its seventy reservists. It was the U.S.S. *Pinta*, a thirty-two year old iron-hulled 550-ton gunboat armed with two cannon and one gatling gun. It was overhauled and sent down from San Francisco. *The San Diego Union* commented: "War fever is running high."

Forty thousand pounds of powder and 38,000 pounds of shells arrived for the big guns. The torpedo casemate was finished and mines were being shipped when the House of Representatives passed the Spanish Intervention Resolution on April 14. The news was received in San Diego with a celebration. The City Guard Band led a procession through the downtown streets playing *The Star Spangled Banner, Dixie, Marching Through Georgia, Yankee Doodle* and *The Red, White and Blue*. There was great cheering for the veterans of the Grand Army of the Republic who carried flags at the head of the line. Young and old alike joined in, even some on canes and crutches. The procession stopped long enough

246

to burn a Spanish flag in front of *The San Diego Union* office and give cheers for President McKinley, Robert E. Lee and for Americans in general. The news of the actual declaration of war was received ten days later, and another parade followed.

Five hundred men volunteered for a "Minute Man" brigade that would defend the city in the event of the appearance of the Spanish fleet. E. E. Capps, city engineer, was named chairman of preparations for defense of the city. Company B of the National Guard immediately went up to full strength of 103 men, and sixty auxiliaries were enlisted. The last one walked in from Ensenada. A Lieut. Meylers, of the Army Engineers, asked for civilian volunteers to assist in laying twenty-one mines in the harbor channel. A hundred volunteered.

Wheelmen's Rifle Corps militiaman

The local chapter of the National Wheelmen's Association, recently reinstated after having been suspended from the national organization for racing bicycles on Sunday, formed the "Wheelmen's Rifle Corps," to act as scouts and messengers for the "Minute Men" in defense of the city. T. J. Storey, deputy county clerk, formed a Signal Corps Auxiliary from the City Guard Band. Reserves drilled daily in the streets though they had no guns. On the Point Loma hillside above the torpedo casemate and overlooking the mine fields, the Army mounted two old obsolete brass Napoleon field pieces whose sole duty was to warn wayward craft away from the mine fields. With frequent regularity the guns boomed, sending round shots splashing off the bow of large and small craft alike, one round usually being sufficient.

Buffington-Crozier 10-inch disappearing gun

On April 30, Admiral Dewey's fleet arrived at Manila, and the "Minute Men" marched from the Plaza to the Armory on Second Street where they heard patriotic speeches and pledged themselves to defend the city. Company B of the National Guard closed its muster roll at ninety-seven men and prepared to go on active duty. The U.S. gunboat *Corwin* patrolled the San Diego coast, while cattlemen and ranchers formed a troop of cavalry and offered their services to the government, volunteering to bring their own horses.

Hotel del Coronado was jammed with tourists and guests, and in San Diego business picked up to a brisk trot.

The Spanish-American War was over quickly. Commodore Dewey's victory at Manila on May 1, forty-eight hours after he had arrived, was the first major action. The charge of Col. Theodore Roosevelt's Rough Riders up San Juan Hill on July 1 and the destruction of the Spanish fleet at Santiago Bay on July 3 were observed at San Diego's Fourth of July celebration on the Plaza.

Heavy 12-inch coast defense mortars planned for Coronado

San Diego was safe from the Spanish fleet. When hostilities ceased on August 12 and the treaty was signed in Paris on December 10, San Diego already had turned back to worrying about water, transportation and real estate sales.

As the Nineteenth Century drew to a close, the conquest of the Colorado Desert was at hand. Many San Diegans, one of them, Ephraim Morse, had been aware of its possibilities, once the waters of the Colorado River could be diverted under control onto the vast basin of silt. The valley was the bed of a long-dead lake and

Salt was mined in the Salton Sink in the Imperial Valley, when it had marshes and lakes, before a Colorado flood formed an inland sea.

its below-sea level depressions were crusted with salt. From time to time in subsequent centuries the low areas would be watered by the overflow of the Colorado. The dry years would expose salt in what became known as the Salton Sink and it was mined by the early settlers of the 1890's. One man virtually died in the cause of the irrigation of the desert. He was Dr. Oliver M. Wozencraft, a United States Indian agent. In 1859 he had obtained from the State Legislature the right to 1600 square miles of the Salton Basin, and then, through the Civil War and afterward, he struggled unsuccessfully to win the cooperation of an indifferent Congress. He died in 1887, having lost his fortune and his home in a seemingly hopeless cause.

The railroads had proved that the desert could be crossed regularly and safely, and the struggle was taken up by C. R. Rockwood, in 1892. Rockwood, who had been both a government and railroad engineer, crisscrossed the United States in search of help and money, until at last he was almost deserted by friends and backers. It was at this point in 1899, when Rockwood had about given up hope, that George Chaffey entered the scene. He had known

Dr. O. M. Wozencraft

248

Wozencraft but had refused to participate in the reclamation of the Colorado Desert as he believed that no white men could ever be induced to live and work in such heat below sea level. He went to Australia as an engineer and saw white men working in a climate as hot as that of the Colorado basin. He returned to this country, and after wandering over the desert wastes with an Indian guide, and losing his hearing because of it, he became convinced that the project was feasible. The California Development Company was organized, and the task of diverting part of the flow of the river into the desert to make one of the world's garden spots, was begun.

For the Indians, the spirit that brought freedom to the Cubans held no assurances for their survival. In their swift decline under the pressures of a White civilization they also carried to their graves the evidence which might have established some proof of their natural longevity. On Warner's Ranch, or Rancho José del Valle, the survivors of the Cupeño Indians, originally only a small

This scenic photo shows a lake in the Salton Sink in 1890. Pioneers knew that someday water would be used to create a farming empire.

249

band of about 500, were under orders of eviction from the Supreme Court of the United States. The heirs of the former governor, John G. Downey, were refusing to sell land to the government for the Indians who lived around the hot springs. The report of the commission related the following conversation with their captain, Cecilio Blacktooth:

We thank you for coming here to talk to us in a way we can understand. It is the first time anyone has done so.

You ask us to think what place we like next best to this place where we always live. You see that graveyard over there? There are our fathers and our grandfathers. You see that Eagle-Nest Mountain and that Rabbit-Hole Mountain? When God made them He gave us this place. It may be good, but it is not ours. We have always lived here. We would rather die here. Our fathers did. We cannot leave them. Our children born here—how can we go away? If you give us the best place in the world, it is not so good for us as this. My people cannot go anywhere else; they cannot live anywhere else. Here they always live; their people always live here. There is no other place. This is our home. We ask you to get it for us. If Harvey Downey say he own this place, that is wrong. The Indians always here. We do not go on his land. These hot springs always Indian. We cannot live anywhere else. We were born here, and our fathers are buried here. We do not think of any place after this. We want this place, and not any other place.

He was asked that if the government was unable to buy the Warner's ranch land, then where would they prefer to go? Captain Blacktooth replied:

There is no other place for us. We do not want you to buy any other place. If you will not buy this place, we will go into the mountains like quail and die there, the old people and the women and the children. Let the Government be glad and proud. It can kill us. We do not fight. We do what it says. If we cannot live here, we want to go into those mountains and die. We do not want any other home.

That was in 1902. The Cupeño Indians were moved onto 3400 acres purchased at Pala. Altogether about 300 were moved, about 200 of them from Warner's Ranch, seventy-eight from San Felipe Valley and eighteen from another nearby area. In less than 150 years the Luiseño, Diegueño, Cahuilla, Cupeño and Yuma Indians of Southern California declined from about 12,000 to about 3000.

In the decade from 1890 to 1900 the population of San Diego County increased hardly at all, from 34,987 to 35,090, in a period when the expansion of the West in general was both persistent and exciting. It was as if nobody had arrived or left, or had been born or died. Many persons abandoned the small boom towns and the marginal farms and drifted into the town. The population of San Diego City increased about 1500, from 16,159 to 17,700.

Under the leadership of President McKinley, the years after the Spanish-American War were prosperous ones, with full production and employment, a gold dollar, high wages and stable prices. There was pride in the nation's new status as a Great Power. The Monroe Doctrine had been reasserted, the Caribbean was an American lake and the United States Navy dominated the Pacific Ocean all the way to Asia. It was called the Age of Confidence.

The Twentieth Century would bring a rebirth to a town that had been left off the path of progress. Alonzo Horton was a symbol of a generation that had expected so much from the spanning of the continent by the railroads. Though in his late eighties, he liked to don his black frock coat and high silk hat and go down to the waterfront and meet the steamers, just as he had done in the days when the railroad barons were arriving and departing and promising so much, and welcome the passengers to "our beautiful San Diego."

Across the bay, a Coronado resident installed a one-cylinder gasoline engine in a buckboard wagon and the first horseless carriage in San Diego County began putting through the streets. Though the struggle for a direct railroad connection with the East would continue, a revolution in transportation was beginning, and roads over the deserts and mountains again would be the foremost challenges, as they had been in the days of the immigrant wagon, to the future of a town that never gave up.

CHRONOLOGY

1865 Lee surrenders at Appomattox; Civil War ends, April 9.

1865 Lincoln assassinated; Andrew Johnson becomes president, April 14.

1865 Second great westward migration begins.

1867 Alonzo E. Horton arrives at San Diego, April 15.

1867 Horton pays $265 for 960-acre city site at auction, May 10.

1868 Kimball brothers buy Rancho de la Nación; lay out National City.

1868 *The San Diego Union* publishes first edition, October 10.

1868 Ulysses S. Grant elected president.

1868 Construction begins on Horton's wharf.

1869 Old Town battles New San Diego to retain county seat.

1869 Central and Union Pacific Railroads meet at Promontory Point, Utah, May 10.

1869 New San Diego has its first major July 4th celebration.

1870 Coleman discovers gold at San Diego River headwaters.

1870 Gold Rush camp named Julian; mining district formed.

1870 Horton House completed and opens, October 17.

1870 San Diego's first bank founded.

1870 New Town's first school building erected.

1870 Western Union's San Diego telegraph line completed.

1870 Immigrants forced out by drouth.

1871 Julian-to-Banner toll road completed.

1871 County seat moved to Horton's Addition.

1871 County Court House constructed.

1871 Texas & Pacific Railroad chartered.

1871 San Diego votes Republican for first time.

1871 *The San Diego Union* begins daily publication.

1872 "No Fence" law repealed.

1872 Reincorporation of city provided by a new law.

1872 Old Town fire destroys business buildings.

1873 Texas & Pacific Railroad work begins at San Diego.

1873 San Diego Water Company formed; first major water system since Mission days.

1873 "Black Friday" stock panic wipes out Texas & Pacific Railroad.

1873 San Diego economy sinks to doldrums.

1874 City's final patent to pueblo lands received.

1875 Bank of California fails; statewide discontent and depression.

1875 Gunfight at Gaskill's Campo store.

1876 President Grant sets up San Diego Indian reservations.

1876 New City Charter adopted; provides five trustees.

1876 Rutherford B. Hayes elected president.

1876 Southern Pacific Railroad connects Los Angeles and San Francisco.

1877 Severe drouth in San Diego County.

1877 Anti-Chinese riots sweep California.

1877 San Diego River dike completed.

1879 New State Constitution formulated, effective January 1, 1880.

1880 James A. Garfield elected president.

1881 California Southern Railroad construction starts.

1881 President Garfield dies in office; Chester A. Arthur becomes president.

1882 San Diego Telephone Company begins operation.

1882 California Southern Railroad service begins.

1883 Mexican colonization law opens Baja California for settlement.

1883 John Montgomery makes world's first controlled airplane flight at Otay.

1884 Flood wrecks California Southern Railroad.

1884 Stephen Grover Cleveland elected president.

1885 A. J. Meyers founds Oceanside.

1885 Babcock and Story buy Coronado.

1885 Transcontinental railroad reaches San Diego.

1885 San Diego Flume Company organized.

1886 First electric street lights installed in city.

1886 New City Charter; San Diego becomes sixth-class city.

1886 First public transit system with horse cars.

1886 Construction of Hotel del Coronado begins.

1886 National City & Otay Railroad incorporated.

1887 National railroad rate war starts westward land rush.

1887 Land stampede begins.

1887 Santa Fe Railroad terminus established at National City.

1887 Vice and corruption grow with the boom.

1887 San Diego & Old Town electric street cars start operating.

1888 Hotel del Coronado opens.

1888 Land boom collapses, population declines.

1888 Benjamin Harrison elected president.

1889 New City Charter; San Diego becomes fourth-class city.

1889 Cable cars begin operating.

1889 San Diego Flume brings mountain water to San Diego.

1891 Coronado secedes from San Diego.

1891 Floods wipe out Temecula railway and Tia Juana City.

1891 California National Bank fails.

1892 Spreckels buys transit systems.

1892	Klondike gold rush begins.
1893	National depression brings bank failures.
1893	Riverside County formed and absorbs large area of San Diego County.
1895	*Evening Tribune* founded.
1896	Kimball brothers go bankrupt.
1896	Harbor fortifications work begins at Point Loma.
1896	William McKinley elected president.
1897	First major Navy celebration held in San Diego.
1898	Battleship *Maine* sunk at Havana, February 16.
1898	Spanish-American War starts, April 24.
1898	Spanish-American War ends, August 12.
1898	"Age of Confidence" begins.

MAYORS OF SAN DIEGO

1850	Joshua H. Bean
1851	David B. Kurtz
1852	G. P. Tebbetts
1852-89	Board of Trustees
1889-91	Douglas Gunn
1891-96	W. H. Carlson
1897-98	D. C. Reed
1899-1900	Edwin M. Capps

CALIFORNIA GOVERNORS

1863-67	Frederick F. Low (Union)
1867-71	Henry H. Haight (Dem.)
1871-75	Newton Booth (Rep.)
1875	Romualdo Pacheco (Rep.)
1875-80	William Irwin (Dem.)
1880-83	George C. Perkins (Rep.)
1883-87	George Stoneman (Dem.)
1887	Washington Bartlett (Dem.)
1887-91	Robert W. Waterman (Dem.)
1891-95	Henry H. Markham (Rep.)
1895-99	James H. Budd (Dem.)

COUNTY TOWNS 1888

San Diego County at this period included much of what is now Riverside County as well as all of Imperial County.

Agua Tibia	Glamis	Perris
Alpine	Helix	Potrero
Anon	Holabird	Poway
Ballena	Howe	Radec
Banner	Jamul	San Diego
Bernardo	Julian	San Luis Rey
Buena	Lakeside	San Pasqual
Campo	La Presa	South San Diego
Carlsbad	Leucadia	Stratton
Coronado	Linda Vista	Temecula
Cota	Menefie	Terra Cotta
Del Mar	Murrieta	Tia Juana
De Luz	National City	Valley Center
Descanso	Nellie	Viejas
Dulzura	North San Diego	Vineyard
El Cajon	Nuevo	West Fallbrook
Elsinore	Oceanside	Wildomar
Encinitas	Olivenhain	Winchester
Escondido	Otay	
Fallbrook	Pala	

COUNTY POST OFFICES 1895

San Diego County at this period included what is now Imperial County.

Alpine	La Jolla	Pala
Banner	Lakeside	Point Loma
Bernardo	La Mesa	Potrero
Black Mountain	La Presa	Poway
Bonsall	Lemon	Rainbow
Bostonia	Lemon Grove	Recluse
Campo	Linda Vista	Richland
Carlsbad	Lusardi	San Diego
Chula Vista	Merle	San Luis Rey
Coronado	Merton	San Marcos
Cuyamaca	Mesa Grande	San Pasqual
Dehesa	Minneapolis Beach	Santa Ysabel
Del Mar	Miramar	Santee
De Luz	Moosa	Sorrento
Descanso	National City	South San Diego
Dulzura	Nellie	Stowe
El Cajon	Nestor	Sunnyside
El Capitan	North San Diego	Tia Juana
El Nido	Nuevo	Twin Oaks
Encinitas	Oak Grove	Valley Center
Escondido	Oceanside	Vineyard
Fallbrook	Ogilby	Virginia
Foster	Olivenhain	Vista
Hedges	Oneonta	Warner
Helix	Orcutt	Witch Creek
Jamul	Otay	Wynola
Julian	Pacific Beach	

PERMISSION CREDITS

California State Library. Excerpts and quotations from the *Correspondence of Ephraim W. Morse, 1866-72.*

Harper & Row, Publishers, Incorporated. Quotation from *Damned Old Crank, a Self-Portrait of E. W. Scripps from His Unpublished Writings,* edited by Charles R. McCabe, 1951.

Henry E. Huntington Library and Art Gallery. Excerpts and quotations from the *Correspondence of David M. Berry; Correspondence of Couts, Pendleton and Stearns; Correspondence of Ephraim W. Morse, 1866-73; City of San Diego,* San Diego Chamber of Commerce, 1874, 1887 and 1888; *A Fight for Health, Life and Happiness,* Citizens of San Diego Association, 1887; *A Grand Scheme to Develop the Eastern Half of San Diego County,* San Felipe and Desert Land & Water Company, 1888; *San Diego, Description of the City and County,* San Diego County Immigration Association, 1885; *San Diego "Our Italy,"* San Diego Chamber of Commerce, 1895; *The Winter of Our Content* by Charles Dudley Warner, 1890-91.

National City Public Library. Excerpts and quotations from the *Diaries* and *Letterbooks of Frank A. Kimball, 1860-1912;* General Files of the *National City Record, 1882-1900.*

San Diego Historical Society. Excerpts and quotations from the *Biographical Files* and *Correspondence* of Alonzo Erastus Horton, Frank A. Kimball, Joseph Mannasse, George White Marston, Ephraim W. Morse, J. A. Shepherd and other San Diego pioneers, 1850-1900; *News Letters* of Rufus K. Porter, 1865-73; *San Diego City Directory,* 1889; *The Golden Era,* 1887-91.

San Diego Public Library. Excerpts and quotations from *Preliminary Report of Warner's Ranch Indian Commission* by Charles F. Lummis, 1902; General files of the *San Diego Bulletin,* 1869-72; General files of the *San Diego Sun,* 1881-1892; *Julian Gold* by Dan Forrest Taylor, 1939; *How Julian Mines Were Discovered* by Horace F. Wilcox, 1926.

University of California Library at Los Angeles, Department of Special Collections. Excerpts and quotations from the *Correspondence of Gen. William S. Rosecrans.*

Whaley House Historical Museum Library. Quotation from the *Correspondence of Thomas Whaley, 1861-68.*

ACKNOWLEDGEMENTS

For professional assistance: Dr. George P. Hammond, Director, and John Barr Tompkins, Head of Public Services, *The Bancroft Library,* University of California; Donald C. Biggs, Director, and James de T. Abajian, Librarian, *California Historical Society;* Allan R. Ottley, California Section Librarian, *California State Library,* Sacramento; Robert Dougan, Librarian, Herbert Schulz, Curator of Manuscripts, Edwin H. Carpenter, Western Americana Bibliographer, and Haydee Noya, Cataloguer in the Department of Manuscripts, *Henry E. Huntington Library and Art Gallery;* Ruth I. Mahood, Chief Curator, *Los Angeles County Museum;* Buford Rowland, Acting Chief, Legislative Branch, *National Archives,* Washington, D.C.; Mrs. Ellen Baeder, City Librarian, *National City Public Library;* Bertram B. Moore, Retired Assistant, *San Diego County Engineer;* Ray Brandes, Director, *San Diego Historical Society;* Mrs. Zelma Locker, California Room, *San Diego Public Library;* Dr. Andrew Szabo, Social Science Librarian, and Mrs. Mildred LeCompte, Library Assistant, Social Science Division, *San Diego State College Library;* Clyde L. Simpson, History Section, *Security First National Bank,* Los Angeles; Richard H. Dillon, Librarian, *Sutro Library,* San Francisco; Harry D. Williams, Head of Library Photographic, James V. Mink, Assistant Head, Department of Special Collections, *University of California Library,* Los Angeles; Dr. Abraham Nasatir, Professor of History, *San Diego State College.*

ARTWORK SOURCES

Arizona Pioneers Society, Tucson. Yuma Crossing; Soldiers on the Desert; Map of Steamboat Landings on Colorado River.

The Bancroft Library, University of California, Berkeley. Los Angeles in 1857; Portrait of Charles Crocker.

California State Library, Sacramento. San Francisco Stock Exchange; Emigrants on the March; Stage Robbers; San Francisco 1863; Cartoon, Two Roads in California; Ready Relief Mine; Stonewall Jackson Mine.

James S. Copley Collection, La Jolla. Painting of Wild and Woolly Days, entitled *The Bar-room Brawl,* by N. C. Wyeth.

Marjorie Reed Creese, Forks of Salmon. Paintings of Grinding Gold; Legend of Gold Discovery; Julian During Gold Rush; "Lost" Town of Banner; Stonewall Mine; Hauling Logs in Cuyamaca Snow.

Hazard Museum, San Diego. Slot Machine; Ore Train; Chuck Wagon; Kimball Brothers' Wagon.

Henry E. Huntington Library and Art Gallery, San Marino. Old Town Plaza; San Diego Presidio Ruins; New Map of California in 1865; Third and D Streets in 1873; San Diego From Across the Bay in 1873; Texas & Pacific Visionary Train Arriving in 1873; Victorian Age at Hotel del Coronado; Imperial Valley Salt Beds; Desert Flood in Salton Sink; Map of Southern California in 1890; Cover Page of *San Felipe and Desert Land & Water Company;* Cover Page of *San Diego "Our Italy;"* Portraits of Thomas Scott and Collis P. Huntington.

Image, Art Division of Frye & Smith, Ltd., San Diego. Paintings of Alonzo Horton, Father of San Diego; Gambling House in Boom-Time San Diego; Woodcuts for Chapter Preface Pages, by David Wayne Millsap. Painting of Campo Gunfight; Dust Jacket Illustration, by Robert Kinyon.

Julian Historical Society, Julian. Portraits of Drury D. Bailey; Horace Fenton Wilcox.

Los Angeles County Museum, Los Angeles. Panorama of Los Angeles in 1869.

National Archives, Washington, D.C. Map of Horton's Addition in 1873; U.S. Army Map of County Roads; New San Diego Barracks.

National City Library, National City. Lithograph of National City in 1888.

New York Historical Society, New York. Poster, California Cornucopia of the World; Painting of Bar Scene with Mexicans, Chinese and Americans, entitled *Mountains and Molehills,* by Frank Marryat.

San Diego Historical Society, Junípero Serra Museum, San Diego. First Edition of *The San Diego Union; Driving of the Last Spike* by Thomas Hill; Map and Railroad Schedule of Southern California Railroad in 1888; Arrival of Wagon Trains in 1869-70; Map of Rancho de la Nación; Cover Page of *The Golden Era,* 1890; Advertisements from *The Golden Era* of Tia Juana City, Oneonta, Otay City, Pacific Beach College of Letters, University Heights College of Fine Arts, San Marcos, San Diego Development Company, Southern California Railroad, and Hotel del Coronado; Engravings from *The Golden Era* of Sweetwater Dam, Richelieu Block, Bank of Commerce, Pierce-Morse Block, First National Bank Block, County Courthouse, Hotel Corona del Cajon, Hotel St. James, and Hotel Brewster; Photographs of Museum Exhibits including Gold Scales, Prospector's Equipment, Rifles, and Pistols; Portraits of Edward W. Bushyhead, John G. Capron, Daniel Choate, Daniel Cleveland, Wyatt Earp, Ed Fletcher, A. P. Frary, Douglas Gunn, J. S. Harbison, Frank A. Kimball, Peter C. Remondino, Louis Rose, Jesse Francis Shepard and Concert Program, J. A. Shepherd, John D. Spreckels, Katherine Tingley, William Tweed, Theodore S. Van Dyke, and O. S. Witherby.

San Diego State College, Social Science Library, San Diego. Horton Bill of Sale, from *Alonzo Horton, Founder of Modern San Diego* by Ward Thomas Donley.

Security First National Bank of Los Angeles, Los Angeles in 1877; Portraits of Benjamin C. Truman and Dr. Oliver M. Wozencraft.

The Society of California Pioneers, San Francisco. Painting entitled *Across the Continent,* by Currier & Ives.

Title Insurance and Trust Company, Historical Collection, San Diego. Chinese Junk; Junks in San Diego Bay; *U.S.S. Monadnock; Orizaba; U.S.S. Philadelphia; U.S.S. Pinta;* Santa Fe Wharf; Ballast Point with Chinese Sail Boat; Point Loma and Ballast Point; Horton's Hall; Knox, Del Mar, Cliffs, Dunnells', Lakeside and La Jolla Park Hotels; Old Town Plaza; Old Town in 1876; Old Town After Fire; Riding Shotgun; Wagon Freight Trains; Wagon Trains Hauling Lumber; Frary & Foster Stage Coach; San Luis Rey Valley Stage Station; Stage Line Advertisements of John Capron, William Tweed and Seeley & Wright; Luiseño Indian; Yellow Sky, Capitán Grande Indian; Cinon Duro, Mesa Grande Indian; Mountain Springs Road; Map of Julian Mines; Original Hays Map; Pueblo Map in 1870; Map of Horton's Addition by Lockling; San Diego in 1871; Seventh and A Streets in 1873; San Diego in 1876; Plaza in 1885; Santa Fe Depot; Temecula Canyon Railroad Trestle; Trestle near Oceanside; California Southern Switch Engine; National City and Otay Train on Trestle; Electric Transit Trolley Cars; Steam Dummies; San Diego and Pacific Beach Motor Train; Horse Car; Cable Railway Car; Double-deck Street Car; Arc Lamps; Otay Watch; Fifth Street in 1888; *The San Diego Union* Office in 1868 and 1870; Pioneer Hook and Ladder Company; Horton's Fourth Home on First Street and Fifth Home on State and Olive; Villa Montezuma; Gaskill Home; Campo Hotel and Store; Los Coches Trestle; San Diego River Flood in 1889; Coronado Rabbit Chase; Circus Parade; Squatter Town; Coronado in 1888; Ocean Beach Balloon Ascension; Advertisement for South San Diego and Imperial Beach; Morena Auction; Oceanside; La Presa; Settlers Leaving San Diego After Crash; Lots for Sale; Frank T. Botsford in Camp; Portraits of E. S. Babcock, Frank Bailey, James O. Bailey, William H. Carlson, Joseph Coyne, S. S. Dunnells, John F. Forward, Gen. John C. Frémont, Lumen and Silas Gaskill, Alonzo Horton at Middleage, Mike Julian, Frank Kimball in Late Years, Warren C. Kimball, M. A. Luce, John J. Montgomery, E. W. Morse as a Young Man and in Late Years, Joseph T. Nash, Pablo the Indian Chief, Louis Redman, Gen. William S. Rosecrans, Chalmers Scott, Kate Sessions, Matthew Sherman, H. L. Story, Rose Hartwick Thorpe, Fr. Antonio Ubach, James Harrison Wagner, and J. J. Warner.

Hugh Tolford Collection, Van Nuys. Map of Santa Fe System in 1892; Pullman Car on Santa Fe Route in 1888; Magazine Advertisement for Santa Fe Route in 1888.

Union-Tribune Publishing Company, San Diego. Maps of Yuma Stage Route and Stations; Mountain Passes; San Diego County in 1893-1907; Texas & Pacific Railroad; California Southern Railroad; National City & Otay Railroad; Coronado Belt Line; San Diego, Pacific Beach & La Jolla Railway; and San Diego, Cuyamaca & Eastern Railroad. Sketches of San Diego County Homesteads and Businesses from *History of San Diego County 1883;* Photographs of Gold Mining Area; Portraits of San Diego Pioneers.

BIBLIOGRAPHY

Adams, H. Austin
The Man John D. Spreckels (San Diego, Frye & Smith, Ltd., 1924)

Ainsworth, Edward Maddin
Beckoning Desert (Englewood Cliffs, N.J., Prentice-Hall Inc., 1962)

Alexander, J. A.
The Life of George Chaffey: A Story of Irrigation Beginnings (London, Macmillan & Company, Ltd., 1928)

Alta California
General Files, 1865-70

Aubury, Lewis E.
Register of Mines and Minerals (Sacramento, California State Mining Bureau, 1902)

Automobile Club of Southern Calif.
Log. . . of Baja California, Mexico (Automobile Club of Southern California, 1962)

Bacon, Edwin M.
Ramblings Around Boston (Boston, Little, Brown and Company, 1914)

Bancroft, Hubert Howe
History of California, Vols. XXIII, XXIV (San Francisco, The History Company, 1888)

Banning, William and George Hugh
Six Horses (New York, London, The Century Company, 1930)

Bartholomew, Ed
Wyatt Earp: The Untold Story (Toyahvale, Texas, Frontier Book Company, 1963)

Baur, John E.
Health Seekers of Southern California (San Marino, California, Henry E. Huntington Library and Art Gallery, 1963)

Beckler, Marion F.
Palomar Mountain—Past and Present (Palm Desert, California, Desert Magazine Press, 1958)

Berry, David M.
Correspondence of David M. Berry to T. B. and Helen Elliott, 1873 (San Marino, Henry E. Huntington Library and Art Gallery)

Biographical Files of San Diego Pioneers
1850-1900 (San Diego Historical Society)

Birkett, Charles V.

The Ready Relief Mine in *San Diego Historical Society Quarterly,* Vol. IX, No. 4 (October 1963)

Black, Samuel F.
History of San Diego County, California (Chicago, The S. J. Clarke Publishing Company, 1913)

Brackett, R. W.
The History of San Diego County Ranchos (San Diego, Title Insurance and Trust Company, 1939)

Browne, J. Ross
Explorations in Lower California, 1868 (Harper and Brothers, 1868; reprinted, Tucson, Arizona, Arizona Silhouettes, 1952)

Bynon, A. A.
San Diego Illustrated in *The Golden Era,* Vol. 38, No. 9 (September 1889)

California Senate Special Committee on Chinese Immigration
Chinese Immigration: Its Social, Moral and Political Effects (Sacramento, California State Office, 1878)

California Water & Telephone Company
The Water Story of the Sweetwater District (Chula Vista and National City, California Water & Telephone Company, 1955)

Carpenter, Ford A.
The Climate and Weather of San Diego, California (San Diego, Chamber of Commerce, 1913)

Carr, A.
Handbook of California (1870)

Caughey, John Walton
California (Englewood Cliffs, N. J., Prentice-Hall, Inc., 1953)

Charter of the City of San Diego with Subsequent Amendments
Adopted March 16, 1889 (San Diego, 1923)

Chickering, Allen L.
San Diego County Wildflowers in *Title Insurance and Trust Company "Title Topics,"* May-June 1949)

Citizens of San Diego Association
A Fight for Health, Life and Happiness (San Diego, Citizens of San Diego Association, 1887)

Cleland, Robert Glass
California Pageant: The Story of Four Centuries (New York, Alfred A. Knopf, 1955)
The Cattle on a Thousand Hills (San Marino, Henry E. Huntington Library

and Art Gallery, 1951)
Drought, Lawlessness and Smallpox in *The Historical Society of Southern California Quarterly,* Vol. XXXV, No. 1 (1953)
From Wilderness to Empire: A History of California (New York, Alfred A. Knopf, 1959)
A History of California: The American Period (New York, The Macmillan Company, 1926)
Transportation in California Before the Railroads in *The Historical Society of Southern California Annual,* Vol. XI, Part 1 (1918)

Cleveland, Daniel
San Diego's Pueblo Lands in *The San Diego Union* (March 14, 1926)

Couts, Cave J.
Correspondence of Couts, Pendleton and Stearns (San Marino, Henry E. Huntington Library and Art Gallery)

Cowan, Robert Ernest
Bibliography of the History of California and the Pacific West, 1510-1906, 3 vols. (San Francisco, The Book Club of America, 1914)

Davis, William Heath
Seventy-five Years in California, 1831-1906 (San Francisco, John Howell, 1929)

Dawson, Muir
Southern California Newspapers, 1851-1876, Part I and II in *The Historical Society of Southern California Quarterly,* Vol. 32, Nos. 1 and 2 (March and June 1950)

De Frate, Julia Flinn
This Was Yesterday, Part I, II and III (San Diego, Julia Flinn De Frate, 1951)

De Voto, Bernard
Course of Empire (Boston, Houghton Mifflin Company, 1952)

Dillon, Richard H.
The Hatchet Men (New York, Coward-McCann, Inc., 1962)

Dixon, Ben F.
Don Diego's Old School Days: The Story of the Beginnings of Public Education in San Diego City and County (San Diego, San Diego County Historical Days Association, 1956)

Dodge, Richard V.
The California Southern Railroad: A Rail Drama of the Southwest in *The Railway and Locomotive Historical Society Bulletin,* No. 80 (San Diego Historical Society)
Rails of the Silver Gate: The Spreckels

San Diego Empire (San Marino, California, Pacific Railway Journal, 1960)

Donley, Ward Thomas
Alonzo Horton, Founder of Modern San Diego (Master's Thesis, San Diego State College, 1952)

Donnelly, Maurice
Geology and Mineral Deposits of the Julian District, Vol. 30 (San Francisco, California Division of Mines, 1934)

Drake, Samuel Adams
History of Middlesex County, Massachusetts (Boston, Estes and Lauriat, Publishers, 1880)

Duke, Donald; and Kistler, Stan
Santa Fe: Steel Rails Through California (San Marino, Pacific Railroad Publications, Inc., 1963)

Dumke, Glenn S.
The Boom of the Eighties in Southern California (San Marino, Henry E. Huntington Library and Art Gallery, 1944)

Englehardt, Fr. Zephyrin, O.F.M.
San Diego Mission (San Francisco, The James H. Barry Company, 1920)
San Luis Rey Mission (San Francisco, The James H. Barry Company, 1921)

Federal Writers' Project, California
California, a Guide to the Golden State (New York, Hastings House, 1939)

Federal Writers' Project, Wisconsin
Wisconsin, a Guide to the Badger State (New York, Hastings House, 1941)

First National Trust & Savings Bank of San Diego
1883-1943: Sixty Years in the Service of San Diego (San Diego, Raymert Press, 1943)

Fitch, Thomas L.
Special No. I, souvenir booklet (Howard & Lyons, 1887)

Fletcher, Col. Ed
Memoirs of Ed Fletcher (San Diego, Pioneer Printers, 1952)

Fowler, Lloyd Charles
A History of the Dams and Water Supply of Western San Diego County (Thesis for the Degree of Civil Engineer, University of California, January 1953)

Frémont, John Charles
Memoirs of My Life (New York and Chicago, Belford, Clarke & Co., 1887)
Notes of Travel in California (New York, D. Appleton & Company, 1849)

Friend, James Edward
1000 Liars (Press of the Recording Co., National City, Calif., 1893)

Gilbert, Anna M.
La Mesa Yesterday and Today (San Diego, City Printing Company, 1924)

Goddard, Frederick B.
Where to Emigrate and Why (Philadelphia, The Peoples Publishing Company, 1869)

Goetzmann, William H.
Army Exploration in the American West 1803-1863 (New Haven, Yale University Press, 1959)

The Golden Era
Advice to Emigrants, Vol. 38, No. 4 (April 1889)
Coronado, Vol. 37, No. 4 (April 1888)
Prospective Fisheries of San Diego, Vol. 40, No. 5 (May 1891)
Roseville, Vol. 37, No. 7 (July 1888)
The San Diego Bay Region, Vol. 37, No. 7 (July 1888) and Vol. 38, No. 4 (April 1889)
The San Diego Flume, Vol. 37, No. 4 (April 1888)
Tia Juana City, Vol. 36, No. 9 (September 1887)

Greenwalt, Emmett A.
The Point Loma Community in California (Berkeley, University of California Press, 1955)

Guinn, James M.
The Great Real Estate Boom of 1887 in *The Historical Society of Southern California Quarterly,* Vol. I, Part 5 (1890)
A History of California and an Extended History of its Southern Coast Counties, 2 vols. (Los Angeles, 1907)
The Passing of the Cattle Barons of California in *The Historical Society of Southern California Annual,* Vol. VIII, Part 1 and 2 (1909-1910)

Gunn, Douglas
Annual Review of Progress of The San Diego Union (San Diego, The San Diego Union, 1895-96)
Picturesque San Diego (Chicago, Knight & Leonard Co., Printers, 1887)
San Diego: Climate, Productions, Resources, Topography... (San Diego, Union Steam Book and Job Printing Office, 1886)

Harmon, John B.
A History of Carlsbad (Carlsbad, "Friends of the Library," ca. 1955)

Haven, Robert Wells
Thomas Whaley (Master's Thesis, San Diego State College, May 1963)

Hebert, Edgar W.
The Last of the Padres in *San Diego Historical Society Quarterly,* Vol. X, No. 2 (April 1964)
Naval Militia of San Diego in *San Diego Historical Society Quarterly,* Vol. IX, No. 2 (April 1963)

Heilbron, Carl H.
History of San Diego County (San Diego Press Club, 1936)

Hensley, Herbert C.
The Memoirs of Herbert C. Hensley, typescript bound in five vols. (San Diego Historical Society)

Herndon, Richard
Boston of Today—a Glance at its History and Characteristics (Boston, Post Publishing Company, 1892)

Hevener, Harold Guy
The Pueblo Lands of the City of San Diego 1769-1950 (Master's Thesis, San Diego State College, 1950)

Higgins, C. A.
California Over the Santa Fe Trail (Chicago, The Santa Fe Railroad, 1910)

Higgins, Shelley J.
This Fantastic City, San Diego (City of San Diego, 1956)

Hill, Joseph J.
History of Warner's Ranch and Its Environs (Los Angeles, Young & McCallister, 1927)

Historical Miscellany
Unclassified historical materials (San Diego Historical Society)

History of San Diego County, California
(San Francisco, Wallace W. Elliott & Co., 1883)

Hittel, John S.
The Resources of California (San Francisco, A. Roman & Company, 1874)

Hittel, Theodore Henry
History of California, Vols. I and II (San Francisco, Pacific Press Publishing House and Occidental Publishing Company, 1885)

Holland, Francis R., Jr.
A Short History of the Cabrillo National Monument in *The Western Explorer,* Vol. II, No. 2 (August 1962)

Hopkins, Harry C.
History of San Diego: Its Pueblo Lands and Water (San Diego, 1929)

Horton, Alonzo Erastus

Biographical File (San Diego Historical Society)

Hortonville Weekly Review
Documentation of Alonzo Horton's second marriage to Sarah Wilson Babe on July 29, 1861 (February 4, 1909)

Office of Public Information, Imperial Irrigation District
Historic Salton Sea (El Centro, Calif., Imperial Irrigation District, 1960)

Jackson, Helen Hunt
A Century of Dishonor (Boston, Little Brown & Company, 1905)
Glimpses of California and the Missions (Boston, Little Brown & Company, 1907)
Ramona (Boston, Little Brown & Company, 1900)

Jackson, W. Turrentine
Wagon Roads West 1846-69 (Berkeley, University of California Press, 1952)

Jahns, Richard H.
The Gem Deposits of Southern California in *Engineering and Science Monthly,* Vol. XI, No. 2 (February 1948)

Jahns, Richard H.; and Wright, Lauren A.
Gem- and Lithium-Bearing Pegmatites of the Pala District, San Diego County, Special Report 7-A (San Francisco, California Division of Mines, 1951)

Jasper, James A.
Trail-Breakers and History-Makers, typescript, Vols. I and II, 1922 (San Diego Historical Society)

Johnson, Crisfield
History of Oswego County, New York (Philadelphia, L. H. Everts Company, 1877)

Julian Chamber of Commerce
Julian Apple Day (Julian, Chamber of Commerce, 1958)

Kimball, Frank A.
Biographical File (San Diego Historical Society)
Diaries 1860-1912 (National City Public Library)
Letterbooks (National City Public Library)

King, Francis X.
Frank A. Kimball, Pioneer of National City (Master's Thesis, San Diego State College, June 1950)

Knox, Donna M.
Old Town Versus New Town—Locating the County Seat of San Diego, 1869-71 (San Diego Historical Society)

Knott's Berry Farm
Calico Ghost Town (Ghost Town, Calif., 1959)

Kroeber, A. L.
Handbook of the Indians of California (Berkeley, California Book Company Ltd., 1953)

La Force, Beatrice
Alpine History (Alpine, Alpine Women's Club Library Benefit, 1952)

Lamers, William M.
The Edge of Glory: A Biography of Gen. William S. Rosecrans (New York, Harcourt, Brace & World, 1961)

Lesley, Lewis B.
San Diego and the Struggle for a Southern Transcontinental Railroad Terminus, 1859-90 (Doctoral Dissertation, University of California, 1933)

Lord, C. C.
Life and Times in Hopkinton, New Hampshire (Concord, N.H., Republic Press Association, 1890)

Los Angeles Express
General Files (1887)

Los Angeles News
General Files (1869-70)

Los Angeles Times
General Files (1884-86)

Loyal, C.
The Squatter and the Don (San Francisco, 1885)

Lummis, Charles F.
Preliminary Report of Warner's Ranch Indian Commission, typescript, 1902 (San Diego Public Library)

McClellan, R. Guy
The Golden State (Philadelphia, William Flint & Company, 1872)

McGhee, Earl Samuel
E. W. Morse, Pioneer Merchant and Co-Founder of San Diego (Master's Thesis, San Diego State College, 1950)

McGrew, Clarence Alan
San Diego and San Diego County, Vols. I and II (Chicago and New York, The American Historical Society, 1922)

McWilliams, Carey
Southern California Country (New York, Duell, Sloan and Pearce, 1946)

Maass, John
The Gingerbread Age (New York, Bramhall House, 1957)

Mannasse, Joseph
Biographical File (San Diego Historical Society)

Marston, George White
Biographical File (San Diego Historical Society)

Marston, Mary Gilman
George White Marston: A Family Chronicle, Vols. I and II (The Ward Ritchie Press, 1956)

Mauzy, Wayne L. (Editorial Director)
Probing the American West (Santa Fe, Museum of New Mexico Press, 1962)

Menzel, Spencer
Paper Railroads of the 90's, typescript, 1943 (San Diego Historical Society)

Merriam, Richard; and Stewart, Richard M.
Geology and Mineral Resources of Santa Ysabel Quadrangle, Bulletin 177 (San Francisco, California Division of Mines, 1958)

Merrill, Frederick J. H.
14th Report of the State Mineralogist 1913-14: Part V. The Counties of San Diego and Imperial (San Francisco, California State Mining Bureau, 1914)

Middlebrook, R. P.
The High Iron to La Jolla: The Story of a Railroad in *San Diego Historical Society Quarterly,* Vol. VII, No. 1 (January 1961)

Millikan, Frank M.
A Survey of the Development of Commercial Banking in San Diego County (Master's Thesis, San Diego State College, 1960)

Military Bounty Land Warrant, No. 5896
Issued to Henry Tons; signed to John T. Schulz; resigned to Alonzo Erastus Horton on February 26, 1848 (Washington, D.C., General Services of the Administration)

Moore, Bertram B.
History of San Diego Roads and Stages, typescript (San Diego Historical Society)
Narrative Describing the Map at the Junipero Serra Museum Entitled: Roads and Trails in Use in San Diego County Between the Years 1769 and 1885, typescript, 1956 (San Diego Historical Society)

Moore, Harvey W.
The Discovery and History of the Stonewall Jackson Mine, typescript

(Cuyamaca Rancho State Park Files)

Morgan, H. Wayne
The Guilded Age, A Reappraisal (New York, Syracuse University Press, 1963)
William McKinley and His America (New York, Syracuse University Press, 1963)

Morrison, Lorrin L.
Warner, the Man and the Ranch (Los Angeles, 1962)

Morse, Ephraim W.
Biographical File (San Diego Historical Society)
Correspondence, Merchandising File 1857-79 (San Diego Historical Society)
Correspondence, 1866-72 (Sacramento, California State Library)
Letters of Ephraim W. Morse 1870-84 (San Diego Historical Society)
Letters of Ephraim W Morse to his father and John S. Morse 1866-73 (San Marino, Henry E. Huntington Library and Art Gallery)

Nadeau, Remi
California, the New Society (New York, Van Rees Press, 1963)
Los Angeles from Mission to Modern City (New York, Longmans, Green and Company, 1960)

National City Record
General Files (1882-1900)

Nevins, Allan
Frémont: The West's Greatest Adventurer (New York, Harper & Brothers, 1927)

Newhall, Beaumont
Image of America—Early Photography 1839-1900, Catalog, Library of Congress Exhibit (Washington, D.C., 1957)

New York Times
General Files (1867)

Nordhoff, Charles
California: A Book for Travellers and Settlers (New York, Harper & Brothers, 1872)

Parker, C. E. and Marilyn
Indians to Industry (Santa Ana, Orange County Title Company, 1963)

Parker, Horace
Anza-Borrego Desert Guide Book (Palm Desert, California, Desert Magazine Press, 1957)

Peterson, J. Harold
The Coronado Story, Twentieth Anniversary Publication (Coronado Federal Savings and Loan Association, 1954)

Porter, Rufus K.
News Letters from San Diego to the San Francisco Bulletin 1865-73 (San Diego Historical Society)

Pourade, Richard F.
The History of San Diego: Vol I, *The Explorers;* Vol. II, *Time of the Bells;* Vol. III, *The Silver Dons.* Commissioned by James S. Copley (San Diego, The Union-Tribune Publishing Company: 1960, 1961 and 1963 respectively)
Notes: Ayer, Boston and Littletown, Massachusetts; Contoocook and Hopkinton, New Hampshire; Oswego County, New York; Oshkosh, Appleton and Hortonville, Wisconsin (1963-64)

Randolph, Howard S. F.
La Jolla—Year by Year (La Jolla, The Library Association of La Jolla, 1955)

Reading, James
Historical Background of Transit in San Diego, typescript, 1962 (San Diego Historical Society)

Remondino, Peter C.
The Mediterranean Shores of America: Southern California (Philadelphia, F. A. Davis, 1892)
The Modern Climatic Treatment of Invalids with Pulmonary Consumption in Southern California (Detroit, George S. Davis, 1893)

Rensch, Eugene and Ethel Grace
Historic Spots in California: The Southern Counties (Stanford, California, Stanford University Press, 1932)

Roadarmel, Gordon C.
Some California Dates of 1860 in *California Historical Society Quarterly*, Vol. 38, No. 4 (December 1959)

Rolle, Andrew F.
An American in California: The Biography of William Heath Davis (San Marino, Henry E. Huntington Library and Art Gallery, 1956)
California—A History (New York, Thomas Y. Crowell Co., 1963)

Romer, Margaret
The Story of Los Angeles, Part V, in *Journal of the West,* Vol. III, No. 1 *(January 1964)*

Rosecrans, Gen. William S.
Correspondence of Gen. William S. Rosecrans (Special Collection, University of California Library, Los Angeles)

Rowsome, Frank
Trolley Car Treasury (New York, Bonanza Books, 1956)

Ruhlen, George
Early Military Forts and Camps in San Diego Area, typescript, 1962 (San Diego Historical Society)
San Diego Barracks in *San Diego Historical Society Quarterly,* Vol. I, No. 2 (April 1955)

Rush, Philip S.
History of the Californias (San Diego, 1958)

Safley, J. C. (Editor)
The Copley Press (Aurora, Illinois, The Copley Press, 1953)

Sanborn, Kate
A Truthful Woman in Southern California (New York, D. Appleton and Company, 1902)

San Diego Board of Education
100 Years of Public Education in San Diego 1854-1954 (San Diego, San Diego Unified School District, 1954).

San Diego Chamber of Commerce
City of San Diego, 1874, 1887 and 1888 (San Marino, Henry E. Huntington Library and Art Gallery)
San Diego "Our Italy" 1895 (San Marino, Henry E. Huntington Library and Art Gallery)

San Diego City Directory, 1889 (San Diego Historical Society)

San Diego County Board of Supervisors
Minutes, 1853-1900 (Records Division, San Diego County Board of Supervisors)

San Diego County Division of Natural Resources
Annual Report, 1952 and 1959

San Diego County Immigration Association
San Diego: Description of the City and County (San Diego, San Diego Sun, 1885)

San Diego, Cuyamaca and Eastern Railway Company
Miscellany Mss (San Diego Historical Society)

San Diego Federal Writers' Project
San Diego, a California City (San Diego, San Diego Historical Society, 1937)

San Diego Land and Town Company
A Guide to the San Diego Bay Region, California (Chicago, Rand, McNally & Co., 1888)
History of the San Diego Land and Town Company (San Diego Historical Society)

San Diego Bulletin
General Files (1869-72)

San Diego Sun
General Files (1881-92)

San Diego Union
General Files (1868-1900)

San Felipe and Desert Land
& Water Company
A Grand Scheme to Develop the Eastern Half of San Diego County, 1888 (Henry E. Huntington Library and Art Gallery)

Schmid, Dorothy Clark
Pioneering in Dulzura (San Diego, Robert R. Knapp, 1963)

Schmitt, Jo Ann
Fighting Editors (San Antonio, Texas, The Naylor Company, 1958)

Scripps, E. W.
Damned Old Crank: A Self-Portrait of E.W. Scripps from His Unpublished Writings (New York, Harper & Brothers, 1951)

Sheldon, Gale W.
Julian Gold Mining Days (Master's Thesis, San Diego State College, August 1959)

Shepard, Jesse A.
Collected Letters (San Diego Historical Society)

Shields, Wilmer B.
Up from San Antonio in *San Diego Historical Society Quarterly,* Vol. IX, No. 1 (January 1963)

Smith, Walter Gifford
The Story of San Diego (San Diego, City Printing Company, 1892)

Smythe, William E.
The Conquest of Arid America (London, The Macmillan Company, 1905)
History of San Diego 1542-1908 (San Diego, The History Company, 1908)

Splitter, Henry Winfred
Newspapers of Los Angeles: The First Fifty Years, 1851-1900 in *Journal of the West,* Vol. II, No. 4 (October 1963)

State of California, Department of Natural Resources, Division of Beaches and Parks
Torrey Pines State Park (California State Printing Office, nd)

State Mining Bureau
Register of Mines and Minerals, San Diego (October 1902)

Still, Bayrd
The West: Contemporary Records of America's Expansion Across the Continent 1607-1890 (New York, Capri-

corn Books, 1961)

Stone, Adolf (Editor)
California, Information Almanac (Lakewood, California, California Almanac Company, 1963)

Stone, Irving
Men to Match My Mountains (Garden City, N.Y., Doubleday & Company, 1956)
The Opening of the Far West (Garden City, N.Y., Doubleday & Company, 1956)

Stratton, James S.
Report of Spanish or Mexican Grants in California, Appendix to the Journals of the Senate and Assembly, California Legislature, 24th Session, Vol. I (Sacramento, Supt. State Printing Office, 1881)

Taylor, Dan Forrest
Julian Gold, Federal Writers' Project, typescript, 1939 (San Diego Public Library)

Telfer, William Booth
Early Transportation Arteries of San Diego County (Master's Thesis, San Diego State College, 1951)

Theosophical Path
Vol. VI (Point Loma, California, June 1914)

Thomas, Sadie M.
Julian, California (Julian Chamber of Commerce, ca. 1929)

Title Insurance & Trust Company
El Cajon, Busy Valley Community San Diego, 1951); *Escondido, Gateway to the Stars* (San Diego, 1951); *La Jolla, the Jewel City* (San Diego, 1951); *National City, Active South Bay City* (San Diego, 1954); *Rancho Santa Fe: Heritage of the Dons* (San Diego, 1951); *The San Diego Story,* 50th Anniversary Publication (San Diego, 1955); *Title Books 1860-1900*

Title Insurance & Trust Company "Title Topics"
Alpine (Jan-Feb 1951); *Aviation History in San Diego: 1883-1952* (Mar-Apr 1952); *Balboa Park: San Diego's All-Year Playground* (May-Jun 1954); *Carlsbad* (Jul-Aug 1949); *Carlsbad, Flower Bower by the Sea* (Mar-Apr 1960); *Chula Vista, The Story of* (Jan-Feb 1953); *Clairemont* (Sep-Oct 1959); *Clean, Crisp Chula Vista* (Jan-Feb 1957); *Del Mar, The Story of* (Jul-Aug 1948); *80 Years of Progress* (Jan-Feb 1950); *82 Years of Growth at a Glance* (Mar-Apr 1951); *Fallbrook... Old and New* (Jan-Feb 1950); *From*

Horse Cars to Modern Busses (May-Jun 1949); *Hotel del Coronado, The Story of* (May-Jun 1948); *Laguna-Cuyamaca...The San Diego County Mountain Area* (Nov-Dec 1952); *Lakeside, Versatile Ranching Area* (May-Jun 1949); *La Mesa, Growing Suburb and City* (Nov-Dec 1949); *National City* (Jan-Feb 1958); *Oceanside, City by the Sea* (Sep-Oct 1957); *Oceanside, The Story of* (Jun-Jul 1947); *Old Campo Store* (Jan-Feb 1950); *Old Coaches* (Jan-Feb 1953); *Old Roads Give Way to Super Highways* (May-Jun 1951); *Palomar, The Story of* (May-Jun 1948); *Point Loma* (Jul-Aug 1951); *Ramona* (Sep-Oct 1958); *Ramona and the Santa María Valley* (Nov-Dec 1948); *Rancho Santa Fe—A Study in Gracious California Living* (Jan-Feb 1949); *San Diego Beach Communities* (Jul-Aug 1950); *San Diego Founders and Builders* (Jan-Feb 1959); *San Marcos* (Jan-Mar 1961); *School Days 1882-1952* (May-Jun 1951); *The Whaley House* (Jul-Aug 1959); *Vista, a Real American Town* (May-Jun 1950); *Warner's Ranch* (Sep-Oct 1950); *Welcome to Vista* (Jan-Feb 1960)

Tout, Otis B.
The First Thirty Years in Imperial Valley, California—1901 to 1931 (San Diego, Arts & Crafts Press, 1931)

Transit Topics
Transportation Progress, Vol. 6, No. 7 (Apr-May 1949)

Truman, Benjamin C.
Semi-Tropical California (San Francisco, Bancroft, 1874)

Turpin, Vicki
San Diego—This Is How It Was (San Diego, Land Title Insurance Company, 1955)

Udall, Stewart L.
The Quiet Crisis (New York, Holt, Rinehart & Winston, 1963)

Underhill, Ruth
Indians of Southern California (Washington, D.C., Department of the Interior, Bureau of Indian Affairs, nd)

Van Dyke, Theodore S.
The City and County of San Diego (San Diego, Leberthon & Taylor, 1888)
County of San Diego, the Italy of Southern California (San Diego, The San Diego Union Company, 1886)
Millionaires of a Day (New York, Fords, Howard & Hulbert, 1890);

Southern California (New York, Fords, Howard & Hulbert, 1886)

Vestal, Stanley
Wagons Southwest: Story of the Santa Fe Trail (New York, American Pioneer Trails Association, 1946)

Walker, Franklin
A Literary History of Southern California (Berkeley, University of California Press, 1950)

Warner, Charles Dudley
Our Italy (New York, Harper, 1892)
The Winter of Our Content in *Harper's New Monthly Magazine*, 1890-91 (San Marino, Henry E. Huntington Library and Art Gallery)

Waters, Frank
The Colorado (New York-Toronto, Rinehart & Company, Inc., 1946)

Weber, F. Harold, Jr.
Mines and Mineral Resources of San Diego County, California, County Report III (San Francisco, California Division of Mines, 1964)

Welch, S. L.
San Diego County (Los Angeles, Warner Brothers, 1887-88)

Wellman, Paul I.
Glory, God and Gold (Garden City, N.Y., Doubleday & Company, Inc., 1954)

Whaley, Thomas
Correspondence 1861-68 (San Diego, Whaley House Historical Museum Library)

Whetstone, Margie L.
The Escondido Story in *San Diego Historical Society Quarterly*, Vol. IV, No. 3 (July 1963)

White, Adaline Horton
The Horton's in America (Seattle, Sherman Printing & Binding Co., 1929)

Wilcox, Horace F.
How Julian Mines Were Discovered, typescript, 1926 (San Diego Public Library)

Wilson, Neill C.; and Taylor, Frank J.
Southern Pacific (New York, McGraw-Hill Book Company, Inc., 1952)

Wood, H. P.
The Port of San Diego, California (San Diego, Frye, Garrett & Smith, 1900)

Wright, Lauren A.
Gem Stones, Bulletin 176 (San Francisco, California Division of Mines)

Wright, William Lawton
The Warner's Ranch Butterfield Station Puzzle (Los Angeles, The Westerner's Brand Book 9, Los Angeles Corral, 1961)

INDEX

273

This fourth volume of the History of San Diego was designed by Jim Millard, Art Director for Image, the Art Division of Frye & Smith, Ltd. Lithography by Frye & Smith, Ltd., on Hamilton Louvain 80 pound text. Typography by Linotron, the Typesetting Division of Frye & Smith, Ltd., using Mergenthaler's Linofilm system. The type face used in this book is Century Schoolbook. Binding is by Cardoza Bookbinding Co.